THE BIRTH OF CHRISTIANITY

AFTER JESUS, VOLUME 1

The Birth of Christianity

THE FIRST TWENTY YEARS

Paul Barnett

William B. Eerdmans Publishing Company
Grand Rapids, Michigan / Cambridge, U.K.

© 2005 Wm. B. Eerdmans Publishing Co.
All rights reserved

Wm. B. Eerdmans Publishing Co.
255 Jefferson Ave. S.E., Grand Rapids, Michigan 49503 /
P.O. Box 163, Cambridge CB3 9PU U.K.

Printed in the United States of America

09 08 07 06 05   7 6 5 4 3 2 1

ISBN 0-8028-2781-0

www.eerdmans.com

For my wife, Anita,
and in thankful memory of
my mother, May Barnett (1912-2005)

CONTENTS

Preface   ix

Abbreviations   x

1. Introduction   1

2. Early Christianity and the Study of History   9

3. Time Borders and Christology   22

4. World History and Christian History   27

5. Mission to Greece: Paul's First Letter to the Thessalonians   42

6. Between Jesus and Paul (1): Paul's Window (Galatians 1)   55

7. Between Jesus and Paul (2): Luke's Window (Acts 1–9)   65

8. "Christians" in Antioch   79

9. Earliest "Teaching": The Influence of Peter   86

10. Into the Land of Israel (A.D. 34-39)   95

11. Between Jesus and Gospel Text   111

12. A Collection Called "Q"   138

13. Primary Gospel 1: Mark   150

14. Primary Gospel 2: John   163

15. Final Reflection: What Cannot Be Denied   180

APPENDIX A: History and Geography in Acts   187

APPENDIX B: Dating Galatians   206

APPENDIX C: Reflections on J. D. Crossan's
Birth of Christianity   211

Bibliography   215

Indexes
    Modern Authors   220
    Subjects   223
    Scripture References   226
    Other Ancient Writings   230

PREFACE

If history writing is true to the original meaning of the word (Greek: *historia*, "inquiry"), it will not be mere narration. This should be as true for the writing of early Christian history as it is for the writing of a history of Russia after 1917.

When historians are true to their craft, they seek explanations for their narratives. For the historian of earliest Christianity the question will always be, Why did it happen? The true "inquirer" will ask what manner of man gave impetus to a movement that soon took his name. This question is not often asked directly in this first volume in the series called After Jesus, but it is implicit on every page.

Once more I dedicate this book to one who belongs to that genus called "an author's spouse." Other authors, and more particularly other authors' spouses, will understand my sentiment. This author's wife, like others (I am sure), lives with a man who is often unhearing and "vacant faced," his mind elsewhere, redrafting an important footnote or struggling to remember a book title. This does not make for good companionship, a matter for regret.

Anita, wife of forty years, is sincerely thanked for patient support and endless encouragement. This book is for her.

ABBREVIATIONS

BAFCS	*The Book of Acts in Its First Century Setting,* ed. B. W. Winter et al. (Grand Rapids: Eerdmans, 1993-96)
BBR	*Bulletin for Biblical Research*
CBQ	*Catholic Biblical Quarterly*
EDNT	*Exegetical Dictionary of the New Testament,* ed. H. Balz and G. Schneider (Grand Rapids: Eerdmans, 1990-93)
ET	English translation
IBR	*Irish Biblical Review*
ICC	International Critical Commentary
JBL	*Journal of Biblical Literature*
JETS	*Journal of the Evangelical Theological Society*
JJS	*Journal of Jewish Studies*
JSNT	*Journal for the Study of the New Testament*
JTS	*Journal of Theological Studies*
LCL	Loeb Classical Library
LXX	Septuagint
NCB	New Century Bible Commentary
NICNT	New International Commentary on the New Testament
NovT	*Novum Testamentum*
NT	New Testament
NTS	*New Testament Studies*
OT	Old Testament
par(s).	parallel(s)
SJT	*Scottish Journal of Theology*
WUNT	Wissenschaftliche Untersuchungen zum Neuen Testament

ONE

Introduction

This book is about the lost years of earliest Christianity, about the thir-
ties and forties of the first century, about those dark ages immediately
after the execution of Jesus.

John Dominic Crossan, *The Birth of Christianity*[1]

This present book is also about the birth or origin of Christianity. It will
tell a different story from Crossan's because its method will be different.

An immediate reaction might be that we already have such a "book"
in the Acts of the Apostles. That, indeed, is what Acts purports to be.[2] Yet
while I have a high regard for the historical reliability of Acts there are
problems that must be faced. Among these we face a narrative that is
highly selective, with surprising omissions. As well, there is an absence of
chronological markers for Paul's early years, which are so important for
understanding this "birth." As it happens, however, Paul's own information proves helpful at points where Acts is either silent or even innocently
misleading.

---

1. John Dominic Crossan, *The Birth of Christianity* (San Francisco: HarperCollins,
1998), ix.
2. See Appendix A.

Jesus and Paul's Letters

The earliest surviving records of Christianity are the letters of Paul, which began appearing twenty years or less after the crucifixion of "rabbi" Jesus. Good historical method suggests that the earliest written evidence is the place to begin one's inquiry. This, however, is not where Crossan and others mentioned shortly begin their analyses.

Remarkably, Paul's letters reveal that the readers had come to worship Jesus as "Christ," "Son of God," and "Lord" and to pray to him to "come back." How can we explain this changed attitude to Jesus whose contemporaries often regarded him only as a "rabbi" or "prophet"?

For simplicity we will confine our interest to Paul's earlier letters, those whose authorship is not in dispute, that is, 1 Thessalonians, 1 and 2 Corinthians, Galatians, and Romans. These are written between the years 50 and 57 (or between 48 and 57 if Galatians was written first).[3]

Paul's view of Jesus ("christology") is pretty much the same throughout these letters from first to last. From this we draw a significant conclusion, that Paul's christology was well formed by the time his letters began appearing. This drives the formation of his christology back into the forties or, as we shall argue, earlier still into the thirties. Indeed, it is our thesis that Paul did not formulate the key elements of his christology but "received" them from his predecessors.

A Perceived Problem and Various Solutions

Fundamental to much NT scholarship is the rejection of Jesus as the miracle-working messianic figure presented in the Gospels. In reality, it is said, he must have been something else. For instance, in 1901, W. Wrede seized the various "secrecy" motifs in the Gospel of Mark, interpreting them as the author's device to retroject divinity upon the altogether human figure of Jesus.[4] R. T. France comments acutely, "For Wrede, Mark's presentation of Jesus as Messiah was not a development from Jesus' own claim but a falsification of it."[5]

---

3. See Appendix B.
4. *The Messianic Secret* (Cambridge: Clarke, 1971 ET).
5. R. T. France, "Development in New Testament Christology," *Themelios* 18 (1992), 5.

If, however, Jesus was merely a "rabbi" or "prophet" or some other figure less than Messiah during his ministry, then how did he come to be worshipped as "Christ," "Son of God," and "Lord" in the Pauline churches within two decades or less? This perceived problem is neatly captured in Maurice Casey's book title, *From Jewish Prophet to Gentile God.*[6]

It is not my intention to review exhaustively the various proposals explaining who Jesus really was and how the early Christians made him something else. In itself that would require a major monograph. Rather, let me mention as examples only some of the approaches that have been made.

A Socio-Anthropological Development

J. D. Crossan believes Jesus was a Cynic-type teacher who subverted political elites and who founded his rural "movement" in Galilee.[7] According to Crossan this movement emphasized "life" issues (e.g., justice). In Jerusalem post-Easter, however, the movement bifurcated and a parallel "death" movement arose. Crossan argues that the truest expression of Jesus' "life" movement has survived in the "Q" document. The "death" movement intervened in, for example, Paul and the Gospel of Mark and all but eclipsed evidence of the "life" movement.

Crossan's work, though erudite, is an idiosyncratic interpretation based on his conjecture about the bifurcation of the Jesus movement. Crossan bypasses NT evidence in Acts, James, and the pre-Pauline tradition, preferring instead the so-called "Q" document and the *Gospel of Thomas.*[8]

Religious Transformation: Hellenization

W. Bousset of the "history-of-religions" school contended that a weakened form of Jewish monotheism in post-exilic Judaism (expressed, e.g., in angelology or belief in hypostases) allowed the nascent Christian move-

---

6. (Cambridge: Clarke, 1991).

7. See D. Crossan, *The Birth of Christianity* (San Francisco: HarperCollins, 1998). Cynics were followers of Diogenes of Sinope (ca. 400-325 B.C.), who urged his followers to live on the barest necessities. Critics called them "dogs" *(kynes)* because of their bitter criticisms of ordinary folk.

8. For a trenchant review of Crossan's *Birth of Christianity* see N. T. Wright, "A New Birth?" *SJT* 53.1 (2000), 72-91. For further comment on Crossan's views see Appendix C.

THE BIRTH OF CHRISTIANITY

ment to find alternative expression in Hellenistic religion.[9] Bousset saw that transition occurring from the "Hebrews" (Palestinian Jewish believers) through the "Hellenists" (Diaspora Jewish believers in Jerusalem) to Gentile believers (notably at Antioch on the Orontes in Syria). It was in a pagan milieu (Antioch) that Jesus came to be seen as the *kyrios*/"Lord" and the *huios*/"Son." Bousset's explanation has been criticized by, for example, M. Hengel ("a syncretistic paganization of primitive Christianity")[10] and L. Hurtado ("a clumsy crossbreeding of Jewish monotheism and pagan polytheism").[11]

Religious Transformation: Hebraization

According to M. Casey[12] the term "the Messiah" was not current among the Jews until after Jesus passed from the scene, so that he could not have applied it to himself. Passages like Mark 8:29-30 and 14:61-62, therefore, and other titles found in the Gospels ("Son of Man," "Son of [God]") were created by the early church.[13]

How, then, did Jesus come to be regarded as he was in the early church? Casey's solution is that the original disciples with Jesus formed a distinctive and separatist Jewish sect that saw in Jesus after his death "the embodiment of Jewish identity."[14] That death proved to be the "catalyst" that immediately led to the new interpretation of Jesus in the early church. Here Casey finds existing ready-made vehicles of thought within Judaism for the attribution of terms like "Lord," "Messiah," and "Son of God" to this ideal martyr figure. Under Paul, but more particularly John, this Jewish prophet became a Gentile god.

9. For Bousset's analysis of Hebrew religion see *Die Religion des Judentums im späthellenistischen Zeitalter* (Tübingen: Mohr, 1926) and for his argument for Hellenization, *Kyrios Christos* (Göttingen: Vandenhoeck und Ruprecht, 1921; ET 1970). For a critique of Bousset's interpretation of alleged Jewish monotheism see L. Hurtado, *One God One Lord* (Philadelphia: Fortress, 1988), 24-27.

10. M. Hengel, *The Son of God* (London: SCM, 1976 ET), 18.

11. Hurtado, *One God*, 100.

12. M. Casey, *From Jewish Prophet to Gentile God: The Origins and Development of New Testament Christology* (Cambridge: Clarke/Louisville: Westminster/John Knox, 1991), 42-43.

13. *Jewish Prophet*, 54.

14. *Jewish Prophet*, 57-75.

There are several problems with Casey's reconstruction. First, through more intense study of Second Temple Judaism we are much more conscious now of various other messianic and prophetic figures of the era (e.g., Judas the Galilean, Theudas, or Simon bar Gioras), none of whom were accorded the kind of status Casey thinks was given to Jesus. Yet in that culture, in which the covenant people lived under occupation by the hated Gentile, more nationalistic figures would have been regarded as worthier than Jesus for such honors. Secondly, Casey seems unaware of the unlikelihood of such a steep reinterpretation of Jesus occurring in so brief a space of time.

Making "Ordinary Religious" Yeshua "Messiah"

According to D. H. Akenson[15] the belief that Yeshua was the Messiah (the Christ) did not originate with Jesus or his disciples during the life of Jesus or subsequently, but later with Saul of Tarsus. Yeshua was "an ordinary religious man of the later Second Temple era" (p. 183). How, then, did Yeshua of Nazareth attract followers during his earthly span and continue to do so after his death? It was due to his "incandescent holiness that burned beyond his burial" (p. 183). He was a man who was "beyond-words holy" (p. 184). For this no evidence is given.

It is important to understand Akenson's conviction of the importance of the destruction of the Temple in A.D. 70 (p. 73). The post-70 era was "totally different" from the pre-70 era of late Second Temple Judaism, to which Yeshua and Saul belonged.

The entire New Testament was written in the post-destruction epoch, with one critical exception, the epistles of Saul. Indeed, that destruction was the raison d'être for those writings (p. 73). The post-70 texts — in particular the Gospels — see Yeshua through the prism of the destruction of the Temple. In the Gospels we find a reinvented Judaism focused on "Jesus" as the Passover lamb, a substitute for the physical Temple (p. 184).

In this post-70 era *historical* access to Yeshua is, therefore, quite "limited" (p. 116). True, Akenson allows the historicity of John the Baptizer, finding corroboration in the writings of Josephus (pp. 79-82). Despite that, however, there is nothing in the teachings of Jesus that was not current in

---

15. D. H. Akenson, *Saint Saul: A Skeleton Key to the Historical Jesus* (Oxford: Oxford University Press, 2000).

late Second Temple Judaism (pp. 186-87). Yeshua was, indeed, an "ordinary" man. In short, according to Akenson, the Gospels' version of Jesus (an extraordinary man) is constructed out of "free floating pieces of theology" from that era of Judaism.

Nonetheless, Akenson contends that "the most likely way to gain access to the historical Yeshua . . . is through the canonical New Testament" (p. 116). This is consistent with his working thesis, that the "New Questors" who seek to find Jesus in pre-70 sources (in particular the "Q" Gospel) are totally misguided.

The only pre-70 source for the historical Yeshua is Saul and he tells us next to nothing about Yeshua. The reason Saul says so little was not because his readers already knew about Yeshua but because "the entire earthly life of the historical Yeshua did not count. Only the post-earthly life did" (p. 173). The historical Yeshua of Nazareth was not the Christ. Nor, indeed, was he even an authority on the Torah since Saul must overrule his judgment on remarriage (p. 205).

How, then, and why did Saul, a Jew of late Second Temple Judaism, come to believe that Yeshua was the Messiah? It was, says Akenson, on account of Saul's resurrection experience of Yeshua that he came to regard him as the cosmic, eschatological, redemptive Christ. Saul's version of Yeshua as the Christ "represented only one version of what was already a multiple-version Yeshua-faith, within the complex of multiple Judahisms" (p. 121).

In short, therefore, D. H. Akenson argues that Yeshua was quite an "ordinary" man of extraordinary holiness whom Saul (pre-70) came to recognize as the Christ, as also did the (post-70) Gospel writers.

Despite its accomplished scholarship, often expressed with shrewd insight, this work has major flaws. First, it does not address the disciples' recognition and confession of Jesus as the Christ that is deeply rooted within the *parallel* traditions of Mark and John (Mark 8:29; John 1:41, 49). Consistent with this, the pre-formed tradition Paul "received" (at his baptism in Damascus?) is centered on one called "Christ" (1 Cor 15:3-7). In other words, Jesus presented himself as the Messiah, his disciples recognized him as the Messiah, and the post-Easter believers preached him as the Messiah.

Second, *Saint Saul* fails to recognize that the Gospels of Mark and John (which Akenson rightly regards as independent)[16] did not appear at the last minute when they were written but each had a prehistory in mis-

16. *Saint Saul*, 99-100.

6

sion activity (primarily in Israel) stretching back to the first Easter and into the ministry of Jesus himself.

Third, Akenson makes a number of inconsistencies and debatable assumptions. (a) He has little regard for Acts as history,[17] but his argument depends on its accuracy;[18] (b) he asserts that the notion of "Messiah" was not current in Second Temple Judaism[19] yet does not adequately explain how Paul's thinking and preaching was dominated by "the Christ";[20] (c) while it's true that the destruction of the Temple in A.D. 70 was a massive event for Jews and Judaism, it is questionable whether this event loomed so large for Christians, including Christian Jews; (d) Akenson, who makes so much of Saul, does not explain how or why he would have a vision of the resurrected Yeshua or why this would launch his radical career change as apostle to the Gentiles. The limp proposal that Saul merely transferred from one form of Judaism (Pharisaism) to another (the Yeshua-faith)[21] does not fit the facts; (e) Akenson does not explain how the post-70 writings should come to recognize Jesus as the Messiah.

Chronology

It should be apparent that chronology is critical in studies in Christian origins. But, surprisingly, many scholars discuss theological terms and ideas rather vaguely, seemingly unaware of the brevity in which these terms and ideas arose. Since Paul's christology and soteriology were in place by the year 50, when his first letter was written (or ca. 48 if Galatians preceded 1 Thessalonians), we are driven to assume that he had settled these matters some years earlier.

This underlines the importance of securing the chronology that, as it happens, is broadly uncontroversial as to the key dates. It is almost as if many have not noticed that the crucifixion is securely dated to 30 (or 33) and Paul's arrival in Corinth to 50. So there was only a very short period between Jesus and God's "call" to Paul.[22] It is my understanding that Paul be-

---

17. *Saint Saul,* 135-43.
18. *Saint Saul,* 177.
19. *Saint Saul,* 40.
20. *Saint Saul,* 74-76.
21. *Saint Saul,* 137.
22. See p. 26 below.

gan preaching Jesus as "Christ," "Son of God," and "Lord" from that time. This means that the christology that he "received" was already pre-formed.

As well as the overall time frame, however, it is important to work out intermediate details such as the dates of Paul's "call" and his first return visit to Jerusalem. Here I am indebted to the thorough research of Rainer Riesner, *Paul's Early Period*,[23] though I regard 33 as more likely than 30 as the date of the crucifixion.

Christology and Christianity

My thesis is that the birth of Christianity and the birth of christology are inseparable, both as to time and essence. Christianity *is* christology. Certainly NT churches grew out of christological preaching and were characterized by christological worship. In time the texts of the NT would arise from christological conviction. Attempts to explain the rise of Christianity by sociological or psychological grounds are doomed to failure. Christ, or should we say christological conviction, was the engine that drove early Christianity.

Chronological inquiry detects the existence of "high" christology in the immediate aftermath of Jesus. Indeed, as we shall argue more than once when we come to consider Paul's letters, we encounter little development in the last letter as compared with the first. Our reasonable assumption is that christology changed little from the first Easter to the end of Paul's letters.

Various labels have been used to describe perceived changes in the doctrine of Christ along the way.[24] The notion of evolution is unacceptable since it implies a series of mutations from lower to higher forms. Not as unacceptable, yet not entirely acceptable is the tag "development." Change, of course, cannot be denied. A better way of describing that "change," however, may be to think of it as "contextual adjustment."

23. (Grand Rapids: Eerdmans, 1998), 52.

24. For discussion see C. F. D. Moule, *The Origin of Christology* (Cambridge: Cambridge University Press, 1977), 6-10.

TWO

Early Christianity and the Study of History

. . . there is a lingering suspicion that the topic of historicity is peculiarly the preserve of a historicist pseudo-scholarship . . . for apologetic ends. . . . This ghost ought to be laid to rest.

Colin Hemer, *The Book of Acts in Its Hellenistic Setting*[1]

One concurs. This book aims primarily to investigate the early years of Christianity, rather than account for its "birth." The investigation, however, inevitably poses questions about the impetus that gave rise to those beginnings,[2] which in turn drive us back to the figure of Jesus himself. Who was this man from whom a movement like early Christianity arose immediately after his life? Any study of Christian origins tends to raise questions like that.

The boundaries for our study are, on the far side, the crucifixion of Jesus (dated to 33 [or 30]) and, on this side, Paul's early westward missions (dated to ca. 48). The later marker was chosen since it "fixes" the historic beginning of the new faith becoming the province of Gentiles. For practical purposes, then, we are speaking about Jewish Christianity of the thirties and forties, a span of twenty years, more or less. Nothing hangs on absolute precision.

---

1. Colin Hemer, *The Book of Acts in Its Hellenistic Setting* (Tübingen: Mohr, 1989), 2
2. See P. W. Barnett, *Jesus and the Rise of Early Christianity: A History of New Testament Times* (Downers Grove: InterVarsity, 1999).

Our word "history" derives from a Greek word *(historēsai)* that meant "inquire into" or "become acquainted with" (cf. Gal 1:18). The work of the historian is to find sources of information, to evaluate their reliability, to make disciplined "inquiry" into their meaning and with imagination to reconstruct "what happened."[3] It follows logically that the sources closest to the event or person in question, in particular eyewitness sources, are of special interest. Sources that merely repeat earlier sources are generally of little value. Much of what follows will involve discussion of sources and the identification of evidence that can be employed in a reconstruction of the events to which they relate.

My Standpoint

Postmodern approaches to history writing have attracted criticism, some of which this author endorses. There are benefits, however, including the issue of the writer's attitudes, biases, and prejudices from which no one is immune. One can detect a degree of fierce enjoyment in those who have laid bare the motives of such notable historians and definers of history as E. H. Carr and G. R. Elton.[4] To spare others the task let me lay my own cards on the table, face up.

I am a creedal believer who, for the greater part of his working life, has been a minister in a mainline denomination. At the same time, a consuming interest in Christian origins has led me to extensive undergraduate studies in the Greco-Roman world and two post-graduate programs centered on first-century Judaism. I have made numerous visits to Israel, where Christianity was born, and to Turkey and Greece, where it quickly spread. Along with more routine ministry activity I have taught ancient history subjects in several universities.

I remain grateful for the rigorous methods, integrity, and skill of my teachers of Classical Greek and Greco-Roman history at the University of Sydney. As an example of academic rigor, as a mere year two (honors) history student I was required to identify and comment on every occurrence of the word clusters for "slavery" and "freedom" in Greek authors from

3. Leopold von Ranke, the father of modern historiography, declared that the aim of the historian was to determine "what actually happened." For discussion see R. J. Evans, *In Defence of History* (London: Granta, 1997), 16-17.

4. See Evans, *In Defence of History*, passim.

Homer to Xenophon. (This was before the advent of computerized concordances.) Our professor met weekly with the one other student and me to review our research; there was nowhere to hide.

Such was the self-discipline and professionalism of our teachers that their own political or religious views were entirely opaque to the student. I imagine many of them would be mystified by the current postmodern preoccupation with subjectivity.

In short, as a creedal Christian I do not claim neutrality. At the same time, however, I am committed to the academic rigor in which I was schooled and to the ideal of objectivity and the professional use of texts. I do not believe empathy and objectivity to be mutually exclusive.

History-Writing Then and Now

If it is impossible historically to establish the present, due to its immensity and complexity, it is no less impossible to do so for the era of the Greeks and the Romans. A major problem is the incompleteness of evidence from antiquity. Papyri perish through dampness and humidity. Precious inscriptions are defaced by earthquakes or lost as recycled masonry. Known histories like Tacitus's *Annals* have gaps; books 7-10 (covering the principate of Caligula) and books 17-18 (narrating Nero's fall) are missing. Claudius's history of the principate of Augustus has not survived.

History-writing now has a different ethos and culture from historiography in antiquity. Today we operate under a universal time regime established by Greenwich mean time and a world calendar. Time then was local, established by the sundial or water clock. There were many calendars, for example, Roman, Macedonian, Syrian, mainstream Jewish, and sectarian Jewish. Our world has been minutely mapped; theirs had only rough sketches. We keep careful demographic records about every conceivable aspect of existence. We know about levels of literacy in Canada, the longevity of Australian aborigines, and the ocular health of children in the Côte d'Ivoire. But we can only guess about literacy in Corinth in Paul's day or the stable population of Jerusalem in the time of Jesus.[5]

5. J. D. Crossan, *The Birth of Christianity* (San Francisco: HarperCollins, 1998) engages in extensive socioeconomic discussion about the Galilee of Jesus' day to establish the environment and character of the Jesus movement. In the absence of empirical data, however, much of his discussion is conjectural.

It is true that a surviving papyrus text or epitaph may cast some light on the daily life of ordinary people. Yet such light tends to be narrowly focused. Today it is possible to write histories of minor movements or "unimportant" individuals in the modern world, but this is rarely possible for the period under review. The extensive data that allows the writing of social and economic histories is not available for comparable works for antiquity. Social histories about village life in Galilee, for example, are necessarily limited to generalizations.

History-writing in antiquity tended to deal with "significant" people who "made it to the top" and left their imprint in official documents, chronicles, and inscriptions. From the historian Tacitus and the biographer Suetonius we know about Roman emperors with occasional passing references to lower-order officials. This information is supplemented by inscriptions (e.g., Augustus's *Res Gestae*) or papyri (e.g., Claudius's *Letter to the Alexandrians*). That so much is known about Pontius Pilate, a prefect of a small province on the margins of the Empire, is a fluke. His predecessors in that office are known to us only by name.

Another major difference between modernity and antiquity is the identifiable motivation of the authors. Today historians and biographers, though having their own interests, generally seek to offer comprehensive and balanced accounts. True, their personal views may be discernible. Yet blatant prejudice evident in manipulation of evidence will meet fierce scorn from reviewers and likely loss of academic reputation.

Overt prejudice, however, is precisely what we encounter in many texts from antiquity. To be sure, authors assured their readers of their integrity. The ideals of Lucian (second century) are faultless:

> Facts must not be carelessly put together,
> but the historian must work with great labor
> and often at great trouble make inquiry,
> preferably being himself present and an eyewitness;
> failing that he must rely on those who are incorruptible,
> and have no bias from passion, to add or diminish anything.[6]

We cannot fail to note the parallels in the prologue of Luke's Gospel, where the author disclaims the status of the eyewitness but nonetheless assures

---

6. *Quomodo* 47. See C. K. Barrett, "Quomodo Historia Conscribenda Sit," *NTS* 28.3 (1982), 303-20.

the reader of the pristine qualification of his sources, who were "eyewitnesses and ministers" of the word no less.

Nonetheless, despite their well-meant assurances, the authors of antiquity were different in that they did not disguise or were unsuccessful in disguising their "interests." We view Roman history and Roman emperors through the jaundiced eyes of Pliny and Suetonius. The great Tacitus does not hide his contempt for the power lust of the Julio-Claudian emperors. Josephus, our only comprehensive source for first-century Jewish history, fails by modern standards of "balance." His *Jewish War* is thinly veiled propaganda. His *Antiquities of the Jews* and *Against Apion* are romantic apologetics for Judaism. His *Life* is sickeningly self-serving. Modern historians of antiquity, however, enjoy identifying Josephus's "tendencies" and noting his omissions, exaggerations, and mistakes. This is all part of the fun! Furthermore, his works are prized, for without them no account of first-century Jewish history would be possible and we would have little sense of the life and times in which Jesus lived and in which Christianity was born.

History from antiquity, then, is recoverable but incomplete due to the limited extent and frequently tendentious nature of the sources. Ancient historiography, more than its modern counterpart, is to a greater degree approximate or provisional. A new discovery may alter previous perceptions. Until the discovery of Claudius's *Letter to the Alexandrians,* written on his accession in 41 but lost until modern times, that emperor's steely resolve could not have been guessed.

In short, evidence from Greco-Roman antiquity is fragmentary, generally devoted to "important" people and events and its texts overtly "interpreted." For these and other reasons ancient historiography should engender humility and a degree of tentativeness. Overconfidence and arrogance are not unknown among historians, but are inappropriate.

Ancient studies are relatively sure-footed in their inquiries into "important" people like emperors. Their respective chronologies, policies, and achievements are understood. Accordingly, when information about lesser people or movements comes to light, a context and environment is at hand in which to locate the smaller thing.

Small Movements

There are several exceptions to the generalization that ancient history knows about the "important" but not about the "unimportant." One is the Qumran movement. The cache of texts discovered in 1947 near the northwestern shore of the Dead Sea and the subsequent excavations of the remains of a settlement nearby created great excitement. These discoveries provide a contemporary window into the small and "unimportant" Jewish sect that occupied the site for about two centuries but that left otherwise small imprints in the histories of the day that have come down to us (mainly Josephus).

The popular view is that the Qumranites were the Essenes mentioned by Josephus and others, a breakaway sect established sometime in the Maccabean era (165-37 B.C.). From archaeologists' investigations it appears that their settlement was destroyed during the Roman invasion of Palestine A.D. 66-70.

There is much, however, that is debated. Were the texts placed in the caves by the sectarians or by other groups for safekeeping in a time of war? Was the settlement a monastery for a sect or a hostel for travelers? Were the Qumranites in fact the Essenes mentioned by Josephus? When and under what circumstances did the sect arise? Who were the "wicked priest," the "man of lies," and the "teacher of righteousness" referred to in some of the texts?

The Qumran discoveries pointing to a community of scholars within Judaism help us imagine the first Christians as a group of Jews who, likewise, scrutinized biblical texts that pointed to recent eschatological fulfillment. These Essenes and the first Christians also likewise shared their goods for distribution to needy members. There were many differences, however.

Like the Qumranites the early Christians are also known from external sources. Josephus and Tacitus refer to a movement begun in Jesus' day that was current in their own times, decades later. Unlike the Qumranites the early Christians survived the dangers of history that might just as easily have destroyed them.

One matter in which an external source from "world history" (Tacitus) and internal sources (Paul and Acts) agree is that the birth of Christianity occurred as a burst of energy soon after the life of Jesus. Tacitus states that following Pilate's execution of Christ the "pernicious superstition *broke out afresh* in Judea" (*Annals* 15.44). Such was its offensiveness to the young Pharisee Paul that he "persecuted the church of God violently and tried to destroy it" (Gal 1:13; cf. 1:22). In persecuting the "church of God" Paul was at the same time persecuting Jesus, so close was the connection between them in time and relationship (Acts 9:5).

"World history" (about "important" people) is important since it provides a more or less stable context into which "unimportant" movements like the Qumranites and the early Christians can be located.

Sources for Early Christianity

There are two main sources for Christianity for the brief period under review (30- or 33-48).

Closest to the events are the letters of Paul, which, for convenience, we limit to 1 Thessalonians, 1 and 2 Corinthians, Galatians, and Romans. New Testament scholars will note that these letters are not disputed and that I have listed them in the commonly agreed historical order. As I will argue later, there is a case that Galatians was Paul's earliest extant work,[7] though the general drift of this book is unaffected either way.

Paul's letters are also interesting since they are not historical narratives but written to correct or reinforce doctrinal beliefs or moral practices in the churches. Nonetheless, the letters, particularly Galatians, do contain historical information about earliest Christianity. Much of this detail is motivated by Paul's need to defend himself from various criticisms. In no way does this minimize the historical importance of what he says, however, since any error of fact on his part would attract even more damning attacks.

The other source is the book of Acts, part two of Luke's seventy-year history beginning with the birth of John the Baptizer and ending with Paul's imprisonment in Rome. This work is undated, though a case can be made that it was completed within a few years of Paul's arrival in Rome ca. 60.

As a source Acts is no less fascinating and challenging to the historian.[8] It is fashionable to regard it as a "secondary" source since the author, unlike Paul, was not personally involved in the events he narrates. This is

7. Appendix B.
8. See Appendix A.

not true if, as I will argue, the author himself takes part in his narrative in the "we"-passages, especially during the five years 57-62 (Acts 20:5–28:31). Given that so much is written in the third person (about Peter, Paul, and their associates), it is hard to believe that the author is not including himself in the narrative when he switches to the first person plural.

The implications are considerable. If the author was Paul's traveling companion for lengthy periods, then he is an *equal primary source* for narratives involving Paul; indeed, as an onlooker his perspective on Paul may be superior to Paul's own. Indeed, we glean more about Paul's early life from Acts than we do from Paul himself.[9] In other words, for events concerning Paul (at least) we must not disconnect Acts from Paul as a source for his earlier life. Furthermore, through Paul the author knew about Peter, James, John, Barnabas, John Mark, and Silvanus. In other words, so far from being the remote writer of religious fiction of much scholarly opinion, this author is an immediate source of evidence for Paul and a good secondary source of information reaching back to the birth of Christianity.

There are difficulties, however, that must be addressed.[10] Scholars point to two apparent errors in Luke's corpus. One is the dating of Jesus' nativity to the time of the census in A.D. 6 "when Quirinius was governor of Syria" (Luke 2:2). Jesus was, however, born in the latter days of Herod, who died ten years earlier. The other (Acts 5:36-37) is Luke's location of Theudas's uprising (ca. A.D. 45), *before* Judas's rebellion (A.D. 6).

The greater challenge in using Acts as a source is that its interests do not coincide with ours. Some sense of chronology for the two-decade period in which Christianity was born is important to us, but not to Luke. The only datable connection he makes with world history is the persecution during Agrippa's reign (41-44).[11] Paul's details in Gal 1:18; 2:1 come to our aid in this regard; Luke provides little help. Such gaps regularly confront the historian of antiquity.

Again, because I need to know about the prehistory of the Gospels, the formation of churches in the land of Israel in which (I presume) the antecedent "traditions" were established is critical. Acts tells me little; its concern is to narrate only those stepping-stones by which the word of God

---

9. For a summary of both see D. Wenham, "Acts and the Pauline Corpus," *BAFCS* I: 216-17.

10. See Appendix A.

11. Acts 12:1-3.

made its way from Jerusalem to the Gentiles. One senses that Luke cannot wait to bring Paul into his story. Once Peter, John, and Philip have advanced the word toward the Gentiles they fade from the narrative. This author is quite selective in the story he tells.

Yet Luke knows that "narratives" about Jesus were formulated during this early period in the land of Israel (Luke 1:1-4). The "eyewitnesses" (of Jesus) became "ministers of the word" (in the land of Israel). They "handed over" "narratives" written by "many" to Luke. Most likely some of this "handing over" occurred in Palestine sometime during Paul's imprisonment (57-60). Luke, however, tells us nothing about how the "many" wrote their "narratives" or their original purpose.

Another shortcoming is the impression Luke creates that Paul's apostolic ministry began with his westward missions in the late forties (Acts 13). Paul's own account is different. He was "called" to be an apostle to the Gentiles from the time of his conversion (Gal 1:16-17) and was engaged in that ministry from the beginning, in Damascus, Arabia, Judea, and Syria-Cilicia. To our dismay, Acts tells us little about Paul during these "unknown years" from Damascus to Antioch.

In short, therefore, because his interests do not coincide with ours Luke fails to provide information to satisfy our curiosity about the critical years under review. As we shall see, however, all is not lost. We will be able to fill in some of the gaps, both in regard to the apostles' ministry in the land and in regard to the activities of Paul elsewhere.

These comments indicate some of the elements involved in a professional historical inquiry into early Christianity. The historian is fortunate to have in Paul's letters and the book of Acts such different and interesting sources for the same period. Moreover, as we will soon indicate, at least one of the sources can be shown to be very close to the events.

Momigliano's "Rule"

The noted historian A. Momigliano was surely correct in his observation: "The whole modern method of historical research is founded on the distinction between original and derivative authorities."

My argument is that Paul and Luke are independent authorities; neither derives his information from the texts of the other. True, they were travel companions for many years. Yet scholars are correct in finding no evidence of literary connection between the book of Acts and Paul's letters. Their parallel — that is, underived — references to the same events or people catch the historian's eye.

First, both authorities mention details in the life of the early church in Jerusalem, though in different ways. From Paul's letters and Acts we know of Jesus' resurrection appearances (Acts 1:3; 1 Cor 15:5-7), that Jesus' brothers were part of the Jerusalem church (Acts 1:14; Gal 1:19), that the Twelve were leaders (Acts 6:2; 1 Cor 15:5), that Peter and John were prominent (Acts 1:13; Gal 1:18; 2:9).

Second, both Paul and Luke have the same sequence for Paul's life in the so-called "unknown years."

Paul's sequence	the sequence in Acts
Paul attempted to destroy the church of God	Paul ravaged the church in Jerusalem
God revealed his Son in Paul	a light from heaven . . . a voice
Damascus	Damascus
Arabia	
Damascus	
Jerusalem	Jerusalem
Syria-Cilicia	Tarsus
[Antioch]	Antioch
Jerusalem	Jerusalem

There are discrepancies, notably the omission from Acts of the Arabia sojourn and whether Paul met all the apostles on his first return visit to Jerusalem.[12] These, however, are exactly the challenges the ancient historian faces. The agreement between parallel authorities in so many other details is striking and supports their historicity.

Urban Environments

Christianity was born in Jerusalem, but soon spread to Damascus and Antioch in Syria, as well as throughout the land of Israel (Judea, Galilee,

12. See Appendix A.

Samaria). We defer for the moment any comment about Antioch, but make brief mention of Jerusalem and Damascus.

Jerusalem

Estimates vary as to the population of Jerusalem at the time. There are grounds for believing there were about 100,000 people permanently living in the city, apart from the times of the great feasts when the numbers may have reached a million.[13] The majority of pilgrims would come from the Diaspora, with rather fewer from Palestine. However, a significant proportion of Jerusalem's stable population were Jews from the Diaspora, who continued to use Greek as their mother tongue and to meet in "Hellenist" synagogues to hear the Scriptures read in Greek and to pray in Greek. It is clear that numerous synagogues existed in Jerusalem at the time. The Talmud suggests as many as 390.[14] A significant number of these were "Hellenist."

Light has been thrown on such synagogues by the discovery in the region of the lower city (the City of David) in 1913-14 of a tablet bearing a dedicatory inscription written in Greek.[15]

> Theodotus (son) of Vettenus, priest and
> archisynagogos, son of an archisynago-
> gos, grandson of an archisynagogos, con-
> structed the synagogue for the rea-
> ding of the law and the teaching of the commandments and
> the guest-room and the (upper ?) chambers and the instal-
> lations of water for the hostelry for tho-
> se needing (them) from abroad, which was foun-
> ded by his fathers and the el-
> ders and Simonides.

The inscription reveals a synagogue established in previous generations that had been rebuilt or enlarged. The dedicator, Theodotus, has a Greek

---

13. See W. Reinhardt, "The Population Size of Jerusalem and the Numerical Growth of the Jerusalem Church," *BAFCS* IV:237-65.

14. *b. Ketubim* 105a. Cf. D. A. Fiensy, "The Composition of the Jerusalem Church," *BAFCS* IV:233-34.

15. R. Riesner, "Synagogues in Jerusalem," *BAFCS* 4:192-201. The spacing and setout of the text above follows Riesner, who in turn reproduces the Greek inscription.

name. His father's Latin name, Vettenus, suggests that his family had migrated to Jerusalem from Italy (Rome?). It is possible that he is an emancipated slave bearing the name of his owner, Vettenus. This family was closely connected both to this synagogue, but also to the Temple; Theodotus is both a priest and an *archisynagogos* ("ruler of a synagogue"). This synagogue provided for regular meetings of local "Hellenist" Jerusalemites, as well as hostel accommodation for pilgrims from the Diaspora. Acts records a dispute between Stephen and the members of five "Hellenist" synagogues in Jerusalem. One was the "Synagogue of Freedmen,"[16] whose members most likely had been emancipated slaves.[17] Is it possible that this synagogue is the one dedicated by Theodotus. Whatever the case, this synagogue appears to have been a "Hellenist" meeting place, where the Greek language would have been used in services. Furthermore, in such a synagogue "Hellenist" Jews and Diaspora Jews would have congregated. It is likely that Saul of Tarsus, as a Greek-speaking Jew of the Diaspora, belonged to, or was a rabbi in, a "Hellenist" synagogue. In short, this inscription is a window into a field of ministry that was important in the rise of early Jerusalem-based Christianity.

Damascus

Paul's onslaught on the church in Jerusalem scattered believers throughout the land of Israel (Judea, Galilee, and Samaria) and also beyond its borders. Some made their way to Damascus, the city closest to the borders of the land, only 150 miles from Jerusalem.

Damascus was located on the fringe between the fertile belt and the Arabian desert. An ancient settlement, Damascus passed through many hands before coming into the orbit of the Hellenistic kingdoms following Alexander's conquests. The city was refounded along Hellenistic lines, on a square grid according to the planning theories of Hippodamus of Miletus, which explains the reference to a "street called straight" (Acts 9:11). The city had well-established Greek institutions of senate house, gymnasia, law

16. Acts 6:9.

17. Such a synagogue is rendered historically plausible by Philo, *Embassy to Gaius* 155-56. Philo refers to the Jewish quarter of Rome, where the Jews were mostly Roman citizens who had been captured by the Romans and brought as slaves to the city, where, for the most part, they had been manumitted. Philo notes that these Jews had kept to their historic faith.

courts, and philosophical schools. Under the Roman settlement of the east in 66 B.C. Damascus became an autonomous city-state, one of the cities of the league known as the Decapolis ("ten cities"). Damascus had a large Jewish population, which was mainly Greek-speaking, and who were distributed among a number of synagogues.[18]

Evidence and Events

After many years I still remember my surprise on two occasions while I was an ancient history undergraduate. First, I found it interesting that Christianity was mentioned only in the third year, as part of a course on third-century Roman history. Upon further reflection, however, I should not have been surprised since only then did the new faith begin to have an impact on the Roman world.

Second, however, I was and remain struck by the closeness in time between the historical Jesus and the earliest evidence about him. Even for the important people like emperors the lead time tended to be much longer. It is likely that fifty years elapsed before Tacitus wrote his account of Nero's assault on the Christians following the fire of Rome in 64. By contrast, the apostle Paul was writing to Christians in northern Greece twenty years or less after the historical Jesus. The proper course for the historian, therefore, will be to investigate 1 Thessalonians, the document many regard as the earliest written source for Christianity, as soon as possible. Beforehand, however, it will be important to establish the time-boundaries of our study with some attempt to identify a chronology within those boundaries. Closely related is the need to locate our brief period within the context of world history. To these matters we now turn.

18. According to Josephus, *War* 2.561, eighteen thousand Jews were massacred on one occasion in the gymnasium in Damascus in A.D. 66, though these numbers have been questioned.

THREE

Time Borders
and Christology

If we look through some works on the history of earliest Christianity we might get the impression that people in them had declared war on chronology.

Martin Hengel, *Between Jesus and Paul:
Studies in the Earliest History of Christianity*[1]

Establishing temporal perimeters is fundamental to history writing, but not, according to Hengel, by all who investigate earliest Christianity.

This book stays within the perimeters of the end of Jesus' historical span, after which Christianity was born (30 or 33), and ca. 48, which marks the end of the phase in which Christianity was overwhelmingly Jewish and the beginning of the phase when it became overwhelmingly Gentile. This is a brief period — less than two decades. After 48 the writings of the NT began to appear, starting with Paul's letters. The Letter of James, however, may have been written before or within the time of Paul's letters.

This raises an urgent issue that will be addressed soon (chapter 5). When, after so brief a period, the NT letters begin to appear they articulate a "high" christology. We might expect a gradual divinization of Jesus over many decades. We are surprised, therefore, to discover that he is called "Lord" in these early documents. Not only so, these texts contain anteced-

---

1. Martin Hengel, *Between Jesus and Paul: Studies in the Earliest History of Christianity* (Philadelphia: Fortress, 1983), 39.

ent traditions that take us back even closer to the historical Jesus. How can this be? Many study chronology and many study christology but few consider the implications of this "high" christology alongside the brevity of the time span in which that christology was formed. It is right, then, to engage the issues of chronology at this early stage of our inquiry.

Our discussion is necessarily brief since NT chronology is notoriously complex and scholarly opinion correspondingly diverse.[2] Nonetheless, the dates that concern us here are secure, at least to within a few years.[3]

The Time Span between Jesus and Paul's Earliest Letters

The Importance yet Limitations of Paul for Chronology

Paul's writings contain significant information about Paul himself and more broadly about early Christianity. Of particular importance are two time notes in Galatians:

> 1:18   "then after *(meta epeita)* three years"
> (from the Damascus "call")
> 2:1   "then after *(epeita dia)* fourteen years"

This is critical though incomplete information. First, we do not know whether the "fourteen years" incorporates or is to be added to the initial "three years"; scholars are divided and the grammar inconclusive. Second, it does not tell us the length of time between Jesus' crucifixion and Paul's Damascus "call."

The one piece of information from his letters that anchors Paul's "call" into world history is his flight from King Aretas's ethnarch in Damascus (2 Cor 11:32-33). Several details here are secure: (1) the escape immediately preceded Paul's first return visit to Jerusalem "after three years" (Gal 1:18), and (2) the "king" was Aretas IV, ruler of the Nabateans.[4] While

---

2. For a survey with critical review see R. Riesner, *Paul's Early Period* (Grand Rapids: Eerdmans, 1998), 3-28.

3. So M. Hengel, *Between Jesus and Paul*, 30.

4. Some matters are unclear: the meaning of "ethnarch" in this context is unresolved, and the hypothesis of a "Nabatean" quarter in Damascus is unproven. See M. Hengel, "Paul in Arabia," *BBR* 12.1 (2002), 47-66; Riesner, *Paul's Early Period*, 84-89.

it is not possible to establish Aretas's precise relationship with Damascus, it is known that he died in A.D. 40, which is therefore the latest possible date for Paul's departure from Damascus and his first return visit to Jerusalem. Accordingly, the latest date for his conversion is 37, three years earlier.

At this point Paul's information takes us no further. We must turn to Luke-Acts to establish the date of Paul's conversion with greater precision.

Establishing a Time Frame from Luke-Acts

We defer for the moment the wider discussion of the reliability of Luke-Acts, except to anticipate a generally positive verdict.[5]

From linkages from Luke-Acts into world history we are able to fix two critical dates: (1) for the time John the Baptizer began prophesying and (2) for Paul's arrival in Corinth. Establishing a marker for the baptizer in turn locates the span of Jesus' ministry. Finding an endpoint for Jesus helps in discovering the earliest possible date for Paul's conversion.

John began to prophesy "in the fifteenth year of the reign of Tiberius" (Luke 3:1). Augustus died August 19, A.D. 14, and Tiberius was proclaimed emperor September 17 of the same year. Regardless of which calendar is used, Jewish, Syrian, or Julian, Tiberius's "fifteenth year" would be A.D. 29,[6] so John began his ministry in that year.[7] As to its duration, it appears that John continued for at least a year. The spread of his fame and the fatal hostility of Herod the tetrarch imply this as a minimum. Since Jesus began his ministry before John's arrest (John 3:22-24) it appears that he, too, began to preach sometime in the year 29.[8]

Due to astronomical considerations, it has been established that Jesus' "Passover of death" must have occurred either in 30 or 33.[9] Thus, un-

---

5. See Appendix A.

6. See H. Hoehner, *Chronological Aspects of the Life of Christ* (Grand Rapids: Zondervan, 1977), 33-37.

7. Some argue that the "reign" refers to Tiberius's appointment as coregent with Augustus in A.D. 26-27. See Hoehner, *Chronological Aspects*, 32 n. 12, however, for evidence from Josephus indicating that the "reign" is to be reckoned from Tiberius's accession in A.D. 14.

8. So Hoehner, *Chronological Aspects*, 45.

9. Following the historical arguments in P. L. Maier, "The Date of the Nativity," in J. Vardaman and E. M. Yamauchi, eds., *Chronos, Kairos, Christos* (Winona Lake: Eisen-

less one takes the view that Jesus' ministry was of only one year's duration (which is scarcely possible), it follows that it extended beyond A.D. 30. Accordingly, the crucifixion of Jesus of Nazareth is to be dated to the Passover of 33.[10] Therefore, Paul's "call" occurred after 33 (Jesus' death) and prior to 37 (Paul's flight from Damascus).

The other critical date is Paul's arrival in Corinth. This is calculated by two linkages from Luke-Acts into world history. The *first* is Aquila and Priscilla's presence in Corinth following Claudius's expulsion of Jews from Rome (Acts 18:2). This connects with Suetonius's reference (*Claudius* 25.4), which by cross-reference to Orosius (fifth century), points to A.D. 49 as the expulsion date.[11] The *second* linkage is the "Gallio" inscription from Delphi (published 1905) establishing summer 51 for the beginning of the proconsul Gallio's year-long tenure.[12] This strengthens 49 as the date for Claudius's expulsion edict. Most likely this meant that Paul arrived in Corinth at the beginning of A.D. 50 and that he withdrew eighteen months later in order to avoid a further trial before the incoming proconsul.[13] This critical reconstruction would not be possible without the two linkages mentioned in Acts tying Paul's visit to Corinth to world history.[14]

These considerations enable us to fix two limits for calculating the date of Paul's "call": 33 for the death of Jesus and 50 for Paul's arrival in Achaia, seventeen years later.

This, however, is as far as Luke-Acts on its own takes us. Indeed, based only on the book of Acts, where the conversion of Paul occurs as late as ch. 9, we might assume (wrongly) that the conversion of Paul occurred much later than it did. Thus we turn once more to Paul's letters.

As noted above, Paul told the Galatians that he made his second visit to Jerusalem "*after* fourteen years," reckoned from (a) his Damascus Road

---

brauns, 1989), 124-26 and the astronomical analyses of C. J. Humphreys and W. G. Waddington, "Date of the Crucifixion," in Vardaman and Yamauchi, 165-81. Riesner, *Paul's Early Period*, 57-58 argues for A.D. 30.

10. This is a minority view; most opt for 30.

11. Some dispute this. For extensive discussion see Riesner, *Paul's Early Years*, 157-211.

12. Riesner, *Paul's Early Years*, 202-11.

13. C. J. Hemer, "Pauline Chronology," in D. A. Hagner and M. J. Harris, eds., *Pauline Studies* (Grand Rapids: Eerdmans, 1980), 6-8. Hemer plausibly suggests that Paul was charged and acquitted soon after Gallio's arrival and left near the end of Gallio's incumbency to avoid a further trial by an incoming proconsul.

14. Riesner, *Paul's Early Years*, 10-25 critiques those scholars who attempt to establish a chronology for Paul apart from the Acts framework, notably Knox and Lüdemann.

"call," or from (b) his earlier visit "three years" after his conversion. Option (b), "fourteen years" + "three years" = seventeen years, seems impossible because it exhausts the available time (seventeen years) between the crucifixion and Paul's arrival in Corinth. Option (a), on the other hand, though tight, is possible.

If we deduct those fourteen years from the remaining seventeen years we are left with a space of three years. If we allow two years for the mission to and from Cyprus and southern Galatia and for Paul's travels to Corinth in 50, we are left with approximately one year. On the hypothesis that the crucifixion occurred in 33 we conclude that Saul the Pharisee was converted about a year later, in 34, and that he fled from Damascus to Jerusalem in 36 (Gal 1:18). The major conclusion we draw is that Paul was, historically speaking, an early convert. Consistent with this is the impression we get from 1 Corinthians that the risen Lord's appearance to Paul followed closely his appearance to those who were apostles before Paul (1 Cor 15:5-8). A corollary is that Paul's (surviving) letters begin to be written less than twenty years after Jesus' earthly ministry, whether 1 Thessalonians, written from Corinth in ca. 50, or Galatians, written from Antioch in ca. 48.[15]

The ramifications are considerable. Paul the early convert is chronologically the first (extant) Christian theological writer, and his christology is as advanced and developed as any within the pages of the NT.

The critical point to establish is whether Paul invented his christology or derived it from others. Our argument will be that while Paul was a "creative" theologian, his christology in all essential points was not of his making but was formulated by those who were believers before him. This would mean that the christology he articulates was formulated within that brief span between the crucifixion of Jesus and the conversion of Paul.

It may be asked why the subject of christology is raised so soon in this, a professed work of history. The answer is clear. It was christology that gave birth to Christianity, not the reverse. Furthermore, Christ gave birth to christology. The chronology drives us to this conclusion.

15. See Appendix B.

FOUR

World History
and Christian History

In Tiberius's reign all was quiet. Then, rather than put up with a statue of Gaius Caesar in the Temple as they had been ordered, the Jews flew to arms, though the rebellion came to nothing owing to the assassination of the emperor. As to Claudius, he took advantage of the death or declining fortunes of the Jewish kings to commit the government of the province to Roman knights.

Publius Cornelius Tacitus, *The Histories* 5.9

Christianity was born and nurtured within the folds of Judaism in a discrete period, between the last days of Tiberius and the early years of Claudius. Before proceeding further let us attempt to discover what was happening in the wider world at that time and try to see how events involving Christians — Christian history — linked with "secular" history.

World and Christian History (33-47)

Christianity was born in turbulent times. The imperial capital experienced a succession of upheavals that disturbed the long years of Roman "peace" under Augustus and Tiberius. After the execution of the praetorian prefect L. Aelius Sejanus in 31, the fury of Tiberius fell upon the supporters of Sejanus in the notorious "treason" trials. In March 37 Tiberius died, to be replaced by mad Caligula, who, after four violent years, was assassinated. The troubles in Rome were to a degree mirrored in the east, especially in matters relating to the Jews. In 41 Claudius, his successor, was proclaimed emperor in unusual and controversial circumstances. Nonetheless, calm was more or less restored under Claudius, including in Judea, for the moment at least.

The "secular" sources make little reference to something as unimportant as the beginnings of Christianity. Tacitus notes that the "pernicious superstition" that had been "checked for a moment" with the execution of Christ, broke out "once more . . . in Judea, the home of the disease."[1] Equally briefly Josephus speaks of the "tribe of Christians" continuing after Christ's resurrection.[2] Apart from these generalizations the "secular" authorities cast no light on the earliest years of Christianity. The movement was small at its birth. Furthermore, it was just another sect within Judaism warranting no attention. Tacitus's passing comment, quoted above, that "under Tiberius" all was "quiet" in Judea *(sub Tiberio quies)* may have been innocent, but in the light of later history (the birth of a great world religion) has proved to be rather ironic.

The Christian sources — Acts and passing references in Paul's letters — say little about external events. Acts is concerned with Christian history and Paul with self-defense. There are one or two details, but the Christian sources are as uninterested in wider events as world history is in Christian origins. Apart from Christ and the spread of the word, nothing else mattered much. Equally, world history barely notices the "birth" of what was destined to become a great world religion.

Yet from this distance both expressions of history are important. If possible to do so, it would be helpful to establish such correlations as existed. This we will attempt to do based on our chronological reckoning of the previous chapter.

Tiberius's Latter Years (33-37)

Among the problems in Palestine in the thirties were the recall of Pontius Pilatus, prefect of Judea, the humiliation and dismissal of Herod Antipas, tetrarch of Galilee, and the replacement of the long-serving high priest Caiaphas.

---

1. *Annals* 15.44.
2. *Antiquities* 18.64. While the integrity of Josephus's "testimony" is to be questioned at a number of points, the reference to the "tribe of Christians" sounds authentic.

Following a number of violent actions against the people of his province, Pilate finally overreached himself. In the year 36 Pilate ruthlessly put down an uprising among the Samaritans at Mount Gerizim. Upon their complaint to Vitellius, the newly-arrived legate of Syria, Pilate was ordered back to Rome.[4]

Herod the tetrarch, for his part, had made few mistakes to this point in his long career, which had begun in 3 B.C. In 36, however, he seriously offended legate Vitellius. At Tiberius's request, the Aramaic-speaking Herod successfully negotiated a settlement between warring factions in Parthia. Unwisely, he sent his account of the proceedings to the emperor before Vitellius had opportunity to do so. Perhaps Herod hoped to curry favor with the emperor and so acquire the adjoining tetrarchy, which had been allocated to Syria after Philip's death in 34. Herod, however, only succeeded in infuriating Vitellius.[5]

Meanwhile, Aretas IV, king of the Nabateans, had been patiently awaiting the opportunity to punish Herod for divorcing Aretas's daughter some years earlier. Possibly that moment came when Herod was in Parthia, or soon after his return. At any rate, in 36 Aretas's forces destroyed Herod's army. Josephus reports that Jews interpreted this as God's punishment for Herod's murder of John the Baptizer (in ca. 30).[6] Tiberius ordered Vitellius to wage war on the Nabateans to avenge his loyal client Herod. To that end Vitellius arrived in Jerusalem with his troops only to receive the news of Tiberius's recent death (March 16, 37). Vitellius forthwith called off the expedition against the Nabateans, to the humiliation of Herod.[7] While in Jerusalem, Vitellius deposed the incumbent high priest, Caiaphas, who had held that office for eighteen years.[8]

At only three points in 33-37 do NT texts intersect with persons also mentioned in world history. (1) Peter and John appeared before *Caiaphas* and other members of the Temple hierarchy (Acts 4:5-6). Although Acts supplies no time note, it is assumed that, since this occurred prior to the trial of Stephen, it would have happened within months of the crucifixion of Jesus in April 33. (2) In a subsequent hearing a noted scribe, *Gamaliel*, offered advice to the Sanhedrin (Acts 5:34-40). And (3) Paul's escape from

4. *Antiquities* 18.89.
5. *Antiquities* 18.105.
6. *Antiquities* 18.116-19.
7. *Antiquities* 18.135.
8. *Antiquities* 18.95.

Damascus from the ethnarch of *Aretas,* king of the Nabateans (2 Cor 11:32-33), which we have reckoned to the year 36,[9] most likely occurred after the Nabatean defeat of Herod's army. Whether before or after, however, we may assume that Jews in general were vulnerable in Aretas's kingdom, especially someone like Paul who was proclaiming the *Jewish* Messiah. Did this influence the timing of Paul's decision to return to Jerusalem (Gal 1:18)?

It is possible that Paul's first return visit to Jerusalem continued into 37, coinciding with Vitellius's critical arrival when the news came of Tiberius's death and the decision made that no action would be taken to avenge Herod. Whatever the precise chronology it is striking that the figures chiefly associated with the death of Jesus each suffered significantly at about the same time. Pilate was dismissed in 36 and Caiaphas the following year. Herod Antipas was defeated in war in 36 and publicly humiliated by Vitellius in 37. As we will see, worse was to follow for the tetrarch. Meanwhile, Tiberius the emperor under whom Christ was executed, died March 16, 37.

Chronology

	Empire	Palestine		Other
33	Jesus crucified			
34		Paul's persecutions	→	Fugitives in Damascus
				Paul in Damascus/
				Arabia 34-36
35				
36		Assault on Samaritans		Aretas defeats Herod
		Pilate dismissed		
37		Paul in Jerusalem		Paul in Syria-Cilicia
	Tiberius's death			
		Caiaphas dismissed		

Christian History in the Later years of Tiberius   The period between the death of Jesus (33) and Aretas's assault on Herod Antipas and Pilate's attack on the Samaritans (36) was one of relative calm in the wider world

9. See above, p. 26; so, too, D. A. Campbell, "An Anchor for Pauline Chronology: Paul's Flight from 'The Ethnarch of King Aretas' (2 Corinthians 11:32-33)," *JBL* 121.2 (2002), 279-302.

of Palestine. Within that brief period Christianity was born. By contrast with the relative peace in Palestine the earliest months of Christianity were anything but peaceful. The apostles' first public announcements of Jesus as Messiah provoked the wrath of the Temple hierarchy. The earliest community of believers soon split into Hebrew-Hellenist subgroups. Stephen, a Hellenist leader, was stoned for attacking the Temple, leading to Paul's campaign against the wider community of believers, most of whom were driven from Jerusalem. The "Hellenists" (Greek-speaking Jewish believers) were "scattered" further afield to less "Jewish" places — Philip to Samaria and Caesarea, others beyond the borders of Palestine, some northward to Phoenicia, Cyprus, and Antioch, others eastward to Damascus.

Paul traveled from Jerusalem to Damascus where, however, he arrived not as persecutor but as preacher of the faith he had been attempting to destroy (Gal 1:23; Acts 9:21). In Damascus, besides the Hellenists he had come to extradite, there were other believers already there on Paul's arrival; Acts gives no clue as to their origin. These events occurred within a year of the death of Jesus.[10]

Meanwhile, it is likely that Jews from Rome influenced by the apostles made their way home, bringing their new faith with them. It appears that they continued as observant Jews with ongoing membership in the synagogues of Rome. Our first certain notice is the reference to Claudius's exile of Jews from Rome, "at the instigation of Chrestus" (Suetonius Claudius 5.4), Priscilla and Aquila among them (Acts 18:1-2).[11] This is usually understood to refer to disputes in the synagogues over the claims that Jesus was the Christ.

According to Acts the conversion of Paul was followed by "a time of peace" so that "the church [of Jerusalem scattered] throughout Judea, Samaria, and Galilee . . . grew in numbers" (9:31). Since the narrative is highly selective, controlled by the missionary program in 1:8, we learn *how* the word came to Samaria and *that* it came to Judea but nothing about its arrival in Galilee.

From Acts we simply meet "the church" in Galilee, "saints" in Lydda, "disciples" in Joppa, "brothers" in Phoenicia and Samaria, a "church" in Caesarea, "disciples" in Tyre, "brothers" in Ptolemais (Acts 9:32, 36; 15:3;

---

10. See above, p. 26.

11. This is opposed by H. D. Slingerland, *Claudian Policymaking and the Early Imperial Repression of Judaism at Rome* (Atlanta: Scholars, 1997).

18:22; 21:4, 7). We know next to nothing of their respective origins except to infer that Philip "the evangelist" and the apostles Peter and John were somehow involved. Paul refers to "the churches of Judea that are in Christ" and "the churches of God in Judea that are in Christ Jesus" (Gal 1:22; 1 Thess 2:14). We assume these arose under the aegis of Peter, apostle to the circumcised (Gal 2:7-8).

To the north, by the mid-thirties the faith was being taught in Antioch among Jews by the first wave of displaced Hellenists. Presumably the Hellenist Nicolaus "the proselyte of Antioch" was among them (cf. Acts 6:5). But we have no further details about the origins of Christianity in what was soon to become the second major center of Christianity. A second wave of displaced Hellenists, men from Cyrene and Cyprus, subsequently arrived in Antioch. These, however, also spoke the gospel to Gentiles. It appears from Acts that these Jews and "Greeks" who believed met together and attracted the attention of the people of Antioch, who called them *Christianoi* (Acts 11:19-26). These developments may have occurred within a short time of Paul's persecutions in 33-34.

While the word of God was spreading in Judea and Antioch, Paul was preaching in Damascus, then in Nabatea, then once more in Damascus. Again, we have no details, including whether or not Paul established churches at this time, though Acts refers to his "disciples" (9:25). Paul's first return visit to Jerusalem would have occurred near the time of Pilate's dismissal and Herod's defeat by Aretas. Whether this visit coincided with Vitellius's arrival we do not know. Nor do we know precisely how long Paul remained in Judea before journeying to Tarsus. Various hints in his letters and in Acts suggest that he remained in Judea for some time before traveling north, out of the land of Israel (1 Thess 2:14-16; Acts 26:20).

It is difficult to overestimate the effects of Paul's assault on Christians in Jerusalem, provoked as it was by Stephen's attack on the Temple and "Moses." Believers from Jerusalem were scattered throughout Judea, Galilee, and Samaria and beyond the borders of the land of Israel to the safety of Damascus and Antioch. Had these events not occurred, Christianity may have remained a Jerusalem-based sect to be swept away in the Roman invasion of 66-70 together with groups like the Essenes and the Sadducees.

The Principate of Caligula (37-41)

As we have noted, in mid-37 Vitellius was in Jerusalem when news reached him that Tiberius had died and that Caligula[12] had been proclaimed emperor. This was well received in the holy city; sacrifices were duly offered in the Temple for the new ruler.[13]

The next year and a half passed quietly enough before events took a dramatic turn. During that period the most significant occurrence was the changed fortunes of Herod Agrippa, grandson of Herod the Great and nephew and brother-in-law of Herod Antipas the tetrarch. Agrippa had been raised in Rome and was a longtime friend of both Caligula and Claudius but not, however, of Tiberius. In a typical act of folly Agrippa had incurred the wrath of Tiberius, for which he was imprisoned for six months. On his accession, however, Caligula not only released Agrippa but appointed him king of the territory of Philip, which, since Philip's death in 34, had been assigned to the province of Syria. This brought insult to the already injured Herod Antipas, who had long brooded over Tiberius's decision not to add this territory to Galilee-Perea and even longer over the failure of both Augustus and Tiberius to give him the title of king.

In 39, goaded now by Herodias, Antipas set off to Rome to plead his case with Caligula for a royal title. Agrippa, however, anticipated this eventuality and wrote to the emperor giving damning details of the tetrarch's enlarged military arsenal and of plots with the Parthians against Rome. For his trouble Caligula forthwith dismissed and exiled Herod Antipas and Herodias, appointing Agrippa as king over the deposed Herod's territory as well. Herod Antipas had gained nothing and lost everything. The unexpected rise of Agrippa as a king under Caligula would later be extended dramatically under Claudius, bringing in turn a wave of persecution against the disciples in Jerusalem.

Meanwhile in the autumn of 38 serious riots began in Alexandria as the wider community attacked the large Jewish population. According to both Josephus and Philo the emperor himself, who now regarded himself as a god, was behind these attacks.[14] Presumably, Caligula's self-deification

---

12. The emperor Gaius is often known by this nickname, given in childhood, "Little Boot."

13. So Philo, *Embassy to Gaius,* 32.

14. Philo, *Embassy to Gaius,* 75-77, 93-118, 346; Josephus, *Antiquities* 18.256-57; 10.4. Cf. Dio Cassius 59.26, 28; Suetonius, *Caligula,* 22.

became widely known by Jews in Palestine and the Diaspora, including by Jews who believed in Jesus as Messiah. Flaccus, the governor of Egypt, who had been evenhanded to the Jews under Tiberius, now facilitated the pogroms under Caligula, once the initial quiet period had lapsed.

The spark that lit the flames of civil war in Alexandria was the visit in 38 of King Agrippa, as he was returning to Palestine from Rome. The Greeks dressed an insane man as a king and, pantomime-like, addressed him as *marin*, "Lord." Then the mob erected statues of the emperor as a god in the synagogues. Flaccus passed edicts depriving Jews of previously held citizenship rights and sanctioned persecution of Jews. Jewish women were compelled to eat pork before a crowd in a theater. Horrific attacks on the Jewish population then followed, including upon the Jewish Council. The crisis reached a climax in 38 and subsided to a degree when Flaccus was replaced by Vitrasius Pollio. Matters remained deeply unsettled in Alexandria, however, until the death of Caligula and the accession of Claudius.

Antioch, capital of Syria, was also affected by serious disturbances at this time. As a large city with a major Jewish component in its population, Antioch was marred by sustained anti-Semitism. Our major source on the troubles during Caligula's years is the *Chronicle* of Malalas, a later authority, whose details are obscure. It appears, though, that many Jews were killed and numerous synagogues put to the torch. According to Malalas a Jewish counter-attack sanctioned by the High Priest in Jerusalem left many Gentiles dead.[15]

Meanwhile, troubles broke out in Judea in the winter of 39 and lasted more than a year.[16] In Jamnia on the coastal plain, Gentiles had set up a statue of Caligula that, however, Jews pulled down.[17] Deeply annoyed, the emperor issued orders that a statue of himself as a god be erected in the Temple in Jerusalem.

Anticipating a hostile reaction, Caligula ordered Petronius, legate of Syria, to bring half his army (two legions plus auxiliaries) to Palestine and to "engage in war without fail."[18] Most likely Caligula's motivation was to provoke war and so destroy large numbers of the Jewish population.[19]

---

15. See M. Hengel and A. M. Schwemer, *Paul between Damascus and Antioch* (Louisville: Westminster/John Knox, 1997), 184-91.

16. Parallel accounts are found in Josephus, *War* 2.184-203; *Antiquities* 18.261-309.

17. Philo, *Embassy to Gaius*, 200.

18. *Antiquities* 18.262.

19. Philo, *Embassy to Gaius*, 201; Josephus, *Antiquities* 18.262.

While the statue was being prepared in Sidon, "tens of thousands" of Jews met with Petronius in Ptolemais pleading with the legate not to proceed. Recognizing that many thousands of Jews faced slaughter, Petronius traveled to Tiberias to assess Jewish attitudes in another place, but with the same result. An equally vast crowd pleaded that they would face death rather than agree to a statue being erected in the Temple.

A delegation led by Aristobulus, brother of Agrippa, persuaded Petronius to write to Caligula pointing out that the killing of many Jews would leave the land unsown so that with no harvest, banditry would follow and no taxes would be paid to Rome. Caligula replied to Petronius by ordering him to take his own life for failing to carry out his orders. Other news intervened, however, informing Petronius of the assassination of Caligula early in 41, averting the crisis.

Caligula's principate brought problems for Jews that were without precedent within the rule of their Julio-Claudian masters. They inevitably saw Caligula's action as a repeat of the assault by Antiochus Epiphanes two centuries earlier. Christian Jews in Antioch would have shared with other Jews significant exposure to violence in a context of severe anti-Semitism. Perhaps their allegiance to the Messiah Jesus, which had earned them the tag *Christianoi,* also attracted hostility from other Jews. At any rate, when Paul came to Antioch with Barnabas in the mid-40s, it is likely that this major city proved to be no easy place to preach Christ, either to Jews or to Gentiles.

Christian Jews in Palestine, however, were different. They were part of a wider community that together shared the crisis of Petronius's invasion and the terrible choice between the desecration of the Temple or genocide. Doubtless this was a time of heightened apocalyptic expression in the synagogues. Jesus' prophecies concerning the End may have been understood as nearing fulfillment in the years 39-40.[20] His words, "When you see the desolating sacrilege standing where he must not (let the lector understand), then let those in Judea flee to the mountains . . ." (Mark 13:14), may have been shaped in their present form by the crisis of 39-40.[21] First, the neuter subject "desolating sacrifice" demands agreement from the participle "standing," which, however, is masculine. Someone has manipulated the grammar to say that the "desolating sacrilege" is a *man.* Sec-

---

20. G. Theissen, *The Gospels in Context* (Minneapolis: Fortress, 1991), 151-65.
21. Contra Hengel and Schwemer, *Paul,* 181.

ond, the words "let the lector understand" instruct the reader in church to explain Jesus' words to the assembled members in light of a current circumstance.[22] Do these words point to the Roman emperor Caligula as that *man?*

Paul's Second Letter to the Thessalonians appears to allude to the same end-time tradition from Jesus,[23] but reflects a more peaceful situation of a decade later. Paul speaks of "the man of lawlessness" who will "take his seat in the temple" (2 Thess 2:4). The Thessalonians have been agitated by reports that the Day of the Lord had come already. Paul assures them against this on the basis that the "man of lawlessness" has not desecrated the Temple, most likely referring to Caligula's failed attempt in 40.

Chronology

Empire	Palestine	Other
37 Caligula proclaimed Agrippa released		Paul in Syria-Cilicia
38		pogrom in Alexandria Agrippa in Alexandria
	Agrippa made king of Gaulanitis	
39	Antipas exiled	
	Agrippa made king of Galilee	troubles in Antioch
40	crisis in Judea	
41 Caligula's death		

Christian History in the Principate of Caligula   We cannot determine the exact time frame for the "growth in numbers" of disciples in Judea, Galilee, and Samaria referred to in Acts 9:31. Clearly it follows the cessation of Paul's persecutions. It is equally clear that Philip "the evangelist" and apostles Peter and John were major participants in this "growth." Again, the conversion of the God-fearer Cornelius and his household marked a major climax in Peter's apostolate in the land of Israel. But when did Peter travel to Caesarea for that critical encounter? Most likely there is a connec-

22. See above, pp. 34-35.

23. D. Wenham, *The Rediscovery of Jesus' Eschatological Discourse* (Sheffield: JSOT, 1984), 295-96.

tion between Peter eating with these Gentiles and the outbreak of persecution under Agrippa that ended the life of James the son of Zebedee as it would have ended Peter's life had he not escaped.

But did the Cornelius event occur before or after the year 40, when Caligula sought to desecrate the Temple? Most likely Peter's visit to Cornelius occurred prior to that nationwide crisis. For Peter to have eaten with a Gentile after 40 would have led to immediate death. It seems more likely that Peter went there earlier (by 38?), but many remembered Peter's action and acted against him when the opportunity arose. That opportunity came with the appointment of Agrippa as king of Judea in the year 41.

The Principate of Claudius (41-54)

Nowhere is the connection between world history and Christian history clearer than in the early years of the emperor Claudius.

Herod Agrippa, grandson of Herod the Great, had grown up in Rome as a boyhood friend of both Caligula and his uncle, Claudius. As we have noted, Caligula made Agrippa king first over Philip's tetrarchy (in 37) and then over Antipas's tetrarchy (in 39). Agrippa happened to be in Rome at the time of the plot that removed Caligula (January 24, 41). While the Roman senators may have hoped for a return to the Republic, the praetorians proclaimed Claudius and imposed their decision on the Senate. According to Josephus, Agrippa acted as Claudius's envoy to the Senate to assure them that Claudius would rule virtuously and not as a tyrant.[24]

Claudius's most urgent task on accession was to bring calm and reassurance to his Jewish subjects. Jews were to be found in large numbers in most cities in the east and may have represented 10 percent of the population of the empire. Alexandria, the major city in the east, had been brought to the brink of civil war. Possibly the situation in Antioch was similarly grave. The people of Judea were prepared to face wholesale slaughter over the desecration of the Temple.

According to Josephus, Claudius issued a decree to Alexandria and "Syria" (that is, Antioch) reaffirming the rights of the Jews as discrete com-

---

24. In *War* 2.206 Agrippa has a passive role and Claudius an active role whereas in *Antiquities* 19.239 the roles are reversed. Most likely the later account is apologetically motivated due to Josephus's association with Agrippa's son Agrippa II (see *Life* 364; *Apion* 1.51).

munities presided over by their own ethnarchs.[25] Josephus stated that the emperor issued a similar decree to "the rest of the world."[26] We are fortunate in having Claudius's own "Letter to the Alexandrians" written in 41 in response to a delegation from Alexandria. Claudius demands that the Alexandrians "dishonor none of the rights observed by [the Jews] in the worship of their god and allow them to observe their customs as in the time of the deified Augustus." As to the Jews, however, Claudius ordered the Jews "not to agitate for more privileges than they previously possessed and in the future not to send a separate embassy as if they lived in a separate city."[27] In short, while Josephus gives an impression that Claudius strongly vindicated the Jews, the emperor's own letter merely maintains their status quo from the time of Augustus with warnings not to seek additional rights.

The emperor's approach to the Jews of Palestine, however, was necessarily different. Judea was their homeland; they were not a minority living in a Jewish quarter presided over by an ethnarch, as in the cities of the Diaspora. Thus Claudius fell back on classical Roman policy. The emperor appointed an indigenous person as a "client" ruler. One person was well qualified for that task in the eyes of Claudius. Herod Agrippa was a member of the Herodian dynasty, he had been educated in Rome, and he was Claudius's trusted "friend" (extant coins bear the words "Great King Agrippa, Friend of Caesar").

Once appointed, Agrippa found it necessary to accommodate both his Jewish and Gentile subjects. For example, at what proved to be a fatal occasion, he presented himself in public as a Hellenistic god-king to the predominantly Greek community of Caesarea Maritima. For the most part, however, Agrippa favored the Jews against the Gentiles. Again, by way of example, he instigated severe action through Petronius against Gentiles who installed a statue of Claudius in a synagogue in Dora.[28] It is difficult, however, to penetrate Josephus's rather romantic account to identify the king's actual attitudes to these respective groups.

There can be little doubt that Agrippa presented himself to his Jewish subjects as an observant Jew. Josephus summarizes Agrippa in glowing terms:

25. Josephus, *Antiquities* 19.279-85.

26. *Antiquities* 19.286.

27. N. Lewis and M. Reinhold, *Roman Civilization* II (New York: Harper, 1955), 366-68 (LCL adapted).

28. *Antiquities* 19.301-8.

He enjoyed residing in Jerusalem and did so constantly, and he scru-
pulously observed the traditions of the people. He neglected no rite of
purification and no day passed without the prescribed sacrifice.[29]

Though much later, a scatter of Talmudic references to Agrippa are likewise favorable.[30] Surviving coins minted under Agrippa point to an observant Jewish king.

Christian History in the Early Years of Claudius's Principate   Three
remarkable linkages between "salvation-history" and "world history" are
found in references in Acts to "Herod the king" (that is, Herod Agrippa I)
and to the emperor Claudius. First, Acts refers to the king's assault on
"some who belonged to the church," including the execution of James the
son of Zebedee. When Agrippa "saw that this pleased the Jews" he arrested
Peter also (Acts 12:1-3). The chronological reference ("about this time") is
vague, though the arrest of Peter at the time of Passover is specific.

The assault on these leaders after the nationwide crisis of the year 40
was not coincidental. James's brother John and Peter had baptized Samaritans six years (?) earlier. More recently, and more pointedly, Peter had entered the house of a Gentile in Caesarea Maritima (cf. Acts 11:3). These
were not crimes under Roman provincial administration, and capital punishment apart from the prefect's jurisdiction was illegal. Under a Jewish
king, however, it was different; he had the power of the sword. Furthermore, that king was appointed to bring peace to Judea, which implied the
freedom to "please the Jews."

After his escape Peter fled, though to which location we are not told.
It is clear, however, that from this moment he was no longer the leader of
the Twelve. Indeed, the Twelve, having lost James the son of Zebedee, were
no more. With Gal 2:1-10 as our guide, it appears that by about 48 the leaders of the Jerusalem church were called "pillars." Three are mentioned —
James (Jesus' brother), Cephas (that is, Peter), and John — though there
may have been others.

Shortly afterward Peter is in Antioch, apparently having permanently left Palestine to be a missionary at large. Gal 2:11-14 mentions an
embassy "from James" to Antioch. This, together with his presidency at the

---

29. *Antiquities* 19.331.
30. *Ketubim* 17d; *Sota* 41b.

Jerusalem Council (Acts 15:6-21), indicates that by then he was a kind of primate of Israel, based in Jerusalem. M. Bockmuehl suggests that his jurisdiction went as far north as Antioch, making Jewish believers in Antioch also subject to him.[31] This would explain his "interference" in the affairs of the church in Antioch.

The second linkage between the two "histories" is the death of Agrippa I. Acts and Josephus record the place and circumstances of his demise in broadly similar terms, though a few critical details are different.[32] The king was making a public appearance in the seaside theater in Caesarea. His self-presentation invited those present to hail him as a god, which they did. Acts states that he was struck down forthwith, while Josephus says that he died five days later.

The blow to Jewish hopes in Palestine and beyond is difficult to imagine. While Agrippa's sincerity as a Jew is open to question, there is no reason to question that the general Jewish perception of him was positive. The Jews had suffered thirty-five years of Roman provincial rule, with great suffering under Pilate. This was followed by massive difficulties under Caligula, first in Alexandria and Antioch and then in 40 in Judea itself. The tyrant's death and replacement by Claudius must have appeared a godsend indeed. Even better was the appointment of a Jewish client king. Now all that was ended with Agrippa's death, aged fifty-four.

Claudius did not appoint Agrippa's son in succession but reannexed Judea and placed it under procurators with a fiscal as well as military role. Under the first such governor, an apocalyptic prophet named Theudas led a multitude to the Jordan with the promise that its waters would part, allowing him to lead his followers to the wilderness.[33] He was cut down by the procurator Cuspius Fadus's legionaries, and a new very bad chapter in Jewish history began.

The third linkage is the "famine" that "occurred in the time of Claudius" (Acts 11:28), which began in about 46-47 and finds explicit and implicit reference in "world history."[34] The famine had catastrophic effect in

---

31. M. Bockmuehl, "Antioch and James the Just," in B. Chilton and C. A. Evans, eds., *James the Just and Christian Origins* (Leiden: Brill, 1999), 155-98.

32. *Antiquities* 19.343-52; Acts 12:20-23.

33. See below, pp. 199-200.

34. Suetonius, *Claudius* 18.2; Dio Cassius, *History* 60.11; Tacitus, *Annals* 12.43; Josephus, *Antiquities* 20.101. See F. F. Bruce, *The Acts of the Apostles: The Greek Text with Introduction and Commentary* (Grand Rapids: Eerdmans, 1990³), 276.

the whole eastern Mediterranean. Yet Acts refers to it for no other reason than the opportunity it provided for Barnabas and Paul to visit Jerusalem.

Conclusion

These were the years in which Christianity was born and grew. Not for these first believers, however, was the protection and nurture of caring parents as for a newly born infant. Events in the wider world, as recorded in "world history," were calamitous. Equally, events in Christian history were turbulent and full of pain which, however, the first Christians met with courage, resolve, and determined leadership.

Through these troubled years the apostles formulated the "faith," proclaimed that "faith," and established "assemblies" of believers inside and outside the land of Israel that belonged to the Messiah, Jesus.

We are struck by this: world history, apart from generalized comments in Tacitus and Josephus, makes no reference to the new "child," Christianity. It is preoccupied with the passing parade of emperors, governors, and high priests. For its part, Christian history in the book of Acts is focused on the continuing works of Jesus, the now-risen Christ. For those first Christians the events of the wider world are largely inconsequential and only noticed if they bear in some way on the progress of the word.

FIVE

Mission to Greece:
Paul's First Letter
to the Thessalonians

Setting sail therefore from Troas, we made direct voyage to Samothrace, and the following day to Neapolis.

Acts 16:11

By broad agreement the earliest (or second earliest) surviving document of Christianity is Paul's First Letter to the Thessalonians, written ca. 50, that is, less than two decades after Jesus.[1] As an early written source for Christianity it is of special interest to historians. Its text is uncorrupted in transmission and its authorship not disputed. Its dating (50), provenance (Corinth), and destination (Thessalonica) are secure. This is the right place to begin historical investigation into Christianity "after Jesus."

Over-familiarity with the NT blunts the interest that the earliness of this document should inspire. Imagine the excitement if 1 Thessalonians had been found for the first time in a Greek monastery. Does this document agree or disagree with the teachings of later ones? In particular, does the letter portray Jesus as a prophet or holy man or as "Lord"? Does it indicate the prehistory of the beliefs taught by the writer? Do we have any sense of what might have happened in the years between Jesus and this letter?

One thing at least is clear from the outset. Though it was written for

---

1. See p. 24 above for the date of the crucifixion and Appendix B for the dating of Galatians.

42

Gentiles, its author, Paul, was a Jew. 1 Thessalonians is Jewish Christianity adapted for non-Jewish readers. Its messianic and apocalyptic categories of thought are thoroughly Jewish.

Echoes of Mission Preaching in Thessalonica

It is evident that Paul had recently engaged in mission work in this Macedonian city. Clearly, the letter is written to deal with issues that have arisen in the meantime.

Echoes of Paul's recent mission preaching include:

You turned to God from idols . . .
and to wait for his Son from heaven,
whom he raised from the dead,
Jesus who delivers us from the wrath to come   (1:9-10)

Later as Paul expands on this "deliverance from *wrath*" it is clear that this teaching too was part of his initial mission catechesis.

God has not destined us for *wrath,*
But to obtain salvation
through *(dia)* our Lord Jesus Christ,
who died for *(hyper)* us. . . .   (5:9-10)

It is worth summarizing the elements of mission teaching that underlie these two brief statements:

God is "Father" (cf. 1:1: ". . . to the church of the Thessalonians in God *the Father*").
Jesus is "Son [of God]" (1:10: *huios autou*), the "Lord," and "Christ" (1:1: ". . . the church . . . in . . . the *Lord* Jesus *Christ*").
In regard to the *past* Jesus died for *(hyper)* us, and in regard to the *future*, deliverance from wrath and obtaining salvation is through *(dia)* him.

In the years to come in both his preaching and writing Paul will repeatedly replay, adapt, and expand these fundamentals in the face of varying pastoral circumstances. Nonetheless, Paul's christology remains uniform throughout. Because the church is "in Christ" *(en Christo)* his vicarious death "for" *(hyper)* its members delivers them from the eschatological wrath "through" *(dia)* him. For Paul, then, salvation/deliverance from wrath is christological from first to last. While the vocabulary of righteousness/justification is not used in 1 Thessalonians, Paul will move to that doctrine whenever it is necessary to counter "works" (man-based) righteousness (see e.g., Rom 3:24-25). According to S. Kim, "the doctrine of justification by grace and through faith is materially present in First Thessalonians as a whole and implicitly contained in the echo of Paul's gospel preaching in 1:9b-10."[2] As we will point out shortly, the range of christological and soteriological terms that appears in 1 Thessalonians appears also, and at greater length, in the correspondence to the church at Corinth, the next major center for the Pauline mission.

Paul preached and wrote that Jesus was the divine Son, whose death delivers his people from the eschatological wrath. What is the origin of this teaching?

This Teaching Was Not Novel

Several things surprise us as we read First Thessalonians.

Its Well-Developed Epistolary "Shape"[3]

Apart from the standard Hellenistic opening "A to B, grace and peace" followed by a "thanksgiving" for the readers, the author[4] devotes the first half of the letter to "narrative" matters.[5] Only then does he address doctrinal and moral issues current in Thessalonica. The concluding prayer, "The *grace* of the Lord Jesus Christ be with you," is liturgically well rounded and probably completes the *inclusio* begun at the opening sentence (". . . to the church of the Thessalonians . . . *grace* to you").

Various suggestions have been offered as to the precise literary genre

2. S. Kim, *Paul and the New Perspective* (Grand Rapids: Eerdmans, 2002), 98.

3. See R. F. Collins, "I Command That This Letter Be Read," in K. P. Donfried and J. Beutler, eds., *The Thessalonians Debate* (Grand Rapids: Eerdmans, 2000), 324-25.

4. Paul attaches the names of Silvanus and Timothy to his own, but he is the author.

5. Forty-three of the eighty-nine verses.

of 1 Thessalonians, including that it is an "epideictic" letter.[6] The point is that the letter is carefully arranged and consistent with known epistolary formats, however it is classified. Later letters, whatever their particular idiosyncrasies, recognizably develop from 1 Thessalonians. A similar observation might be made about Galatians if it were recognized as the first-written of the extant Pauline corpus.

Here, then, we make an important comment. This author is no novice in his mode of communication to a distant church in its troubles. We know of no letters from Paul's "unknown years." It is remarkable that such an early letter is so polished a medium for its judicious pastoral, theological, and ethical advice. Possibly there were earlier letters by Paul (now lost), more experimental and less well developed in form and content.

Its Presupposition of Recent and Earlier Mission Work

This letter presupposes extensive mission work in the provinces of Greece, Macedonia, and Achaia. The "apostles of Christ" (2:6) had come from *Philippi* to *Thessalonica* (2:2). In *Athens* Paul dispatched his coworker Timothy back to *Thessalonica* (3:1); Timothy has now joined Paul in *Corinth* (cf. Acts 18:5). From Acts we know of churches in Philippi, Thessalonica, Berea, and Corinth. Clearly there had been extensive mission work in the provinces of Greece. 1 Thessalonians also mentions Jewish *ekklēsiai* ("the churches of God in Christ Jesus that are in *Judea*," 2:14). These messianic assemblies had been in existence from the mid-30s, that is, for at least a decade and a half when Paul wrote the letter (see Gal 1:22; cf. Acts 9:31-32).

Paul Reminds the Thessalonians of His Mission Teaching

Paul begins the "moral" section of the letter with "we beseech and exhort you in the Lord Jesus" (4:1). What follows, however, is not new teaching but

---

6. So Donfried (citing F. W. Hughes) in K. P. Donfried and I. H. Marshall, *The Theology of the Shorter Pauline Letters* (Cambridge: Cambridge University Press, 1993), 3-7. See also Collins, "I Command," 325-26.

a reinforcement of the instruction "delivered" during the mission "entry" (*eisodos*, 1:9; 2:1) to Thessalonica.

> . . . that
> just as you *received (paralabete)* from us
> how you ought to *walk (peripatein)* and to please God,
> just as you are doing,
> you do so more and more.
> For you know what *instructions (parangelias)* we *gave (edōkamen)*
> you through the Lord Jesus.

This well-rounded statement, expressed in rabbinic terms ("received," "walk," "instruction," "gave"),[7] suggests mature practice in church founding. By the time Paul visited Thessalonica he had been a missioner for a decade and a half.

It is not possible to reconstruct fully the apostles' initial teaching. The only items mentioned are those Paul must revisit, based on Timothy's report to Paul in Corinth about current problems and questions[8] in Thessalonica. These include:

> the inevitability of suffering as the Lord did (inferred from "as we told you *beforehand*," 3:3-4; cf. 1:6; 2:15),
>
> the necessity of sexual fidelity (inferred from "you know what instructions we *gave* you," 4:2, and "as we told you before and *forewarned* you," 4:6),
>
> the necessity to work so as to be self-supporting (inferred from ". . . to work with your own hands, even as we *charged* you," 4:11), and
>
> the timing of the parousia (inferred from "you have *no need* [for me] to write to you," 5:1, and "you yourselves *know* well that the day of the Lord will come like a thief . . . ," 5:2).

---

7. See also 1 Cor 7:10; 11:23; 15:1, 3; Gal 1:9; Phil 4:9; Col 2:6; 1 Thess 4:11; 2 Thess 3:6.

8. From 1 Thess 4:9 it appears that the Thessalonians sought guidance through Timothy to Paul (orally or by letter) regarding "love of the brothers." Paul encourages them that their love is in such evidence that there is no necessity for him to write anything (cf. 5:1). This is contra Collins ("I Command," 320-22), who argues that the words "you do not need" were a rhetorical technique used for emphasis *(praeteritio)*.

We only know about these items since they needed repeating and reinforcing at the time. In no other letter does Paul so often appeal to what the readers already "know" (1:5; 2:1, 2, 5, 11; 3:3, 4; 4:2; 5:2) because of earlier catechetical instruction. Clearly there was an extensive pattern of teaching, doctrinal and moral, that Paul and his associates gave at the time of their mission "entry." It is unlikely that Paul formulated these instructions only at the time of the mission in Macedonia and Achaia.

His appeal for the members to "respect those who . . . are over you in the Lord" and to those leaders to "admonish and encourage" various groups (5:12-13) presupposes that Paul or his coworkers established a structure of "order" in the Thessalonian assembly. Equally, Paul's appeal was necessary because of some current functional failure in their "order." As with other matters presently discussed we assume that such arrangements were not new but went back earlier in Paul's apostolate.

The parousia of the Lord is conspicuous in 1 Thessalonians (2:19; 3:13; 4:15; 5:23).[9] In one passage it is closely connected with Jesus' death and resurrection (4:14). Most likely Paul's words pastorally adapt a preformed credo, as evidenced in that it is introduced by "we believe," it is introduced by the citation convention "that" *(hoti),* and it is expressed symmetrically. Its original form may have run as follows:

> We believe
> > that
> > > Jesus died and rose again
> > and that
> > > God will bring with Jesus
> > > those who have fallen asleep.

As with other teachings given at the mission "entry" *(eisodos)* in Thessalonica, it is reasonable to assume these were formulated earlier and used in earlier missions.

In this regard, we cannot fail to notice the many references in 1 Thessalonians to "the gospel."[10] The apostles "spoke," "proclaimed," and "shared" the gospel (2:2, 9; 3:8) which had been "entrusted to" them by

---

9. See J. R. Harrison, "Paul and the Imperial Gospel in Thessaloniki," *JSNT* 25.1 (2002), 71-96.

10. The cognate verb occurs in a different sense in 3:6.

God (2:4) whom they "served . . . in the gospel" (3:2). The gospel as a personalized subject "came to them . . . in power" (1:5). Likewise the synonym "word" occurs often, whether as "word of God" (2:13), "word of the Lord" (1:8; 4:15), or simply "the word" (1:6). There is an existent, clearly formulated theology of the "the gospel"/"the word of God" and its contents underlying these references.

When and Where Did Paul Formulate These Teachings?

Our thesis is that the teaching revisited in 1 Thessalonians was not of recent formulation but must predate the letter.

When and where did Paul establish his catecheses? Was it Antioch? Some argue that Paul was influenced by the theology of the Antiochene church through his ministry there from the mid-40s.[11] Further, if, as Fitzmyer holds, Luke was based in Antioch,[12] his journey with Paul from Troas to Philippi (Acts 16:10-16) as well as their likely association beforehand would have provided further opportunity for an Antiochene influence on Paul.

If Acts was our only guide we might think Antioch was the center of Paul's world mission, at least initially. After narrating Paul's persecutions and conversion in Palestine, Acts firmly locates him in Tarsus and Antioch, from which he went forth westward in his missions to the Gentiles. This would tend to support the view that the author of Acts was Antioch-based and lend weight to the possibility that Paul was influenced by the theological ideas of that church.

When we turn to Paul's letters, however, there is a different perspective. According to Paul it was "from *Jerusalem* in an arc to Illyricum that he fulfilled the gospel" (Rom 15:19). Paul dates God's mission call to "proclaim the Son [of God] to the Gentiles" from the Damascus event (Gal 1:16). To that end, he immediately "went away to Arabia" (Gal 1:17). In Jerusalem in the mid-40s the "pillars" James, Cephas, and John recognized that he had been entrusted with the "gospel for the uncircumcision." Paul im-

---

11. Contra Donfried, *Shorter Pauline Letters,* 65-66, 72, who argues that 1 Thessalonians is "early" Paul, as influenced by the Hellenistic church and the church in Antioch.

12. See p. 192 below.

plies that they confirmed the legitimacy of that "apostolate" to Gentiles in parallel with Peter's "apostolate" to Jews (Gal 2:7-9). According to Paul, they declared that he had "not been running in vain" (Gal 2:2), that is, his christology was consistent with theirs.

This is confirmed in the preformed tradition Paul "received" that he quotes in 1 Cor 15:1-3. That tradition lists those to whom the risen Lord "appeared," including Cephas, the Twelve, and James (15:5-7). These men preach the same gospel as Paul himself (15:11). Paul is implying that the Christ-tradition he "received" and "preaches" was formulated originally by apostles before him.

Where, then, did Paul "receive" this preformed tradition about the death and resurrection of Christ? Most likely Paul equates that tradition with "the faith" he had "set out to destroy" as a persecutor of "the church of God" (Gal 1:13, 23). There are two possibilities, both of them Jerusalem-based, originating soon after the first Easter.[13] The first is Damascus at his baptism, as the basis of his proclamation of Jesus as "the Son of God" (that is, as "the Christ") in the synagogues (Acts 9:20, 22). In this case, the tradition had been formulated in Jerusalem beforehand and brought to Damascus. Alternatively, Paul received the tradition from Cephas and James on his first return visit to the holy city three years later (Gal 1:18-20). This, however, is less likely than Damascus since he first began to fulfill his missionary "call" in and from Damascus.

Perhaps it will be objected that the tradition Paul quotes is in Greek whereas the earliest Jerusalem church members (the "Hebrews") were Aramaic-speaking. This, however, is not a telling objection since there were also Greek-speaking Jewish believers ("Hellenists") in Jerusalem. Most likely, too, among the "Hebrew" Jewish believers were those like Barnabas and Silvanus who spoke Greek. Paul himself, though a "Hebrew of Hebrews," was accomplished in the Greek language, both spoken and written.

Paul traces the beginnings of his "apostolate" to Damascus, to an event that must have been quite close in time to the first Easter.[14] His exposure to the church in Antioch occurred a decade after his initial "call" and in any case was relatively brief. In any case, the foundation members of the church in Antioch were "Hellenists" from Jerusalem (Acts 11:19). Bousset

---

13. See M. de Jonge, "Original Setting," in R. Collins, ed., *The Thessalonian Correspondence* (Leuven: Peeters, 1990), 234.

14. See p. 26.

and Bultmann portrayed Antioch as a Gentile-dominated church where polytheistic ideas were generated and by which Paul was influenced. Paul's references to Jesus as "Lord" *(kyrios)* and "Son (of God)" *(huios)* are deemed to have arisen there. This view is, however, without basis, as Hengel has demonstrated.[15]

In sum, then, the evidence points to a Jerusalem source of the pre-formed traditions about the death and resurrection of the Messiah and the institution of the Lord's Supper. Most likely, too, Paul's knowledge of various "words of the Lord" echoed in 1 Thessalonians[16] went back to this earliest period. The Jerusalem-based influence was early and significant and the Antioch-based influence was late and arguably minimal. Paul shaped and re-shaped these primal traditions as catecheses for the churches of his mission, including those in Thessalonica and other cities of the Greek mission.

The Christology of the Corinthian Correspondence

Our argument is that the christology of 1 Thessalonians was not recently established, but went back to the Damascus event, when Paul received the *apokalypsis* (revelation) of Christ from heaven and the *paradosis* (tradition) from those who had been instructed by his apostolic predecessors. By this reasoning Paul's thinking was effectively settled by the time he arrived in the Greek provinces.

Very soon after his mission in Macedonia Paul preached in Corinth and wrote several letters to that church. It follows that his preaching and letters to the Corinthians would be consistent with his preaching and letters to the Thessalonians. Paul's theological understanding deepened but did not change fundamentally over the next few years between 1 Thessalonians and 2 Corinthians.

Suggestions that Paul's theology underwent considerable theological development at this time should be heard with caution. First, it is easy to forget that Paul had been an apostle for many years before his mission to Greece. During that period he had preached extensively in Damascus, Ara-

---

15. Between Jesus and Paul (Philadelphia: Fortress, 1983), 30-47.

16. 1 Thess 4:15 (Matt 24:27); 4:16 (Matt 24:31); 4:17 (Mark 13:36; Matt 25:6); 5:3-7 (Luke 21:34-36; Mark 13:35-37). See S. Kim, "The Jesus Tradition in 1 Thess 4:13-5:11," *NTS* 48 (2002), 225-42 for the argument that Paul must write these words because the Thessalonians misunderstand his original transmission of words of the Lord about the parousia.

bia, "Jerusalem and throughout all the country of Judea,"[17] Antioch, and Cyprus; established churches in Cilicia[18] and southern Galatia; and engaged in vigorous debates with church leaders. By the time he came to Greece Paul was an experienced theologian, preacher, and missionary.

Moreover, he showed evidence of a degree of evangelistic flexibility in addressing Jews as opposed to Gentiles, as seen in speeches in Acts to Jews, on one hand, and to Gentiles, on the other. Pastorally, a similar secure adaptability can be seen *within* letters like 2 Corinthians and *between* letters, for example, Galatians and 1 Corinthians. Differing emphases within and between letters is evidence of a mature mind applied to changing pastoral contexts rather than to evolution in his ideas.

Further, Paul's letters are not straightforward Pauline constructions. We know of different co-senders and amanuenses, though their precise roles in the letter-writing is uncertain. It is possible they may have given letters different shapes, emphases, and "texture." Changes in content are more likely to be due to differing participants in the letter-writing rather than intellectual rethinking.

Finally, analysis of mission preaching in Greece echoed in 1 Thessalonians and 1 and 2 Corinthians indicates direct correspondence with echoes of gospel preaching.

	1 Thessalonians	1 Corinthians	2 Corinthians
Son of God	1:10		1:19
Lord	1:1	16:22	4:5
Christ	1:1	1:23; 15:1, 3	2:11

Clearly, Paul proclaimed Jesus as "Son," "Lord," and "Christ" in Corinth as he had proclaimed him a few months earlier in Thessalonica. The Corinthian letters arose out of the mission to Greece and were written for the churches that were established in that mission. Furthermore, because of their greater length they amplify the ideas and teaching about the "Son," the "Lord," and the "Christ" more briefly stated in 1 Thessalonians. In the first place, we must assume that the brief reference "Christ died for us" (1 Thess 5:10) points to the fuller catechesis "Christ died for our sins according to the Scriptures" that Paul "delivered" in Corinth a few months later and which he repeats more fully for pastoral reasons in 1 Corinthians.

17. Acts 26:20.
18. Acts 15:23, 41.

That catechesis also included Christ's burial, resurrection, and fivefold appearances (1 Cor 15:1-7). The gospel Paul "delivered" in Corinth he would have "delivered" beforehand in Thessalonica and, doubtless, in earlier mission contexts.

Secondly, in 1 Corinthians Paul's statements about "one God" and "one Lord" presuppose prior catechetical instruction, as inferred by "we *know* that we all have *knowledge*" (8:1) and "We *know* that 'an idol has no real existence' and that 'there is no God but one'" (8:4). Paul's "we know" serves to remind of initial catechesis now being reinforced.

The words "no God but one" are adapted from the *Shemaʿ*.[19]

> Hear O Israel, the LORD our God, the LORD is one
> Love the LORD thy God. . . . (Deut 6:4)

Paul restates this as

> . . . there is one God,   the Father,
> > from whom are all things
> > for   whom we exist
>
> and   one Lord, Jesus Christ,
> > through whom are all things
> > through whom we exist.

So far as Paul is concerned the confession "Jesus in *kyrios*" is the sign of the *pneumatikos*/the Spirit-filled person (1 Cor 12:3). Later (16:22) Paul writes

> If anyone does not love the Lord let him be cursed.
> *Marana tha* (Lord [Jesus], come back).[20]

In these catechetical echoes Paul (1) identifies the "God" of the *Shemaʿ* with "the Father" and (2) the "LORD" with Jesus, who (a) is to be "loved"

19. This is but one of a number of christological adaptations of the *Shemaʿ* in the NT, for example, "There is *one* God and Father of us all" (Eph 4:5) and "There is *one* God and *one* mediator between God and men, the man Christ Jesus" (1 Tim 2:5).

20. See J. Fitzmyer, "New Testament KYRIOS and MARANATHA and Their Aramaic Background," in *To Advance the Gospel: New Testament Studies* (Grand Rapids: Eerdmans, 1998), 218-35 who understands *Marana tha* as imperatival and derived from a Palestinian liturgical setting.

and (b) is the returning *kyrios.* Confession of this *kyrios* is the mark of the Spirit. R. Bauckham calls this "a Christology of Divine identity."[21]

Paul's reminder to the Thessalonians that they "turned from idols" to "God" whose "Son" (the "Lord") they "await from heaven" corresponds closely with the *Shema*-adapted catecheses of Paul's first Corinthian letter (8:4-6; 16:22). We reasonably assume that the "knowledge" restated by letter in 1 Corinthians had been communicated orally at Corinth and prior to that in Thessalonica.

1 Thessalonians as a Window into Early Christianity

Based on this discussion we reach several conclusions.

> 1 Thessalonians is securely datable to 50 and was written from Corinth a few months after Paul's mission in Thessalonica.
>
> The confident epistolary style and mature contents of the letter imply that Paul and his colleagues were by then experienced missioners. Paul "received" the main elements of the gospel from Jerusalem sources and not from Antioch.
>
> The letter points to mission work in Judea in the mid-30s and to recent mission work in the Greek provinces. By that time there were Jewish churches in Judea and Gentile churches in Greece.
>
> Paul's reminiscences of his initial mission *eisodos* (arrival) in Thessalonica establish that he proclaimed Jesus as "Son [of God]," "Lord," and "Christ." And it is clear that the same threefold proclamation occurred also in Corinth shortly afterward.
>
> Since Paul's theology was settled by the time of the mission to Greece we assume that the lengthier exposition of catechesis in 1 Corinthians about (1) Christ's death and resurrection (15:3-7) and (2) idols, the Father, and the Lord (8:4-6) approximated closely

---

21. According to R. Bauckham, *God Crucified* (Grand Rapids: Eerdmans, 1998) Paul is "including the Lord Jesus Christ in the unique divine identity" and "redefining monotheism as Christian monotheism" (38). L. Hurtado, *At the Origins of Christian Worship* (Grand Rapids: Eerdmans, 1999), however, speaks of the "two-ishness" of God and Christ within an exclusivist monotheism. In his view, the "shape" of Christian worship is "binitarian" (70). See also M. L. Y. Chan, *Christology from Within and Ahead* (Leiden: Brill, 2001), 269 n. 21.

to Paul's initial mission preaching in Corinth and earlier in Thessalonica.

In short, 1 Thessalonians is a window into Christian beliefs in the year 50. This teaching, however, predates its written form by many years and goes back to the earliest period "after Jesus." Understood in this light, the various attempts to reconstruct the "birth of Christianity" along other and minimalist lines are historically misdirected.[22]

22. See pp. 2-7 above.

SIX

Between Jesus and Paul (1):
Paul's Window (Galatians 1)

Because [the letters] of Paul are innocent of any attempt to convey new information about the historical Jesus, such information as they do contain, being incidental, is the more valuable and must be taken carefully into account.

Paul Barnett, *Jesus and the Logic of History*[1]

By any calculation the period between the crucifixion of Jesus and the Damascus "call" of Paul was brief. According to my reckoning (see p. 26 above) only a matter of about a year interposed "between Jesus and Paul."[2]

Clearly the period "after Jesus," in which the "birth of Christianity" occurred, was critical. The main sources are Paul's letter to the Galatians (ch. 1) and the Acts of the Apostles, which allocates no less than nine chapters to this period. Given the reservation of so many regarding Acts, Paul's own work, in particular Galatians, is especially important.

Care is called for in handling sources from such different genres. Acts was written retrospectively, more than thirty years later, by which time Jewish rejection of Christ was more or less an accomplished fact. The letters are much closer to the events and written at a time when the degree to which Jews would reject the gospel and Gentiles would welcome it was not

---

1. Paul Barnett, *Jesus and the Logic of History* (Grand Rapids: Eerdmans, 1997), 25.

2. Cf. the suggestive title of M. Hengel, *Between Jesus and Paul* (Philadelphia: Fortress, 1983).

anticipated. By the time Paul wrote to the Romans (ca. 57), however, the trend was becoming clear (see Rom 9:30-33; 10:18-21).

Galatians

Although a mid-length letter (about 2500 words), Galatians is far and away the most historically detailed of the Pauline corpus.[3] Furthermore, it is universally accepted as an authentic letter of Paul, though the debate continues as to its date and provenance. As it happens, its value to the historian is unaffected by these issues.[4]

Historians place special value on a document like Galatians. Its historical information is "defensive" in character rather than intentionally written narrative history.[5] True, Paul heavily interprets his information in line with his own apologetic interests.[6] Yet the raw facts are most likely true since, as he knew, his opponents in Jerusalem and Anatolia would use any inaccuracy against him. The intensity of the dispute would have secured his attention to detail.

Several elements make Galatians important in the study of early Christianity. First, it makes it clear that Paul did not invent Christianity; "apostles" were there "before" him, and so, too, were "the church of God" and "the faith" objects of his persecution (1:13, 17, 23). Second, we are able to measure Acts against Paul's own account since both texts narrate a number of common items (see pp. 77-78 below). And third, Galatians provides details not found in Acts. It gives the time notes "after three

3. Rhetorical criticism directed toward Galatians has issued in several theories as to the form of the letter, for example: (1) H. D. Betz, "The Literary Composition and Function of Paul's Letter to the Galatians," *NTS* 21 (1974-75), 353-79; *Galatians* (Philadelphia: Hermeneia, 1979) classified Galatians as a legal defense; (2) B. H. Hungerford, *Galatians — Dialogical Response to Opponents* (Chico: Scholars, 1982) regarded Galatians as an "apologetic speech" directed to the Galatians; (3) G. W. Hansen, *Abraham in Galatians: Epistolary and Rhetorical Contexts* (JSNT Supplement series 29; Sheffield: Academic, 1989), saw Galatians as a "rebuke-request" form of epistle.

4. See Appendix B.

5. Barnett, *Jesus and the Logic of History,* 25-26. Cf. D. Lührmann, *Galatians* (Minneapolis: Fortress, 1992), 20-27.

6. B. R. Gaventa, "Galatians 1 and 2: Autobiography as Paradigm," *NovT* 28.4 (1986), 309-26 argues that Galatians 1–2 is not so much apologetic as autobiographical, intentionally written to seek imitation by the readers.

years . . . after fourteen years" (1:18; 2:1) and mentions Paul's visit to Arabia (1:17; cf. 2 Cor 11:32-33).

Christ in Galatians

The name "Jesus" does not appear on its own in Galatians, but always with "Christ," whether as "Jesus Christ" or, less frequently, "Christ Jesus." The name "Christ," however, occurs alone quite frequently, without "Jesus." But since Galatians is an early letter, it is likely that Paul's use of the word "Christ" still carried the idea of a title, *the* Messiah/*the* Christ. In the fullness of time, God sent forth his Son, *the Messiah* Jesus (4:4; 3:13; 1:1).

Presumably when Paul preached he provided personal details about Jesus of Nazareth. While for us "Christ" and "crucified" have become almost exclusively theological terms, the curiosity of the original hearers must have provoked many questions. Who was he? Where did he come from? Who were his parents? These would have been addressed to the missionaries to Pisidia and Lycaonia, so it was unnecessary to revisit them in the letter.

Nonetheless, Galatians does give the readers some glimpses of the historical Jesus. As "Christ" Jesus was both the *messianic* Son and the *filial* Son of God ("*his* Son," 1:16; 4:4, 6); believers call God "*Abba*, Father," and so, too, most likely, did Jesus (4:6; cf. 1:1, 3, 4). Jesus' family circumstances were known: he was "born of a woman" (doubtless her name was known) and "born under the law" (into a family of observant Jews), and James was his brother (1:19). Jesus was killed by crucifixion (3:1; 5:11, 24; 6:12, 14). God the Father raised him from the dead (1:1).

"The Faith"

Paul reports that after he went to Syria-Cilicia in ca. 36-37 the churches of Christ in Judea "had been hearing, that 'he who was once persecuting us is now proclaiming *the faith* that he was once trying to destroy'" (1:23). In other words, "the faith" was an established entity not only by ca. 36, but earlier, in the brief time span "between Jesus and Paul." Paul's persecutions attempted to destroy "the faith." Clearly, then, "the faith" (which must have been a *christological* faith) had already been formulated in the months between the crucifixion of Jesus and the conversion of Paul.

Paul's reason for mentioning this is to insist that he is now proclaiming the same "faith." Let the Galatians know that his present ministry enjoys the imprimatur of the Jerusalem "pillars" (2:2; also 1 Cor 15:11). Paul is preaching "the faith"; he is not "still preaching circumcision," as his opponents claim (5:11).

Are we able to determine from Paul's letter the contours of "the faith" he taught when present with the Galatians? His reminder that he publicly portrayed Jesus Christ as "crucified" points to the centrality of the crucifixion of the Christ (3:1). Further, one passage at least, has the marks of a tradition Paul taught the Galatians when present with them.

> When the time was fulfilled
> God sent forth his Son
>   born of a woman
>   born under law
> to redeem those under law
> that we might receive the adoption as sons.   (4:4-5)

The eschatological note ("When the time was fulfilled"), with the christological ("God sent forth his Son . . . born of a woman"), supports the notion of an early creed.[7] Paul would scarcely write like this unless there had already been extensive teaching to the Galatians about God's "Son."

As we have already noted Paul preached the Son of God in Thessalonica and Corinth (1 Thess 1:10; 2 Cor 1:19). His reference in Galatians to "[God's] Son" shows that he preached him also among the Galatians. According to Acts Paul's earliest proclamation was that Jesus is "the Son of God . . . the Christ" (Acts 9:20, 23). Presumably, this "faith" was established at Paul's baptism in Damascus, in further explanation of Christ's appearance to him on the road to the city.

It appears, then, that Jesus as "Son of God" was central to "the faith" that Paul now preached, that he had previously attempted to destroy.

Further, that Paul proclaimed Jesus as "[God's] Son" explains why God is now known as "the Father" (1:1, 3; cf. 1 Thess 1:1; 1 Cor 8:6). Prayer is offered to "God the Father" as "abba" (4:6). It is striking that speakers of

---

7. Paul, however, appears to add his own glosses in epistolary reminiscences for the pastoral situation of the moment (cf. 1 Cor 11:23-26 and 15:3-8). In the face of current judaizing attempts among the Galatians, we ponder whether "redeem those under Law" was a pastoral gloss on an original tradition. "Redeem" appears also in 3:13.

Greek should pray to God using a word from a language foreign to them.[8] The most likely explanation is that "abba" originated with Jesus' own address to God (Mark 14:6) and that his disciples passed it on to others (cf. Rom 8:15; 1 Pet 1:17) including Paul, who in turn taught it to the churches of his mission.

Paul also taught that Christ died "for *(hyper)* our sins" (1:4; 2:20; 3:13), echoing the "tradition" repeated more fully in another letter (1 Cor 15:3; cf. 1 Thess 5:10). Here, then, we are very close to "the faith" of "the church of God" in its early months.

This "faith," as Paul calls it, must be closely related to "the teaching of the apostles" in Acts (e.g., 2:42). To anticipate, "the teaching of the apostles" appears to be catechesis formulated by the apostles for the baptismal instruction of new believers (see pp. 69-70 below). "The faith" Paul attempted to destroy was one and the same thing as "the teaching of the apostles," in short, christology.

Apostles in Jerusalem

Paul first revisited Jerusalem three years "after" the "Damascus event." Counting part years as whole as was customary, this means that Paul was back in Jerusalem two years and some months after his dramatic conversion.

The purpose of this visit was "to become acquainted with" *(historēsai)* Cephas. Paul also "saw James the brother of the Lord" (Gal 1:18-19). There were also "other apostles" in Jerusalem. Paul does not explain why he sought out Cephas and James. Most likely he did so to identify himself as a fellow believer to the known leaders in Jerusalem.

Here is a window into Christianity not more than four years after the historical Jesus. Already we see "apostles" in Jerusalem, led by Cephas and James.

Peter, Apostle to Israel

In Galatians Cephas (Aramaic, "rock") is also called Peter (Greek, "rock"). This Cephas was "entrusted" by God "with the gospel to the circumcised."

8. M. Hengel, *The Son of God* (London: SCM, 1976), 63.

"[God] worked through him in the apostolate *(apostolē)* to the circumcised" (2:7-8). According to Paul, then, God commissioned Peter with a "mission" to the Jews. Furthermore, that the "pillars" then agreed to "go" to the circumcised implies that Peter's ministry to that point had been confined to the land of Israel.

From Galatians we learn that Peter was the "apostle to the circumcised" in the land of Israel, based in Jerusalem, most likely beginning sometime before the fourteen-year span of Paul's ministry that began with Paul's "Damascus event." Thus Galatians confirms the picture from Acts, where Peter is the leading apostle in Jerusalem from the time of the crucifixion and has a wider ministry to Jews in the land of Israel.

Mention of John as the third of the "pillars" (2:9) suggests that he, too, had been involved in ministry to the circumcised of Israel throughout the same period, very probably working alongside Cephas in his "apostolate." Whenever John appears in Acts he is always with Peter. In the fourth Gospel the "beloved disciple" and Peter appear to be specially connected.

Paul, Apostle to the Gentiles

The autobiographical details Paul mentions throughout his appeals to the Galatians serve the apologetic case Paul is arguing. These references appear to be in chronological sequence.

"Former Life in Judaism" (1:12-13)

Paul speaks of his "former way of life in Judaism" in which he "was advancing beyond many of his own age from his nation." He was "more exceedingly zealous than them in the traditions of [his] fathers." This, however, did not mean mere scholarship. His preeminence among his contemporaries, evident in zeal for the traditions, was concretely expressed in his persecution of the church of God with the intention of destroying it. Consistent with this extreme "zeal," Paul at that time also "preached circumcision" (5:11). Presumably this was to close off from proselytes an easy route into the covenant of the God of Israel.

Paul gives this brief autobiographical note in 1:12-13 for a purpose, to show that his radical turnabout owed nothing to any human and everything to God. He is preparing the way to show that he owed his authority to preach to the Gentiles to God and not to humans, including the apostles in Jerusalem.

The Damascus Road "Call" (1:15-17a)

Sometime during or after this persecution of "the church of God" (he does not say when or where) God "called" Paul to proclaim "[his] Son" to the Gentiles. At that time God revealed "his Son in [Paul]." God's revelation of his Son in Paul and his "call" for Paul to engage in mission to Gentiles occurred at the same moment; they are inseparable parts of the one event.[9] Previously the prophetic hope was for the Gentiles to stream *into* Zion; through Paul the movement centered on Paul was to be *away* from Zion.

Paul adds that he "did not immediately confer with flesh and blood," that is, "go up to Jerusalem to those who were apostles before [him]."[10] Later, indeed, when he met with the three "pillars" they "added nothing" to his message (2:2, 6, 9).

Paul manages to leave several impressions with his readers. First, he affirms the human primacy of the Jerusalem leadership, initially Cephas and subsequently the three "pillars" led by James (1:18-19; 2:1-10). It was important to be able to cite their approval of his "apostolate." However, secondly, he did not owe his "call" to them, nor was he above opposing them if the (Law-free) "truth of the gospel" was threatened (2:11-13).

Damascus, Arabia, Damascus (1:17b)

Paul relates in the briefest terms that he "went away into Arabia and came back again to Damascus." Thus God "called" Paul prior to or at Damascus, from which he went away to "Arabia" and then returned to Damascus. This

9. M. L. Y. Chan, *Christology from Within and Ahead* (Leiden: Brill, 2001), 270-75.

10. G. Lüdemann, "The Content and Occasion of the Jerusalem Conference," in *Paul, Apostle to the Gentiles* (Philadelphia: Fortress, 1984), 64 argues that Gal 2:7-9 attributes apostleship only to Peter. For a critique of this view see B. McLean, "Galatians 2:7-9 and Paul's Apostolic Status," *NTS* 37 (1991), 67-76.

occupied a period of two years and some months (1:18), the greater part of which was probably in Arabia. A passing reference elsewhere suggests that Paul's activities in "Arabia" provoked Aretas, king of the Nabateans, to seek Paul's arrest in Damascus (2 Cor 11:32). This suggests that Paul had been preaching the Son of God among the Nabateans. God "called" Paul to "proclaim his Son to the Gentiles," and he set about doing this immediately initially in "Arabia." Paul may have reached as far as the capital, Petra, within this two-to-three-year period.[11]

Bitter relations between Nabateans and Jews followed Antipas's divorce of Aretas's daughter and remarriage to Herodias (in the late 20s). "Arabia" would have been a dangerous place for Paul the Jew preaching a Jewish Messiah to Nabateans.[12] This would explain Aretas's attempt to arrest Paul in Damascus.

Galatians: Further Considerations

Several other matters must be considered from this letter. First, by his reference to his "eminence" in his "former . . . life in Judaism" it appears that Paul was an accomplished biblical scholar. Most likely as a Greek-speaking Jew from the Diaspora this meant he was a synagogue teacher well versed in the Septuagint and other Greek versions.[13] At the time of his "call" to proclaim the Messiah Jesus to the Gentiles he was familiar with the biblical text and its citation and glossed exegesis according to current Jewish practice.

Second, from the beginning of the fourteen "unknown years" Paul is known to have preached to Gentiles, as well as debated with Jews. By the time he came to write Galatians he had identified key texts from the LXX and worked out a reasoned exegesis of them based on Christ, Son of God and redeemer. The middle chapters of Galatians express the fruits of Paul's scholarship.

Third, Paul's passion is evident in this letter, including at the end when he takes the pen from the amanuensis and adds his own fiery conclusion (6:11-18). This is readily imaginable in terms of the Damascus event

11. Cf. J. Murphy-O'Connor, "Paul in Arabia," *CBQ* 55 (1993), 732-37, who suggests that Paul may not have penetrated very far down into Nabatea.

12. M. Hengel and A. M. Schwemer, *Paul between Damascus and Antioch: The Unknown Years* (Louisville: Westminster, 1997), 111-12.

13. M. Hengel, *The Pre-Christian Paul* (London: SCM, 1991), 67.

when it became evident that the crucified Son of God, not the Law of Moses, lay at the heart of God's redemptive purposes for the world.

A striking feature of Paul's reasoning is that not only Gentiles but God's historic people Israel also must find "righteousness" from God in Messiah Jesus alone.

> We ourselves who are Jews by birth and not Gentile sinners, yet who know that a man is not justified by works of the law but through faith in Jesus Christ. . . . (2:15-16; cf. Acts 13:39)

> For even those who receive circumcision do not themselves keep the law. . . . (6:13)

Paul argues that the need of redemption from the Law applied first and foremost to Jews prior to the application of the message of salvation to Gentiles.[14]

Galatians gives no basis for the "new perspective," that Paul's gospel is only addressed to the "inclusion of Gentiles," as if Israel had no such need. The members of the historic people of God are equally "sinners," law-breakers under the curse of God. Jews must find deliverance from "the curse of the Law" only in Christ, who became a "curse" to redeem "us" (i.e., Jews) from that curse (3:13). "Righteousness by faith," then, is not something devised later by Paul for his mission to Gentiles. From the time of the Damascus event Paul understood that the need for redemption applied equally to the covenant people. The measured argument in Romans 2–3 about Jewish law-breaking states what Paul the Christian had always believed.

Conclusion

Paul's Letter to the Galatians is important in the study of earliest Christianity. In the opening chapters, where Paul defends his apostleship he pro-

---

14. As argued by D. W. B. Robinson, "The Distinction between Jewish and Gentile Believers in Galatians," *Australian Biblical Review* 13 (1965), 29-48. Robinson draws attention to the distinct and separate nature of the missions to Jews and Gentiles and therefore to separate and distinct Jew and Gentile clusters of assemblies. Yet these distinct groups had a common ground of righteousness — attachment by faith to the Messiah Jesus, crucified and risen. Nonetheless, Robinson may have overdrawn the distinction. The Gentile churches established by Paul had Jewish members.

vides invaluable historical information, though incidentally. It is evident that Paul did not invent Christianity. Indeed, he set out to destroy "the church of God" (1:13); he set out to destroy "the faith" (1:23). There were apostles "before him," including Peter and James (1:17-19).

Accordingly Galatians provides a template by which we can measure the other main source for the brief period between Jesus and Paul, Acts 1–9. To that source we now turn.

SEVEN

Between Jesus and Paul (2):
Luke's Window (Acts 1–9)

... attempts to free ... chronology from the framework of Acts, attempts that have become more prominent during the past ten years, have resulted in a new level of confusion rather than in any more precise specification.

Rainer Riesner, *Paul's Early Period*[1]

Acts and History

The book of Acts provides the only sequential narrative of the first years "after Jesus," yet it presents the historian with such major problems that many scholars approach this text with caution if not skepticism. Clearly it was written at least thirty years after the events it narrates. Furthermore, there are several apparent errors of fact. As well, the author's approach seems quite biased.

These problems are real and must be addressed, as they will be later (in Appendix A). For the moment we make one observation that in our view does allow us to use Acts 1–9 as a window into the brief "corridor" between Jesus and Paul. This is that Paul was the companion of the author of Luke-Acts for many years, from ca. 57 to ca. 62. This is evident from the so-called "we" passages in Acts (16:10-16; 20:5–21:18; 27:1–28:16)[2] and from Paul's Second Letter to Timothy (2 Tim 4:11).[3]

---

1. Rainer Riesner, *Paul's Early Period* (Grand Rapids: Eerdmans, 1998), 29.

2. While some scholars argue that the "we" passages are merely stylistic it is far from

This is an important consideration due to the widely held view that Paul's letters are "primary" evidence and must be preferred to Luke's "secondhand" information. Since, however, Luke was Paul's companion for many years, it is not possible to relegate his data in this way. Rather, Luke must be regarded as an *equal primary source* with Paul for information about Paul. Furthermore, through Paul's contacts with Peter, James, and John (see Gal 1:18-19; 2:7-9) Luke also had access to information about these early leaders and the events that occurred between Jesus and Paul. In short, Paul's long association with Luke prior to the time Luke wrote Acts encourages confidence in Luke's capacity to write accurately about this critical period.

There is, however, at least one major shortcoming in Luke's account. Acts devotes nine chapters to the period between Jesus and Paul, implying a considerable lapse of time. In reality only a year or so passed between the first Easter and the dramatic event that overtook Paul near Damascus. True, the author ties the period to the high priesthood of Caiaphas, which ended in A.D. 37 (Acts 4:6), but he gives us no sense of the overall passage of time.

The Future Direction of Christianity in Israel

The future directions of Christianity were set within the first year of its life. Within that brief space the "sect of the Nazarenes" was formed (Acts 24:5). Within those early months two streams of disciples emerged, the "Hebrews" and the "Hellenists."

For a period persecution scattered members of both groups from Jerusalem. The "Hebrews" likely took refuge in Aramaic-speaking centers in Judea and Galilee and the Hellenists in Greek-speaking towns and cities throughout the land of Israel, including Samaria. In time members of both groups returned to Jerusalem. Some of the Hellenists, however, emigrated permanently to Antioch and became foundation members of the church there.

Within Israel, however, Saul's persecution appears to have left the "Hebrews" and the "Hellenists" permanently separated. After the persecu-

---

clear what is meant by this. The most obvious inference is that the author was then part of the narrative.

3. Whether or not one accepts Pauline authorship does not affect the likelihood that Luke was with Paul near the end of his life.

tion the church in Jerusalem appears to be an increasingly "Hebrew" church, whereas the "Hellenists" in Israel more or less disappear from sight. Hints of their continuing life, however, are to be seen in the church of Caesarea led by Philip the "evangelist" and in Mnason the Cypriot, with whom Paul stayed in Jerusalem rather than with James (Acts 21:16).

In my view, the believers addressed by the letter to the Hebrews are most likely to have been continuing Hellenists in Israel.[4] The "Hebrews" like James, the son of Zebedee, and Peter suffered under persecution (by King Agrippa) but this appears to have been sporadic. The readers of Hebrews, however, seem to have suffered permanent marginalization. But this is to run ahead.

The "Birth" of Christology

Christianity depends upon beliefs about Jesus, that is, christology. Historically speaking we encounter christology first in Paul's earliest letter, whether 1 Thessalonians or Galatians. Nonetheless our contention is that christology was born within the earliest period of Christian history, A.D. 33-34.

This is based on three connected observations: (1) Paul's christology remains unchanged throughout his letters from first to last. (2) Accordingly his christology must have been resolved by the late 40s before he commenced letter writing. (3) Paul's christology was formulated by others from whom he "received" it (1 Cor 15:1-7; cf. Rom 1:1-4).

The critical questions are where, when, and from whom did Paul "receive" the christology he and others preached. "When" is answered by Gal 1:23, where Paul refers to the astonishment of Judean churches in the mid-30s that Paul was by then preaching "the faith" he had attempted to destroy. This pushes the time back even further to the brief space between Jesus' resurrection and the beginning of Paul's persecutions and virtually guarantees that the place where he grasped the truth about Christ was not Jerusalem but almost certainly Damascus. Indeed it was, he states, at or near Damascus that God "revealed his Son" so that he might proclaim him to the Gentiles (Gal 1:16).[5]

---

4. See later, pp. 106-9.

5. F. F. Bruce, *Paul: Apostle of the Heart Set Free* (Grand Rapids: Eerdmans, 1977), 83-94 argues that Paul received the tradition from the apostles in Jerusalem on his first return visit.

Leadership of the Apostles (Acts 2–5)

One Community, Two Groups

After the Pentecostal outpouring, the senior apostle, Peter, bore witness to the exaltation of Jesus son of David to God's right hand as Lord and Messiah. Three thousand accepted baptism from the hands of the apostles in the name of Jesus the Messiah. To the few hundred Galileans who had now settled in Jerusalem were added many hundreds who were for the most part Jews from the Diaspora on pilgrimage in Jerusalem. Most would return to their homelands. Some (a minority?), however, most probably were "Hellenist"[6] Jews living permanently in Jerusalem (Acts 6:1).

These Greek-speaking Jews living in Jerusalem attended the five or more "Hellenist" synagogues in Jerusalem (6:9).[7] From archaeological research it appears these synagogues were located in the "City of David" area.[8] Most likely the Hellenists lived nearby.

It seems that the "Hellenists" were more numerous than the "Hebrews." Jerusalem was their home; the Galileans were recent arrivals, as yet without permanent residence. This would explain why the "Hellenist" widows were missing out in the daily food distribution.

Against those who argue for two discrete groups the evidence at hand points to *one* community composed of "Hebrews" and "Hellenists" presided over by "the Twelve" (6:2), whose leader was Peter (2:13). "All who believed," that is, both "Hebrews" and "Hellenists," were "together" *(epi to auto)* and drew from a common pool of goods and food, which was supported by the proceeds of property sold by landowners (2:44-45; 4:32, 37).[9] The seven almoners, though all "Hellenists," were elected by the whole community and were responsible for the daily distribution to the widows of both groups. Hengel is doubtless correct in observing that these distinct linguistic groups were "bound together by their bilingual members" (e.g., Barnabas). Nonetheless, it must not be overlooked that

6. See Hengel, *Between Jesus and Paul*, 8-11 for discussion of the identity of "Hebrews" and "Hellenists."

7. See R. Riesner, "Synagogues in Jerusalem," in *BAFCS* 4:179-210.

8. Riesner, "Synagogues," 211.

9. On the proximity of the Jerusalem Essenes to the "upper room" and their likely influence on the new sect see P. Barnett, *Jesus and the Rise of Early Christianity* (Downers Grove: InterVarsity, 1999), 199-200.

the apostles led by Peter provided overarching leadership, especially as teachers.

The Apostles' "Teaching"

The whole community of believers were subject to "the teaching *(didachē)* of the apostles" (Acts 2:42; 4:33). At that time the apostles "filled Jerusalem" with their "teaching," as the high priest complained (Acts 5:28). What did they teach? It is clear from Acts that their "teaching" was centered on the man "Jesus"[10] "the *Nazōraion*"[11] who was crucified at Gentile hands.[12] Overwhelmingly that "teaching" was christological.

Jesus "the Christ"　On many occasions the apostles declare "this Jesus" to be "the Christ" (2:31, 38; 3:18, 20). He was of the "seed of David" (2:30), the Lord's "anointed" (4:26). Remarkably, Peter identified this "anointed" one as God's "holy servant" *(pais,* 4:27, 30). Since, as Peter said, "God *glorified* his servant" (3:13), it is clear that he was referring to the "servant" referred to in LXX Isa 52:13 ("my servant *[pais]* . . . will be *glorified*").

In short, the apostles' "teaching" was that "the Christ" of Davidic descent was also the "servant" who suffered vicariously for his people. It is evident that the apostles "searched the Scriptures" finding Jesus to be the fulfillment of prophecy as the "servant" (Isa 52:13–53:12; cf. Acts 8:32-35) and the "accursed" of God on the "tree" (Deut 21:22-23; cf. Acts 5:30; 10:39).

Jesus "the Son of God"　In Luke's account of the apostles' "teaching" there is no reference to Jesus as "Son of God." How, then, do we account for the appearance of the "Son of God" in Paul's Damascus preaching months later (Acts 9:20)? As indicated earlier,[13] God "revealed his Son in" Paul at that time (Gal 1:16). There is abundant evidence that the "Son of God" lay at the heart of Paul's mission preaching (1 Thess 1:10; 2 Cor 1:19). Were there any antecedents for "Son of God" in the "tradition" Paul "received" in Damascus?

10. Acts 4:2; 5:30; 5:42.

11. Acts 2:22; 3:6; 4:10. The early believers became known as the "sect of the *Nazōraiōn*" (Acts 24:5).

12. Acts 4:10; cf. 3:15; 5:30.

13. See p. 61.

The appearance of the "Son of God" in a creed-like passage at the beginning of Romans (1:1-4) and subsequent appearances of "Son" references in Romans (1:9; 5:10; 8:3, 29, 32) to readers not evangelized by Paul suggests a pattern of teaching independent of and earlier than Paul. Did Roman Jews who were instructed and baptized by the apostles bring a teaching of the "Son of God" back to their city of origin?

Here, too, we point to the Aramaic "abba" in Romans (8:15; cf. Gal 4:6) that must have come to Paul from a "Hebrew" source and that Paul's Roman readers already knew. That Paul employs "abba" to those whose Christian faith was not learned from him indicates that this way of approaching "the Father" was widespread in early Christianity, predating Paul. Indeed, based on the Gospel tradition it is clear that "abba" came first from the mouth of Jesus (Mark 14:36 pars.). Most likely, therefore, the "abba" tradition was part of the earliest "teaching" of the apostles (cf. 1 Pet 1:17).

Jesus the "Lord"   The apostles' "teaching" was that Jesus was "Lord" (Acts 2:36; 4:33), exalted to God's "right hand" (2:33-34; 5:31). Clearly this assertion flows from Ps 110:1 and from Jesus' own application of that text to himself as the Christ, the son of David (Mark 12:35-37). Paul's citation of Aramaic *marana tha* in a passage calling for the "love of the Lord" in terms echoing the *Shema'* (1 Cor 16:22)[14] most likely draws us back into the earliest weeks of the new sect.

In short, what brought about the "birth" of Christianity was christology, the apostles' "teaching" that Jesus was "the Christ," "the Son of God," and "the Lord." These elements were formulated as part of the apostolic *didachē* and informed Stephen's understanding for his preaching in the "Hellenist" synagogues of Jerusalem as well as for the fugitive believers like Philip who took this "teaching" to the Samaritans and the Ethiopian as well as to the coastal cities. Unnamed disciples took this teaching to Damascus, where the persecutor "received" it at his baptism. As well, the apostles were the fountainhead for preachers like Barnabas, John Mark, Silvanus, and others who carried the gospel far afield. Ultimately the NT itself arose from this earliest christology.

---

14. See earlier, pp. 52-53.

Division in the Community (Acts 6–7)[15]

The "Holy Place"

It soon became apparent, however, that differences of emphasis were emerging between the two groups. The point at issue was not christology but eschatology in relationship to Jerusalem and the Temple.

The apostles continued to attend the Temple services (Acts 3:1) and were content to teach in the temple precincts, in Solomon's colonnade, where Jesus had taught (3:11; 5:12; cf. John 10:22-23). Furthermore, priests serving in the Temple joined the community without difficulty (6:7). When persecution fell on the church, only the apostles remained in Jerusalem (8:1). Perhaps the apostles, remembering Jesus' recent words about the destruction of the Temple and the coming of the Son of Man, believed that this would occur soon and that they, the Twelve, were to be the foundations of that new Sanctuary.

It was otherwise, however, with the "Hellenists."

Division

Two factors provoked the division. One was the influx of priests into the community (6:7). Most likely they were pro-Temple. The other was the election of Hellenist almoners, led by Stephen, who began preaching in the Greek-speaking synagogues of Jerusalem. Signs and wonders accompanied his preaching (6:8), as they had the apostles' preaching. Clearly Stephen had become an evangelist among fellow Hellenists in Jerusalem. His preaching, however, was expressed in anti-Temple terms (6:13).

Twice previously the Temple authorities had arrested and imprisoned various apostles, releasing them with a warning on one occasion and with a beating on another (Acts 4:1-3, 5-22; 5:17-40). Stephen's attack, even if exaggerated by the complainants, was more serious.

What now followed (Acts 7) was a Sanhedrin trial, with witnesses from the Greek synagogues accusing Stephen of blasphemy, the accused defending himself, and finally the judges deciding Stephen's guilt of the theological crime of blasphemy, for which he was stoned.

15. Hengel, *Between Jesus and Paul*, 3-4 based on unusual vocabulary suggests that Acts 6–7 is derived from an Antiochene source.

Acts makes it clear that Stephen's immediate offense was not preaching Christ, but speaking against "the holy place and the Law" (Acts 6:13). These were the sacred symbols of Israel's covenant faith, along with circumcision, the religious calendar, and the dietary laws. From the time of Alexander the Great and the spread of Hellenism, Israel's covenant was under theological and moral threat; Hellenism was aesthetic, intellectual, and enticing. Successive devout scribes had clung to Law and Temple as symbols of Yahweh's covenant. So now a *Hellenist* Jew was attacking these two sacred emblems. This was an assault against God, no less.

Influences on Stephen

Various explanations have arisen for Stephen's surprising emphasis. Was he influenced by the Qumran/Essene opposition to the Temple? But the sectaries had withdrawn from the Temple community because of the impurity and corruption of the Hasmonean High Priests and were not, like Stephen, opposed to the Temple *in principle.* Moreover, Stephen was also accused of being against Moses, which the sectaries were not. Was Stephen merely a liberal Jew like some others from a Diaspora background, rather aloof from the intense commitment to these "Jerusalem" symbols? It is possible that Stephen as a Diaspora Jew who sustained faith in the synagogue may have been unpersuaded by the importance attributed to the Temple. This, however, does not explain the strength of his polemic against the Temple. Nor does it take into account his proclamation to his fellow Hellenists. The almoner second to Stephen was Philip, who came to be called "the Evangelist" (Acts 21:8). The same title could have been given to Stephen; he was not merely a polemicist.

The driving force behind Stephen's preaching about the Temple and the Law of Moses must have been something else. Stephen had grasped something the Galilean Hebrew apostles had not yet comprehended. Jesus prophesied his death and resurrection after three days and also that the Temple would be destroyed only to be reconstituted "in three days" as his body (John 2:19-21). Jesus' death would secure its "death" and his resurrection would secure its "resurrection," that is, a new people of God founded on the Twelve and joined to Jesus the messianic king independently of Jerusalem and its Temple. But the Galilean disciples did not fully understand this at the time. They continued to teach and worship in the Temple, and when Saul's onslaught occurred they did not leave Jerusalem (8:1). The Temple remained part of their eschatology.

Saul's Assault on the Church

It is likely that Stephen's chief accuser was another "Hellenist" Jew, the "young man," Saul of Tarsus. This eminent younger scribe appears to have been a rabbi in the Hellenistic synagogues of Jerusalem.[16] As a youth he had come from Cilicia to Jerusalem, first to study the Torah and then to teach it there. He was outraged by Stephen's rejection of the Temple and his affirmation of God's new plan to redirect his purposes to the Jews of the Dispersion. Saul of Tarsus rightly saw, however, that Stephen's polemic was not merely his preference for the Diaspora over Jerusalem and its "holy place." Saul discerned that Stephen's radicalism was inspired by Jesus the false Messiah.

What was Saul's role? Did the Sanhedrin commission him to investigate and act upon Stephen's activities in the Hellenist synagogues? Or, more probably, was it Saul who alerted the authorities to Stephen's preaching? That "those from Cilicia" were among those who disputed with Stephen in the synagogues[17] may be Luke's hint preparing us for the dramatic introduction of the persecutor. This is the "young man" at whose feet Stephen's clothes "were laid," who was "consenting to his death," and who immediately became the high priest's agent in the assault against the church in Jerusalem (Acts 7:58; 8:1, 3).

While the arguments of Stephen the Hellenist provoked the crisis, it does not appear that Saul's assault was limited to the Hellenist believers. Acts and Paul's letters are in agreement that his persecution was against the whole community. He "persecuted the church of God . . . and tried to destroy it" (Gal 1:13; cf. Phil 3:3). "A great persecution arose against the church in Jerusalem . . . *all* were scattered" (Acts 8:1). True, the apostles did not leave Jerusalem. But this must not be taken to imply that the "Hebrews" in general remained. The statement that the church in Jerusalem was "scattered throughout Judea and Samaria" should be taken to mean that both "Hebrews" and "Hellenists" were driven out.[18]

---

16. Hengel, *Pre-Christian Paul,* 67.
17. Acts 6:9.
18. Contra Hengel, *Between Jesus and Paul,* 24.

The severity of Saul's assault emerges at a number of points in Acts and is corroborated Paul's own letters. Although Acts is an apologia for Paul, its author does not spare him. Saul "was breathing threats and murder . . . was in raging fury . . . ravaging the church"; he "persecuted" "the way" "unto the death" (Acts 9:1; 26:11; 8:3; 22:4). In his own words, he "persecuted the church violently and tried to destroy it" (Gal 1:13). In "zeal" for Yahweh he "was a persecutor of the church" (Phil 3:6; cf. Gal 1:13).[19] Acting on the authority of the high priest and the Sanhedrin in Jerusalem (Acts 26:9), he entered the houses of believers, dragged out men and women, and handed them over to prison (8:3; 22:4). When these prisoners were brought to the synagogues for trial, Saul was their accuser. He instigated their flogging and voted for their execution (Acts 26:10).

Twenty-five years later he was able to appeal to the memory of the high priest and the Sanhedrin about his violent actions (22:5). He effectively destroyed the messianic community in Jerusalem, at least for the time being. His task in Jerusalem thus completed, Saul traveled to Damascus to retrieve disciples fleeing from Jerusalem.

Stephen's Teaching

Why did the teaching of Stephen so provoke Saul, Pharisee and zealot? No doubt Saul took offense at Stephen's attack on the Temple and the Law of Moses. Yet the Jews from the Diaspora were not alone in their negative views about the Temple; the Essenes stood aloof from the Temple. Nor were their criticisms of the Law without parallel; many Jews of the Diaspora also had a weak grasp of the covenantal faith. Stephen held a "decentralized" view of God's purposes for the Diaspora rather than the focus on Jerusalem; so did many Jews from the Diaspora. Stephen's views had most probably been heard before, in one form or another. It is unlikely that his criticisms of Temple and the Law by themselves explain the violence he provoked. Stephen's special quality may have been to bring all these criticisms against Temple and Law together and articulate them so passionately.

For his part, Saul may have discerned that Stephen's worldview was informed by something else, or, rather someone else, Jesus the *Nazōraios,* the false Messiah. Saul appears to have had special insight about what was at

19. Barnett, *Rise,* 223-25 for discussion of zealotry and Paul as a "zealot."

stake in the messianic claims made for Jesus of Nazareth. He must have known that Jesus had been recently crucified as "king of the Jews." Caiaphas's accusation against Jesus had left the Romans with no alternative except to crucify him for treason as a self-professed "king." As the high priest well knew, being impaled on "a tree" meant that the victim bore Yahweh's "Deuteronomic" curse, providing an automatic rejection of his messianic claims.[20] The young zealot, outraged that the claims of a false Messiah lived on in his followers, saw it as his religious duty to stamp it out.

What inner processes were occurring as Saul pursued his course against the believers of Jerusalem? On one hand, by then he must have discovered further information about the historical Jesus through his interrogations of the disciples. He could not have been uninformed about Jesus as he set out for Damascus. And he may also have been shaken by the non-vindictive behavior of Stephen and others as they met their deaths in the name of Jesus (Acts 7:60). Something of the love and mercy of the One he pursued may have been revealed in the behavior of his victims as he punished them.

As one who had learned the apostles' "teaching" Stephen knew that the Lord's "Christ" was at the same time the Lord's vicariously suffering "servant" (see above). The "breaking of bread" in the "Hellenist" households must regularly have reminded the believers that Jesus' death was *for* others.[21] Stephen may have grasped before the apostles that the death of the Christ-Servant made the priest's sacrifices in the Temple redundant and the scrupulous observation of the Torah unnecessary. Conceivably such a theological view underlay Stephen's attack on Temple and Torah,[22] even though Acts does not establish that precise connection. Nonetheless, Stephen most likely did teach this in the "Hellenist" synagogues of Jerusalem and, equally likely, Saul of Tarsus heard this teaching. The seeds of Saul's Damascus revelation were sown in Jerusalem.

Stephen's Influence

It is impossible to overestimate the importance of Stephen, his teaching, and his death for the birth of Christianity. Without his radical insight the

20. M. Hengel, *The Atonement* (London: SCM, 1981 ET), 39-44.
21. Acts 2:46; Hengel, *Atonement*, 73.
22. Hengel, *Atonement*, 44-47, 54.

"sect of the Nazōraiōns" would have continued as a messianic Temple cult founded by an obscure Galilean. Like the Essenes they may have attracted the attention of Jewish and Roman historians. Like the Essenes, but also the Pharisees and Sadducees, they would have disappeared after the Roman invasion of 66-74.

Stephen's attack on Temple and Torah, likely based on his radical grasp of the expiatory death of the Christ, paved the way for Gentiles accepting the Messiah without becoming Jewish proselytes. True, Paul the apostle formulated this in his preaching and letters, but it appears that Stephen had begun to think this way before him. Further, the mission of Stephen's successor Philip outside Jerusalem to Samaritans and an Ethiopian God-fearer, which was overtly blessed by God, demonstrated to Peter the impossibility of his Temple-centered eschatology.

The Origin of Earliest Christology

Our earliest window into NT christology is the letters of Paul, where his views are more or less uniform throughout. Accordingly that christology was established when his earliest letters began to appear ca. 50. Earlier still, it is evident that by the mid-30s he was preaching in Syria-Cilicia "the faith" he had attempted to destroy in Judea (Gal 1:23). Again from his own pen we are pointed to Damascus as the place God revealed his Son in him, that is, by ca. 34 (Gal 1:16).

Two elements contributed to Paul's christology: "revelation" from heaven (*apokalypsis,* Gal 1:16) and "tradition" from predecessors (*paradosis,* 1 Cor 15:1-3).[23] It is not possible to determine the relative weight of one as against the other.[24] Since we acknowledge that each had a significant contribution, it is important to include the information that Paul "received" from his Christian predecessors. Most likely, this transmission of christology occurred in Damascus at the time of his baptism.

So far as we can tell Paul's instructor was Ananias, a disciple of Damascus who was a conservative Jew (Acts 9:10; 22:12). It is likely that the

---

23. Bruce, *Paul: Apostle of the Free Spirit,* 86-93.

24. In our view S. Kim, *The Origin of Paul's Gospel* (Grand Rapids: Eerdmans, 1981), 113-14 does not provide sufficiently for the contribution of the christology Paul "received." Kim's reconstruction is too one-sided in its "vertical" theory of the origin of Paul's christology.

christology he "handed over" to Saul had been formulated in recent times in Jerusalem and brought to Damascus from the Jerusalem apostles, whether by "Hebrews" or "Hellenists." It is not known by whom or by what means "the teaching of the apostles" made its way to Damascus.

It is not clear whether the tradition Paul "received" was in Aramaic or had already been formulated in Greek. Here we note that the "Hellenists" were the recipients of the apostles' "teaching," not its formulators.[25] Nonetheless, they may have been responsible for rendering it in the Greek forms[26] we encounter embedded in the Pauline texts (notably 1 Cor 11:23-25; 15:1-7).

From whence, therefore, did the earliest christology arise? In our view all fingers point to Peter. As we shall note, Philip's preaching of Jesus as "the Christ" and by implication "the Servant *(pais)*" in fulfillment of Isaiah 53 (Acts 8:4, 35) coincided with — because it was derived from — the "teaching" of the apostle Peter (Acts 2:31; 4:27). Furthermore — again as we shall note — Paul's christology in Rom 1:1-4 (Christ's Davidic descent) and 1 Cor 15:1-7 (Christ's resurrection) closely resembles Peter's preaching in Acts 2:30 and 10:40. Paul's reference to "the Deuteronomic tree" (Gal 3:13; Acts 13:29) is likewise Petrine in origin (Acts 5:30; 10:39; 1 Pet 2:24). Moreover, it is likely that Saul the persecutor heard the anti-Moses, anti-Temple teaching of Stephen, catechumen of Peter the apostle. We must not diminish the influence on Paul of the Damascus christophany. At the same time, however, we must recognize the didactic role of the original apostles, led by Peter, and in particular the pre-resurrection influence of Jesus in the very recent past.

Conclusion: Between Jesus and Paul (Galatians and Acts)

We have now looked through the "windows" provided by Paul (Galatians 1) and by Luke (Acts 1–9) to catch glimpses of Christianity "between Jesus and Paul." Let us set these side by side.

---

25. Contra Hengel, *Between Jesus and Paul,* 40-42 who attributes the influence on Paul to the early "hellenist" missioners.

26. Contra Hengel, *Between Jesus and Paul,* 11; D. A. Fiensy, "The Composition of the Jerusalem Church," in *BAFCS* 4:235 who (following Moule) states that the Hellenists would have understood little or no Aramaic. Yet the practical necessities of life would have demanded some linguistic adaptation by the Greek speakers residing in Jerusalem.

Year	*Galatians 1*	*Acts 1–9*
33 Jesus' crucifixion		
	Peter leader	Peter leader
		teaching of apostles
		trials of apostles
		division of community
		preaching of Stephen
		execution of Stephen
	Paul's persecutions	Paul's persecutions
34	Damascus conversion	Damascus conversion
	Paul in Damascus	Paul in Damascus

Despite the difference of genre between Galatians and Acts, the overall sequence is similar. This is due to Luke's knowledge of Paul, his persecutions and conversion, and to Paul's knowledge of the early leaders Peter and James. The items peculiar to Acts should not be dismissed. They credibly explain future developments, in particular the early development of christological thought and the impetus for the rise of Christianity in Antioch.

EIGHT

"Christians" in Antioch

The Jewish race, densely interspersed among the native populations of every portion of the world, is particularly numerous in Syria, where intermingling is due to the proximity of the two countries. But it was at Antioch that they especially congregated, partly owing to the greatness of the city, but mainly because the successors of King Antiochus had enabled them to live there in security . . . and moreover granted them citizenship rights. . . . The Jewish colony grew in numbers. . . . Moreover they were constantly attracting to their religious ceremonies multitudes of Greeks, and these they had in some measure incorporated with themselves.

Josephus, *The Jewish War* 7.43-45

And in Antioch the disciples were for the first time called Christianoi.

Acts 11:26

Antioch was the greatest city of the Levant, Rome's military sentry-post to the east. The city had a large Jewish population and many Gentile sympathizers with Judaism who attended the synagogues.

Paul's assault on the church in Jerusalem scattered the members from that city, except the apostles. It is likely that the "Hebrew" believers fled to safe places in Judea and Galilee where, seed-like, they took root, and from them the "churches of Judea" grew up (1 Thess 2:14; Gal 1:22; Acts

9:31-43). Many, however, returned to Jerusalem once Paul's "reign of terror" had passed.

Doubtless some "Hellenist" believers took refuge in the more Hellenized parts of Israel. Philip, for example, took up residence in Caesarea Maritima, a predominantly Gentile city. Other "Hellenist" believers appear to have fled further afield, beyond the historic borders of the land of Israel. The two closest cities outside the land, as scripturally defined, were Damascus and Antioch. It is possible that both were regarded as part of the land, depending on biblical exegesis (Ezek 47:15-17; 48:1).[1] In that case, the choice of these cities was not merely a matter of convenience.

"Christians" in Antioch

According to the Acts of the Apostles, the message of the Christ of Israel came to Antioch in two waves. First, there were Hellenists displaced by Paul's assault, some of whom may have returned to their places of origin.

There is no reason to doubt that this occurred ca. 34 as an immediate consequence to Saul's persecution in Jerusalem. Some Hellenists went inland to Damascus while others traveled north along the coast, some settling along the way in Phoenicia, others going offshore to Cyprus, others again coming to rest in the northern metropolis, Antioch (Acts 11:19). These, however, confined their preaching of the Christ to fellow Jews in the synagogues.

A second wave, also composed of unnamed people, who, however, are more closely identified as being from Cyprus and Cyrene, also came to Antioch. These took the bold step of preaching the Christ to "Greeks," that is, to Gentiles. The date they came can only be conjectured, but it may have been by the late 30s. The impression created by Acts is that the "great number that believed and turned to the Lord" were Gentiles. It is likely that these were, in the main, "God-fearers." As noted above, Josephus commented that "through their worship [the Jews] attracted a large number of Greeks and in a way made them part of themselves." The Acts account of Paul's missions suggests that it was not among Jews or outright pagans but among "God-fearers" that early Christianity chiefly took root.

1. See M. Bockmuehl, "Antioch and James the Just," in B. Chilton and C. A. Evans, eds., *James the Just and Christian Origins* (Leiden: Brill, 1999), 169-79.

It may have been at this time that the preaching of these disciples, from both waves, came to the attention of the authorities, who then referred to them as *Christianoi*/Christians, adherents of the Christ.[2] This word, like *Herodianoi*/Herodians (Mark 3:6; 12:13), points to those who were followers of a noted ruler.

The Crisis under Caligula

After a few years the fortunes of Christianity in Antioch were caught up in the turbulent principate of Caligula and the furor among Jews created by his policies, which threatened to erupt into open war in the Greek cities of the eastern Mediterranean.

Simmering hostility in Alexandria broke out into a bloody pogrom against Jews following the Greek mob's mockery of Herod Agrippa as he passed through the city in 38. Jews in Alexandria were now herded into one quarter of the city, the first ghetto in history.

Soon afterward Jews in Judea demolished an altar to Caligula in the coastal town of Jamnia, which had been built by the Greek citizens to celebrate his recent victories in Germany. The emperor responded with the directive that a statue of himself as the god Jupiter be erected in the Temple in Jerusalem. In effect, Caligula was seeking to convert the holy sanctuary into an imperial shrine.

The situation in Israel, but also in Greek cities with large Jewish communities, now became acute. Jews in Palestine were on the brink of declaring war on Rome. Inflamed over Jewish citizenship demands, the Greeks in Caesarea, Damascus, and Antioch were poised to attack the Jews as the Greeks in Alexandria had done. Significantly, Antioch held Caligula and his father Germanicus, who had died in the city, in particular honor. There are medieval accounts of a Greek assault on Jews in Antioch, including the burning of their major synagogue.[3]

For their part, Jews in these cities were ready for conflict. At the death of Caligula in 41 Jews took up arms in Alexandria against their persecutors. In Antioch in the 60s the Jews planned to burn the whole city and were se-

---

2. See p. 32 above.

3. M. Hengel and A. M. Schwemer, *Paul between Damascus and Antioch: The Unknown Years* (Louisville: Westminster/John Knox), 183-91.

verely punished when the conspiracy was revealed. The crisis under Caligula must not be underestimated. It revealed how profound and extensive was the antipathy between Jews and Greeks in the Gentile cities of the eastern Mediterranean. Twenty-five years after Caligula's death, Jewish and Greek hostility was again breaking out, in Caesarea Maritima in Judea. The war between Rome and the Jews would follow as Roman legions marched into Judea, encircling Jerusalem and then destroying the sacred shine after desecrating it in 70.

Clearly, then, cities like Antioch in the late 30s and early 40s witnessed severe hostility on the part of Greeks against Jews and on the part of Jews against Greeks. It is against this background that we must understand how alarmed the Greeks and Romans of Antioch must have been on hearing the reports that a Messiah/Christ of Israel was being proclaimed in the synagogues by recently arrived Jews. Jews everywhere could be united under this leader, who might even rival the emperor himself. This explains why these preachers and their supporters were called *Christianoi*, "adherents of [the] Christ." At the same time we can only reflect on the turmoil within the synagogues of Antioch in the knowledge that these preachers, fellow Jews as they were, were treacherously offering the salvation of the God of Israel to *Greeks!* We may not easily imagine how explosive for Greeks, Romans, and Jews the arrival in Antioch of these preachers of the Christ must have been.

Ministers in Antioch

Thanks entirely to the Acts of the Apostles, we know how, in broad terms, the gospel came to the Syrian capital, the Roman sentinel to the east.

Acts does not mask the resistance of the Jerusalem church to the incorporation of Gentiles into the community of the Messiah. The apostles dispatched Peter and John to the Samaritans following Philip's visit. The Jerusalem brotherhood expressed concern at the report that Peter had preached to the Gentile Cornelius (Acts 8:14; 11:1). When the report from Antioch reached Jerusalem that Gentiles had become believers they reacted characteristically, by sending an envoy to Antioch to investigate, but also to exercise prudent ministry while there.

Barnabas was a trusted member of the Jerusalem church, a Greek-speaking Cypriot who would be welcomed in Antioch and a man of proven pastoral ability, in short, a suitable ambassador from the mother church. Yet Barnabas was a "Hebrew" rather than a "Hellenist" and well able to represent the concerns of the Jerusalem church. His role, however, proved to be not merely that of diplomatic emissary on a sensitive mission. He was shaken by what he saw in Antioch so that immediately he threw himself into ministry in this growing community, which expanded as a consequence. No time note is given, but we suggest that Barnabas arrived in the early 40s. The demands of the community were beyond his resources. Assistance was needed, so he set out for Tarsus. He had heard of Paul's ministry. In ca. 44 Barnabas found Paul in Tarsus and brought him to the metropolis where he, too, ministered, for "a whole year" according to Acts. Again, further growth is noted.

Acts also gives us a window through which we see something of the internal life of the community of *Christianoi* in Antioch of a few years later. Warned by the prophet Agabus of impending famine in Judea, Barnabas and Paul journeyed to Jerusalem (in ca. 47) with famine relief sent by members of the church of Antioch. Accompanying them was Titus, a "Greek," most probably a Gentile convert of Antioch.[4] While in Jerusalem they met the "pillars" of the Jerusalem church who in a private meeting agreed that Barnabas and Saul would take the gospel to the Gentiles. On their return to Antioch, in the light of this dramatic development in Jerusalem, the church was worshipping the Lord and fasting, seeking the guidance of the Spirit.

Five men from the church of Antioch are named: Barnabas, Simeon called Niger, Lukios of Cyrene, Manaen from the court of Herod the tetrarch, and Paul.

These five names are listed like the twelve names of the original apostles and the seven leaders of the Jerusalem Hellenists.[5] Luke's listing of these men's names may indicate the significance with which he viewed this church as the launching point for westward mission to the Gentiles.

Simeon and Lukios have Gentile names — the first Greek, the second Roman — though both were probably Jews. That Simeon was called Niger implies that he was a black man, or perhaps a man from northern Africa, a place associated with black people. Lukios from Cyrene in North Africa may have been one of those who had been expelled from Jerusalem and

---

4. Gal 2:1-3; cf. Acts 11:27-29. Titus may have been a God-fearer.
5. Acts 1:26; 6:5.

who, according to Acts, first preached to Greeks in Antioch; there is no good reason to identify him with the Loukas who became Paul's companion, the noted NT author.[6]

Another of the five leaders was the Jew Manaen (Hebrew Menachem), the associate of Herod Antipas, tetrarch of Galilee (Greek *syntrophos* could mean "boyhood friend" or "courtier").[7] Questions abound. How was this man now a Christian? Did Joanna, wife of Chusa (a steward of Antipas), provider for the Lord in Galilee and witness of the empty tomb (Luke 8:3; 24:10), point Manaen to the Christ? Was he a member of the early church in Jerusalem, only to be scattered with others to Antioch? Or, did he migrate to Syria after Antipas's exile in 39? Answers are not forthcoming; we may only conjecture.

These three men, with Barnabas the leader (his name is given first) and Saul (whose name is given last), are called "prophets and teachers" in the church at Antioch.

Westward to the Gentiles

A prophet (so it seems) now spoke in the assembly in Antioch, directing the church to "set apart" Barnabas and Saul and to "release" them for ministry to the Gentile world. The Acts account of the first westward mission to the Gentiles now follows.

This marks the end of the period which I have called the "birth of Christianity." To this point most believers were Jews, with few exceptions. Gentiles who became believers appear to have been mostly "sympathizers" with Judaism, God-fearers. From now on, however, the response of Jews appears to diminish and the response of the Gentiles to increase.

Antiochene Christology

The "history-of-religions" school argued that Paul's view of Jesus as "Son of God" and "Lord" was Hellenistic in character, derived from Gentile Antioch. According to this interpretation the historical Jesus was a prophet

6. Cf. Col 4:14; 2 Tim 4:11; Phlm 24.
7. See p. 83 above.

or holy man, not the Messiah. After Hellenistic Jews founded the church in Antioch, so the argument goes, the Gentile believers began to see Jesus as a "god" or a "Lord."

The material from previous chapters, however, points to "the faith" (= "the teaching of the apostles") that Jesus is "Christ," "Lord," and "Son" having been formulated exceedingly early, between Jesus' crucifixion and Paul's conversion. Furthermore, the founders of the church in Antioch were not Gentiles but Jews whose message was centered on Christ/the Messiah, hence the name given the believers, *Christianoi*. Doubtless in the next half-century the Gentile influence increased and the Jewish influence diminished. But this was after the Pauline mission, during which Paul wrote his letters setting out his christology, which had been formulated beforehand. In short, the arguments of the "history-of-religions" school are anachronistic.

NINE

Earliest "Teaching": The Influence of Peter

Simon Peter: *"You are the Christ, the Son of the Living God."*
Jesus: *"You are Peter. . . . On this rock I will build
my church. . . ."*

Matthew 16:16, 18

The most urgent question relating to earliest Christianity is to ascertain what the first disciples believed and said about Jesus. Did they think of him minimally, in one or another of the ways suggested by, for example, Crossan, Bousset, or Casey (see pp. 2-7 above)? In that case, Jesus came to be viewed in more exalted ways with the passage of time. Alternatively, was the christology of the first believers "advanced" from the beginning so that there is no great difference between it and the formulations in the literature as it began to appear?

In this chapter we examine three statements about Christ from the earliest period and seek to trace them to their source.

The Preaching of Philip (Acts 8:4-40)

Acts calls Philip the Hellenist Jew the "Evangelist" (21:8). Having been driven from Jerusalem by Paul's attacks, Philip is seen first in Samaria, second on the road from Jerusalem to Gaza speaking to an Ethiopian, and third preaching to all the towns on the coastal strip from Azotus to

Caesarea. We hear echoes of his preaching. To the Samaritans he said that Jesus was "the Christ" (8:4), and in response to the Ethiopian reading Isaiah 53 (the Servant passage) he preached to him Jesus (8:35).

It is surely no coincidence that Philip's preaching echoed the teaching of Peter in Jerusalem. In the summaries of sermons in Acts we hear Peter say many times that Jesus is "the Christ" (2:31, 38; 3:18, 20) and that Jesus is of the "seed of David" (2:30), the Lord's "anointed" (4:26). We can understand why Philip preached Jesus as "the Christ."

Furthermore, we know why Philip identified the "Servant" of Isaiah 53 with Jesus. The Greek text of Isaiah 53 uses the word *pais* ("servant"), the word Peter had employed for Jesus as God's "holy servant" (Acts 4:27, 30). In Isa 53:13 God says "my servant/*pais* will be glorified"; Peter says "God glorified his *pais* Jesus" (Acts 3:13). In other words, Peter understood Jesus as the Lord's vicariously suffering *pais*. Since the "apostles' teaching" (2:42; 5:28; cf. 4:2, 18; 5:21, 25, 28, 42) led by Peter impacted on a disciple like Philip, it is no surprise that Philip immediately identified the *pais* the Ethiopian read about in Isaiah 53 as Jesus.

This suggests that the apostles formulated their christology on the basis of their involvement with Jesus and his death and resurrection, now seen through the lens of Spirit-led reflection on OT texts. Philip the "evangelist" instructed others in the faith he had learned from the apostles.

A Pre-Pauline Tradition (1 Corinthians 15:1-7)

As an introduction to his teaching on the end-time resurrection Paul reminds the Corinthians of the resurrection tradition he "handed over" to them when the church was formed. Paul did not formulate that tradition, but "received" it from others. Although he does not identify the time or place he received it, this likely occurred at Damascus at the time of his baptism when, according to Acts some instruction at least probably occurred (Acts 9:18; 22:16). This likelihood is strengthened by the fact that in Damascus Paul immediately began to preach Jesus as Son of God and the Christ, which he also did in "Arabia" prior to returning to Damascus and Jerusalem (Gal 1:16-17; Acts 9:28; 26:20; cf. 1 Thess 2:15). By the time Paul first returned to Jerusalem, when a further opportunity arose to "receive" the tradition (from Peter and James) Paul had been preaching for three years. Damascus is the preferred option.

When we place this "received" tradition alongside Peter's preaching in Acts we note a number of parallels.

1 Corinthians 15:3-5	Acts 10:40-41, 43
Christ died for our sins according to the *Scriptures.*	To him *all the prophets* bear witness that everyone who believes in him receives *forgiveness of sins through his name.*
He was raised [by God] on the third day *(tȩ̄ hēmerạ tȩ̄ tritȩ̄).*	God raised him on the third day *(tȩ̄ tritȩ̄ hēmerạ).*
He appeared to *Cephas* . . . the Twelve. . . .	God gave him to be manifest . . . to *us* . . . witnesses.

In these two passages we see a convergence of ideas, but also of words, that teach (1) the vicarious death of "[the] Christ," (2) whom God raised "on the third day," whereupon (3) he appeared alive to various witnesses.

Historically, Peter's "teaching" *(didachē),* expressed here in Luke's summary, was likely the source of the "tradition" that Paul "received" (secondhand) in Damascus and then taught to the churches of his mission. A further point of contact may be seen in Ananias's words to Paul to "be baptized and wash away your sins, calling on his name" (Acts 22:16). The forgiveness of sins is found in (1) the pre-Pauline tradition in 1 Corinthians, (2) Peter's sermon in Caesarea, and (3) Ananias's baptismal instruction in Damascus, which in turn derives from the vicarious sufferings of the *pais* in Isaiah 53.

Origins of the Teaching in Rome

Paul did not write to the believers in Rome to initiate their faith. Rather he wrote to "strengthen"[1] their existing Christ-centered faith against those who were seeking to make it Torah-centered. This is evident (1) by the frequency of references (mostly negative) to "Law" *(nomos)*,[2] (2) by Paul's

---

1. Rom 1:11; 16:25.
2. After "God" the most frequently appearing word in Romans is "Law."

"exchanges" with his Jewish "interlocutor,"[3] and (3) by his warnings at the end of the letter against those who "create barriers to the teaching [they] have learned."[4] In fact, Paul has nothing but praise and encouragement for the faith of the Roman believers and their leaders,[5] which others are currently attempting to subvert.

In the final chapter of Romans Paul encourages the readers to "greet" eleven persons or groups of persons. Most likely those greeted represent house meetings of believers known to Paul at the time he wrote, ca. 57. Paul appears to have been informed about the circumstances of the church in Rome; only a few weeks' travel separated the cities of Rome and Corinth.[6]

The first persons to be "greeted" are Paul's "fellow workers" Prisca and Aquila, who had been forced from Rome to Corinth in ca. 49 by Claudius's expulsion of the Jews from Rome.[7] It appears that they had been Christians in Rome going back into the 40s. Their grasp of the faith seems to have been acceptable to Paul from the beginning, adding to the impression that Paul was generally encouraged by the doctrines of the Roman believers.

Apart from Prisca and Aquila there are no names in Romans 16 that we know were believers back into the 40s, to say nothing of the 30s. It has been plausibly suggested, however, that Roman Jews and proselytes[8] baptized under Peter in Jerusalem at Pentecost brought Christianity home with them. If so, they may have continued their association with the synagogues, not forming distinctly Christian assemblies. Paul does not direct his letter to "the church in Rome"; the only "church" mentioned is the one meeting in the house of Prisca and Aquila.

The Genuineness of Roman Faith

Whatever the origins of the faith in Rome Paul does not question its genuineness. Twice he appeals approvingly to the catechesis that undergirded their faith.

---

3. Rom 2:1-5, 15-29; 3:27–4:2; 9:19-21; 11:17-24.
4. Rom 16:17-20.
5. See, e.g., Rom 1:8-12; 15:14; 16:3-16.
6. So Philostratus, *Life of Apollonius of Tyana* 7.10.
7. Acts 18:1-2; cf. Suetonius, *Claudius* 25.4.
8. Acts 2:10-11.

> Thanks be to God . . . that . . .
> you became obedient from the heart
> to the pattern of teaching *(typon didachēs)*
> to which you were handed over. (6:17)

> I appeal to you, brothers,
> to take note of those who create divisions
> and who raise barriers
> against the teaching you learned *(tēn didachēn . . . emathete).*
> (16:17)

These passages presuppose a context of baptism (6:3-11) and catechetical instruction: "handed over to . . . a pattern of teaching," "teaching which you learned." This vocabulary is technical, in fact "rabbinic" in character. It appears in many places in Paul's letters, for example, in regard to the institution of the Lord's Supper (1 Cor 11:23-26) and the gospel of the death and resurrection of Christ (1 Cor 15:1-7). Paul himself had been the "traditor" of preformed teaching he "received" (most likely in Damascus) and in turn "passed on" to the newly formed churches. Paul, however, does not specify from whom the Romans "learned . . . the pattern of teaching."

The Christology of Romans 1:1-4

At the head of the letter Paul sets out this weighty statement of faith.

> . . . the gospel of God which he promised beforehand
> through his prophets in the Holy Scriptures
> concerning his Son,
> who came from the seed of David
>   according to the flesh,
> who was set apart as Son of God in power
>   according to the Spirit of holiness
> through his resurrection from the dead,
> Jesus Christ our Lord. . . .

The creed-like format and content of this text have often been noted.[9] There are two balancing yet contrastive phrases, both of which "concern

9. See, e.g., M. Hengel, *The Son of God* (London: SCM, 1976), 59-66.

his Son." As to content we note the archaic-sounding "Spirit of holiness" (found nowhere else in the NT).

This passage has the marks of a preformed teaching that Paul "received" at some earlier time. Its prominent place at the head of the letter may well indicate the "pattern of teaching" the Romans "learned" and which Paul deliberately quotes as a fundamental shared belief.[10] Here Paul seems to be establishing at the outset his oneness with them in the fundamentals of christology.

The Antecedents of Romans 1:1-4

This tightly compacted formulation corresponds quite closely with Peter's proclamation on the day of Pentecost (Acts 2:14-36). Both affirm:

	Romans	Acts
fulfillment of Scripture	1:2	2:25-26
Jesus' descent from David	1:3	2:20
Jesus' special relationship with God	1:2 ("his Son")	2:31 ("the Christ")
Jesus' resurrection	1:4	2:32
Jesus as Lord	1:4	2:36
the coming of the Spirit at that time	1:4	2:17

The combination of elements in common is too striking to be coincidental. These passages seem to be connected in some way. Furthermore, both are connected with baptism (Rom 6:3, 17; Acts 2:41-42).

The early chapters of Acts refer many times to "the teaching of the apostles" *(hē didachē tōn apostolōn).*[11] It is reasonable to assume a close connection between Peter's Pentecost sermon and this "teaching" to those being baptized. Arguably, such teaching was cast in summary form similar to that reproduced by Paul in the opening lines of Romans. In this case, by different routes the "teaching of the apostles" reached both newly baptized Jews returning to Rome from Jerusalem and Paul at his baptism at Damascus.

Upon his baptism in the synagogues of Damascus Paul proclaimed

---

10. So Hengel, *Son of God,* 59-60.
11. See p. 90 above.

Jesus as "Son of God . . . proving that Jesus was the Christ" (Acts 9:20, 22). The connections between Paul's post-baptismal preaching and the credo of Rom 1:1-4 are so close as to demand some explanation like the above.

Romans 1:1-4 as Typos for Paul's Synagogue "Teaching"

Indeed, it is likely that "the teaching of the apostles" summarized in the credo of Rom 1:1-4 became a template for preaching elsewhere to Jews in the synagogues.

Paul's preaching in the synagogue in Thessalonica is stated in brief terms (Acts 17:2-3).

> Paul . . . argued with them from the Scriptures, explaining and proving that it was necessary for the Christ to suffer and rise from the dead . . . saying, "This Jesus whom I proclaim to you is the Christ."

Placed alongside Rom 1:1-4 we note the coincidence of fulfillment of Scripture, Jesus' messianic status (i.e., Davidic descent), and his resurrection from the dead. The Lukan summary refers to the necessity of the Christ's sufferings which, though not found in Rom 1:1-4, is set out in symmetrical creedal form later in the letter (e.g., Rom 4:25: ". . . Jesus our Lord, who was put to death for [*dia*] our trespasses and raised for [*dia*] our justification").

The more expansive report of Paul's preaching in Colonia Antiocheia also bears close resemblance to Rom 1:1-4:

	Romans	Acts
fulfillment of Scripture	1:2	13:32-33
Jesus' descent from *(sperma)* David	1:3	13:23
Jesus' special relationship with God	1:2 ("his Son")	13:33 ("my Son")
Jesus' resurrection	1:4	13:37

There are differences. The Acts account has no reference to the Spirit and provides extensive historical reference to Jesus not found in Romans. A striking common element is the promise of forgiveness from sins and freedom from the law of Moses to those who believe (Acts 13:39), which bears close similarity to Paul's exposition of "justification by faith" found throughout Romans.

In short, references in Acts to Paul's synagogue preaching bear striking similarity to the credo in Rom 1:1-4, as well as to various expansions of that teaching later in Romans. That credo in turn appears to have arisen from "the teaching of the apostles" as it was passed on to those who were being baptized.

Romans 1:1-4: From and for Jews

The opening lines of Romans are profoundly "biblical" in character as seen in the strong note of fulfillment of the Scriptures and the Davidic descent that marked Jesus as Messiah/Christ. This solemn credo could only have arisen in a self-consciously Jewish setting (most likely Jerusalem). Any proposal that this teaching was formulated in Antioch in Syria must be regarded as unlikely. Furthermore, these words were crafted for Jews. They are *from* and *for* Jewish concerns, as reflected in Paul's dialectic teaching in synagogues in Colonia Antiocheia and Thessalonica. Here we note a clear contrast with the preaching of Paul to Gentiles, where the call is to turn from the manmade gods to the true and living God and to wait for the return of God's resurrected Son from heaven, the eschatological deliverer Jesus (1 Thess 1:9-10). True, there are references to Gentiles and Gentile concerns in the apostle's letter to Rome (e.g., 6:12-23; 11:13; 14:1), yet these are secondary. The burden of the letter is to confirm Jewish believers in the "pattern of teaching" *(typos didachēs)* and to resist any impetus toward Law-based, as opposed to Christ-based, dependence for salvation.

Understood in this light Paul's strategy becomes plain. In reminding the (mainly Jewish) readers at the head of the letter of the baptismal credo he and they share, he reinforces his unity with them against those who now attempt to move their faith in another direction. The remainder of the letter is, in effect, an exposition of a credo that Paul has proclaimed many times in the synagogues along the way but which is now conditioned by the new situation in Rome.

Conclusion: The Influence of Peter

We have briefly studied three passages, one from Acts narrating the preaching of Philip "the evangelist" and two from Paul. One of these is an explicitly preformed tradition, the other implicitly preformed. In each Pauline text it is possible to detect the influence of "the teaching of the apostles," in particular the teaching of Peter. If this is correct, then Peter must have been the prime formulator of the didactic outlines that were taken and applied by others, whether by Ananias, who instructed Paul, or by Philip, who instructed the Samaritans and the Ethiopian.

Peter's significance emerges clearly from the literature. According to Acts Peter is the first-named apostle and the only public spokesman in Jerusalem, and he later travels extensively as leader within the land of Israel (Acts 9:31-32). We have the same clear impression from Paul, who notes that Peter is the first witness of the resurrection (1 Cor 15:5) and the leader of the Jerusalem church (Gal 1:18), having his apostolate to the circumcised from God (Gal 2:7-8). This role of Peter post-Easter is consistent with his relationship with Jesus pre-Easter, where as confessor he is named as the "rock" (Matt 16:18) on which the church is to be built, the one who is to feed Christ's lambs (John 21:15-17).

TEN

Into the Land of Israel
(A.D. 34-39)

It was also striking that — in complete contrast to the later romance-like acts of apostles — Luke usually uses exact geographical information only when it is there in the tradition and is significant for the narrative or for his own theology. He does not need to invent it for novelistic elaboration, since he does not want to display specialist learned knowledge nor does he have the delight of later pilgrims in satisfying curiosity by depicting "holy places."

Martin Hengel, "The Geography of Palestine in Acts,"[1]

So the church [of Jerusalem scattered] throughout all Judea, Galilee, and Samaria had peace and was built up; and walking in the fear of the Lord and in the comfort of the Holy Spirit it was multiplied. Now as Peter went here and there among them all. . . .

Acts 9:31-32

The Years 34-39: Overview

The persecutions of Saul of Tarsus in ca. 34 effectively drove the surviving members from Jerusalem, except the twelve apostles. The now-sharpened division between "Hebrews" and "Hellenists" determined the future direc-

1. Martin Hengel, "The Geography of Palestine in Acts," in *BAFCS* 4:67.

95

tion of these groups. The "Hebrews" were "scattered" throughout the land of Israel ("Judea, Galilee, and Samaria"), where they established churches. By the time Paul the believer returned to Jerusalem three years later, however, church life in Jerusalem had been restored (Acts 9:26-36).

It was otherwise with the "Hellenists." Philip, the second of the "seven," preached in Samaria and then along the coast of Judea from the south, before settling in Caesarea, a predominantly Gentile city. Many other "Hellenists" moved outside the land of Israel altogether beyond the reach of the high priest. Was this why the remnant "Hebrew" believers hastily sent Paul from Jerusalem to Tarsus (Acts 9:30)?

In time the apostles Peter and John (and others?) traveled outside Jerusalem throughout the land of Israel, demonstrating their hegemony over the churches that had been established recently. The conversion of the Samaritans shook their eschatological conviction that the Temple was the epicenter of God's future.

Meanwhile the persecutor himself became a convert in Damascus to the faith he had been attempting to destroy. For the next three years Paul, believer and apostle, was outside the land of Israel, in Damascus, "Arabia," and then Damascus again.

These events occurred within the wider river of world history.[2] The first few years after the persecution of 34-36 were, to our knowledge, relatively uneventful. The next years (36-37), however, were marked by serious disturbances. Aretas, king of the Nabateans, inflicted a crushing defeat upon Herod Antipas, tetrarch of Galilee. Pilate massacred numerous Samaritans, unleashing a chain of events that eventuated in his own dismissal in 37. In that year Caiaphas, the high priest under whom Jesus had been executed and the first believers persecuted, was replaced. Also in 37 Tiberius died and Caligula, the new emperor, took actions that were to shake the whole eastern empire, including Judea.

The book of Acts mentions none of this. Nonetheless, the "peace" following Saul's conversion coincided with the quiet years in the land of Israel. Then, however, the troubles in Galilee and Samaria (in 36-37) may have retarded the "multiplication" of ministry in those parts of the land of Israel. Quieter times returned for the years 37-38, after which, however, the anti-Semitic policies of Caligula brought the land to the brink of disaster.

2. See pp. 27-41 above.

In his Gospel's preface Luke refers to "eyewitnesses and ministers of the word," by which he means the apostles mentioned at the beginning of Acts. These were the apostles, led by Peter, who formulated and "handed over" their "teaching" *(didachē),* as Acts notes on many occasions.[3] Later, according to Luke, they authenticated written texts (some of which they may have written) that they "handed over" to Luke. Luke does not inform us when oral teaching began to be committed to written text. This may have begun soon after the first Easter and been given significant impetus by Saul's persecution. If the apostles had been killed, their oral *didachē* would have died with them.

The "Scattering" of the Jerusalem Church (34)

The Growth of the Church

The church of God in Jerusalem grew rapidly. The early chapters of Acts are dotted with generalized references to this growth (2:47; 5:14; 6:7) as well as to specific numbers (1:15; 2:41; 4:4).

After the ascension, the initial group of disciples, followers, and family was enlarged to one hundred twenty "persons"[4] (1:15). After the Pentecost event "about three thousand souls were added" (2:41), many of whom were pilgrims from the Diaspora visiting Jerusalem for the great feast. Sometime later about five thousand "men" heard the apostles' word and believed (4:4). Possibly the "five thousand," like the "three thousand," were visiting pilgrims who had remained in Jerusalem for a period and then returned to their homelands. Whatever the case, it is possible that by this early stage in the church's history there were many hundreds of believers, who may have represented a visible group in Jerusalem.[5]

3. See pp. 69-71 above.

4. Acts 1:15 distinguishes between "brothers" *(adelphoi)* and "persons" *(onomata).*

5. Most estimates of the population of Jerusalem vary between 60,000 and 100,000. See W. Reinhardt, "The Population Size of Jerusalem and the Numerical Growth of the Jerusalem Church," in R. Bauckham, ed., *BAFCS* 4:237-65.

The Scattering of the Church

The combined evidence from Paul's letters and Acts points to the severity of Saul's persecution of the church. Paul states that he "was persecuting the church of God violently and attempting to destroy it" (Gal 1:13).[6] Acts declares that "Saul was ravaging the church" (8:3). The numerous members of the church were scattered throughout Judea and Samaria and — we suppose — also Galilee (9:31); only the apostles remained in Jerusalem (8:1).

Without saying so, Luke intends the reader to understand that both "Hebrews" and "Hellenists" were driven out. He refers to these dispersed believers as "scattered" (as of seed, 8:1, 4; 11:19). After adding that they "went throughout[7] preaching the word" (8:4), he introduces Philip the "Hellenist" who "went . . . and proclaimed . . . the Christ" in Samaria and Judea (8:5, 27, 35, 40). Most likely the scattered "Hebrew" believers also "preached the word" and, seed-like, took root as churches in Judea, Galilee, and Samaria.

The Rise of Jewish Churches in the Land of Israel

In this brief statement Luke refers to dispersion of the Jerusalem church throughout the biblical "land of Israel": "So the church [of Jerusalem scattered] throughout the whole of *Judea* and *Galilee* and *Samaria* . . . was multiplied" (Acts 9:31).

Churches in Judea

Twice Paul refers to "the churches of Christ in Judea." These churches must have arisen by the mid-30s or sooner since Paul reports their amazement as they "kept hearing"[8] about the former persecutor "preaching the faith" in Syria-Cilicia (Gal 1:23). Paul also mentions the example of "the churches

---

6. The imperfect tense *eporthoun* is conative: "I was attempting to destroy." See E. de W. Burton, *The Epistle to the Galatians* (ICC; Edinburgh: Clark, 1980), 45.

7. *Dierchomai*, "go throughout," is used often in Acts, suggesting systematic itinerant preaching (e.g., 9:32).

8. This is the force of the periphrastic *akouontes ēsan* (Gal 1:23).

of God in Christ Jesus . . . in Judea . . . who suffered . . . from the Jews . . . and who . . . drove us out . . ." (1 Thess 2:14-15). The expulsion of Paul from Judea occurred soon after his first post-conversion return to Jerusalem in ca. 36 (Acts 9:28-30; Gal 1:21). By that time those churches were sufficiently established to attract persecution by their fellow-Jews. Evidently these Judean churches were composed of Aramaic-speaking "Hebrews."

Who established these Judean congregations? Since the apostles remained in Jerusalem (8:1), it appears that the founders were unnamed "Hebrews" who preached the word of Christ in Aramaic in the synagogues of Israel. Only later did Peter (and other apostles?) leave Jerusalem to consolidate these Judean churches.

We know little of the ongoing history of these communities. Doubtless they deferred to the Jerusalem apostles led by Peter. Later the mantle of leadership passed to James, the Lord's brother.

Churches in Galilee

There is only one mention of "Galilee" in the book of Acts, as noted above. Following the cessation of Saul's persecutions, "the church throughout . . . Galilee . . . was built up . . . and multiplied" (9:31). It is reasonable to suppose that many of the original hearers of Jesus were drawn into churches in Galilee through unnamed "Hebrew" preachers. True, the "core followers" with the family of Jesus had settled in Jerusalem. Yet there would have been many who had been prepared as seedbeds by Jesus' own teaching and miracles and by the mission of the Twelve, who were "reaped" by the newly arrived preachers.[9]

The passage quoted above concerning the church of Jerusalem "scattered" in Judea, Galilee, and Samaria (8:4; 9:31) continues with "Now Peter went in and out among *them all.*" So believers in Galilee, the northernmost part of the land of Israel, were also visited by Peter.

In the early 40s, during the persecutions under King Herod Agrippa I, Peter was forced to flee from Jerusalem to "another place." Various suggestions about this "other place" have been made, including Rome and Caesarea. But those cities may be eliminated. Rome was too distant; Peter was back in Jerusalem only a few years later (Gal 2:7-9). Caesarea was

---

9. Cf. John 4:45.

predominantly a Gentile city and soon became the home of the king who had originally arrested Peter. A more likely place of refuge is Galilee, Peter's own homeland. If correct, Peter had further opportunity for ministry in Galilee.

Churches in Samaria

The Samaritans, as descendants of the apostate northern kingdom, had developed a distinctive temple cultus on Mount Gerizim as an alternative to Mount Zion. They had also established their own canon of Scripture and an idiosyncratic eschatology with lively expectations of the appearance of their Messiah, the *Taheb* ("Restorer").

During the Hasmonaean era the Idumeans were converted to Judaism and the Galileans were reconverted. It was otherwise with the Samaritans. There is evidence that Galileans encountered difficulties[10] traveling through Samaria to Jerusalem for the major feasts.[11] A Samaritan village refused to receive Jesus and the disciples because they were journeying to Jerusalem (Luke 9:51-53).

Although Jesus instructed his disciples to "enter no town of the Samaritans" (Matt 10:5), he had contact with individual Samaritans (Luke 17:16). The most prominent of these was a woman at Shechem (John 4:7-26). His discussion with her reached its climax when she raised the subject of the Samaritan Temple. It is possible that "Rabbi" Jesus' ministry to this "woman of Samaria" prepared the way for missions to the Samaritans after Easter. John's comment that "many Samaritans in that city believed in [Jesus] because of the woman's testimony" suggests that some of these Samaritan believers continued beyond that time.

The first mission came via the Hellenist Philip, who preached "the Christ" in a "city of the Samaritans" (Shechem?).[12] Those to whom he came were most likely Hellenized city dwellers rather than indigenous rural Samaritans. In a subsequent mission Peter and John confirmed these Samaritan city dwellers in their new faith. Thereafter Peter and John also

---

10. Josephus, *War* 2.232-34; cf. *Antiquities* 20.118.

11. Josephus, *Antiquities* 20.118.

12. So F. F. Bruce, *The Acts of the Apostles: The Greek Text with Introduction and Commentary* (Grand Rapids: Eerdmans, 1990³), 216.

preached the gospel to "many villages" in Samaria (Acts 8:25). Most likely these were indigenous Samaritans.

The net effect of these successive missions (to Hellenized Samaritans and then to indigenous Samaritans?) was that a major city and "many villages" were evangelized and churches established. This is confirmed by Luke's words that "the church [of Jerusalem scattered] throughout . . . Samaria . . . was built up and . . . was multiplied" (Acts 9:31). This is in line with Jesus' command to the apostles to bear witness to his resurrection "in Jerusalem and in all Judea and Samaria" (Acts 1:8). Less than twenty years after these initial missions, Paul and Barnabas passed through Samaria traveling from Antioch to Jerusalem, where they reported the conversion of the Gentiles to "the brothers" there (Acts 15:3).

Greek Churches in the Land of Israel

The book of Acts is interested in Philip, the second of the "seven" "Hellenist" almoners, whom it calls "the evangelist" (21:8). The author, as Paul's companion, stayed with Philip in Caesarea two decades after Philip's first mission (21:10), affording opportunity to hear firsthand of those earlier endeavors. Luke, as probably an Antiochene,[13] would have felt a special bond with the "Hellenists," who were also founders of his home church.

At any rate, Luke narrates in some detail Philip's ministry to Samaria and to the Ethiopian treasurer while commenting generally that "passing through, he preached in all the towns from Azotus to Caesarea" (Acts 8:40). Among these were probably Lydda and Joppa, where churches were established. Based in Caesarea, Philip was probably also responsible for the creation of churches in the Hellenistic cities of Ptolemais, Sidon, and Tyre (21:3-7).

Peter's Apostleship in the Land of Israel

Not Acts but Paul is the source for critical information about Peter's ministry to Jews at this time.

---

13. See p. 48 above.

> . . . Peter had been entrusted [by God]
> with the gospel to the circumcised.
> > [God] worked through Peter for the mission *(apostolē)*
> > to the circumcised. (Gal 2:7-8)

Acts, in stating that Peter "went throughout them all," refers to the members of the church of Jerusalem who had been "scattered" "throughout the whole of Judea, Galilee, and Samaria" (8:4).

Luke, however, tends to underplay Peter's role as "Apostle to the circumcised in the Land of Israel." Luke's interest is to tell the story of the word of God coming away from Jerusalem to the Gentiles. Accordingly Peter has a secondary role, following that of Philip among the Samaritans. Thereafter Luke briefly narrates events in Lydda and Joppa only as steppingstones to the great moment when Peter witnesses the Spirit coming to the Gentile Cornelius. Peter now fades from Luke's story. Peter's ministry throughout the land of Israel may have been far more extensive than Luke's radical selectivity allows.

That wider ministry, however, only began when the apostles confined hitherto in Jerusalem heard that the Samaritans had received the word of God (Acts 8:14). The journeys of the Hellenist Philip outside Jerusalem forced the apostles to reconsider their opinion that the holy city was the epicenter of God's end-time plans. The apostles, led by Peter and John, had to demonstrate their hegemony over the land of Israel, which they did by following in Philip's footsteps.

Samaria

Peter and John went north for ministry to (Hellenized?) Samaritans. They witnessed the coming of the Spirit to Samaritans by outward ecstatic manifestation, as in Jerusalem on Pentecost. The unusual delay in the coming of the Spirit *after* the welcoming of the word and baptism was unambiguously intended to show the apostles that God was active outside the holy city and with people who were not the pure heritage of Israel. Thus convinced, Peter and John then proceeded to preach the gospel among "many villages" of ethnic Samaritans (Acts 8:25).

There were probably also Jewish believers now living in Samaria and establishing churches. Acts speaks of Jerusalem church members who were "scattered" in Samaria (8:1) and who "took root" as churches in Samaria, where they were visited by Peter (9:31-32) and years later by Paul and Barnabas (Acts 15:3).

Judea

Saul's persecutions also scattered "Hebrew" believers from Jerusalem to wider Judea (Acts 8:1). The clear inference is that many but not all returned to Jerusalem after the cessation of persecution, but that churches came into existence through these dispersed Jerusalemites (9:31).

It is likely that as Peter and John visited Samaria to confirm and consolidate the new churches there, they went also for the same purpose throughout Judea (9:31-32). While Peter would have gone primarily with a pastoral intention, it is almost certain that he would also have engaged in evangelism, as he had done in Samaria (8:25). Most likely this evangelism occurred in the synagogues of Judean villages and towns.

Galilee

It seems likely that when Peter came to oversee the churches established by scattered church members from Jerusalem (Acts 9:31-32), he would also have engaged in direct evangelism, as in Judea.

The Coastal Plain

Peter went also to Lydda on the coastal plain for ministry to the believers. His healing of Aeneas brought news of his presence to Joppa on the coast, where he was summoned to minister to the deceased widow (?) Tabitha/Dorcas. At Joppa he stayed with Simon, a tanner, from which, in a series of supernatural events, he was brought to the house of the Gentile Cornelius in Caesarea. Although Acts makes it clear that Peter was involved in extensive ministry at Lydda and Joppa, it describes only those events that brought Peter to Cornelius. Furthermore, it is evident that by the time of Peter's visit the churches in Lydda and Joppa were well established. But Luke shows little interest in these Jewish churches. His concern is to demonstrate the role of the Hellenists leading to world mission springing from Antioch.

The climax of the miraculous episodes in Lydda, Joppa, and Caesarea was the ecstatically manifested coming of the Spirit upon Gentiles in Caesarea. It was now beyond dispute for Peter that Jerusalem and its Temple were not God's eschatological endpoint, but that Gentiles, Gentiles *outside* Jerusalem, were now to be incorporated into the divine plan.

Historically speaking it is probable that Philip had evangelized these cities on the coastal plain ahead of Peter, as in Samaria. The coastal cities were Hellenized and bilingual, appropriate to the cultural and linguistic background of Philip the Hellenist Jew. It may not be coincidental that Aeneas, Dorcas, and Simon, believers from Lydda and Joppa respectively, all have Greek names. Certainly, Caesarea was a predominantly Gentile city and Greek was its major language, in all likelihood even for Jews living there.

Peter was linguistically equipped for this ministry in Hellenized regions. His original name was the Greek Simon, and he came from Bethsaida in Gaulanitis, a Hellenized region. To be sure, he was no "Hellenist" as Stephen, Philip, and the others were. Nonetheless, he could at least understand and speak Greek.

Jesus' threefold commission to Peter to "feed" Jesus' sheep (John 21:15-19) should be read in the light of the "oversight" Peter exercised over the churches in the land of Israel in the years 34-41.

Peter's "Word" in the Land of Israel

Acts portrays Peter teaching and preaching in Jerusalem and in Judea, Galilee, and Samaria (cf. 9:31-32). Whereas in Jerusalem we hear four "sermons,"[14] we hear Peter's words only once outside the holy city, to the God-fearer Cornelius in Caesarea (10:34-43).

Peter's Jerusalem preaching, as summarized by Luke, accuses the Jews for their rejection of Jesus while asserting that God has vindicated Jesus in resurrection and exaltation as Messiah/Christ and Lord at God's right hand. Only once does Peter refer to the earlier activities of "Jesus of Nazareth" as "a man attested by God to you by miraculous wonders and signs which God did among you . . ." (2:22).

---

14. 2:14-41; 3:12-26; 4:8-12; 5:29-32.

The single sermon of Peter outside Jerusalem is less polemical and may reflect the development of a preaching format that had become typical of his preaching in the land of Israel (Acts 10:34-43). True, Cornelius was a God-fearer, not a Jew. Nonetheless, Peter could address him as if he were a Jew, pointing to the fulfillment of prophecy in Jesus. The striking difference from the Jerusalem sermons is that this "word" is so comprehensively biographical. Peter narrates Jesus' "story" from John's baptism, through ministry in Galilee and the country of the Jews, to Jerusalem, where he was killed. But God raised him from the dead and caused him to be seen, whereupon he commissioned his witnesses to proclaim him to the people (of Israel).[15]

James, Brother of the Lord

A good example of the way Paul's letters and the book of Acts complement and confirm each other is their witness to James, brother of Jesus. This is not acknowledged sufficiently by scholars, as it deserves to be.

James was thrust into prominence by the publication in 2002 of an inscription on an ossuary of "James, son of Joseph, brother of Jesus." Despite substantial doubts as to its authenticity, this artifact may be genuine.[16] It is likely, however, that the genuineness of the "James" ossuary will remain in dispute.

Chronologically the first reference to James is in Paul's Letter to the Galatians. There we meet James in Jerusalem ca. 36 as "the Lord's brother" and, it would appear, second in seniority to Cephas among the apostles (Gal 1:18-19). By ca. 47, when Paul revisits Jerusalem, things have changed. The college of apostles has been replaced by a troika, called the "pillars," among whom James is preeminent (Gal 2:9). In Antioch Cephas and Barnabas must bow before James's decree, though Paul resists it (2:11-13).

This broadly coincides with Acts. The Gospel of Luke does not mention James by name; he is one of "[Jesus'] brothers" mentioned alongside Jesus' mother as unsympathetic to Jesus' ministry (8:19-21). We meet Jesus' mother and brothers next in Jerusalem, where they are now in company with the Twelve (Acts 1:14), though no explanation is offered for their new sympathy to Jesus.

15. See pp. 152-54 below.
16. See C. A. Evans, "Jesus and the Ossuaries," *BBR* 13.1 (2003), 39-49.

Acts passes over the brothers of Jesus in silence for the next decade. Only when Peter is forced to flee from Herod Agrippa in the early 40s do we meet them again. Now, for the first time in Luke-Acts James, a brother of Jesus, is mentioned by name (Acts 12:17). By the time of the Jerusalem council ca. 49, James is clearly the leader (15:13), as he remains when we see him again in the late 50s (21:18).

Luke does not explain why James left Galilee to reside in Jerusalem, taking his place with the apostles. The preformed tradition cited by Paul (1 Cor 15:7) most likely supplies the clue. The risen Jesus appeared to James.

Despite the prominence of James evident by the late 40s there is no reason to believe that he shaped the understanding of the earliest Jerusalem disciples. According to the book of Acts, the teaching of Peter was critical in this regard.

The Author and Readers of the Letter to the Hebrews

The only name mentioned in the Letter to the Hebrews is Timothy (13:23). The identity of the writer and the readers and the circumstances of both are therefore unresolved.

Nonetheless the letter may be dated between ca. 49, when Timothy joined Paul as a coworker, and 70,[17] when the destruction of the Temple ended the sacrifices of the levitical priesthood, against which the letter is so opposed (13:10, 12). Much of the argument of the letter would be irrelevant if the sacrifices by the priests in the Temple were no longer occurring (11:7-28). The readers appear to belong to a house church (3:6; 10:21) or a network of house churches with leaders (13:24; cf. 13:7). Their wider context is an urban setting (13:14).

---

17. The greater number of introductions and commentaries argue for a post-70 date. For critical discussion see J. A. T. Robinson, *Redating the New Testament* (London: SCM, 1976), 200-205. Various arguments for a later date are not substantial: (1) The "forty years" of Israel's disobedience (3:7–4:11) offers no basis for the view that the readers had been resistant to God for a comparable period, thus setting the dating of the letter well after 70. (2) There is no evidence that the sacrifices continued after the destruction of the Temple, but rather the evidence is that the sacrifices were discontinued (see Robinson, *Redating*, 202-3). (3) That the *scriptural* Temple is described (9:1-7) rather than the actual Temple built by Herod is no reason to regard the references as entirely symbolic. "Our altar is one from which the priests who serve the tent have no right to eat" (13:10) speaks of the real Temple.

Timothy, who is soon to be released from prison in Italy or else-where, will accompany the writer in visiting the readers. The author sends greetings from "those from Italy" (13:24). This could mean that he was in Italy at the time of writing. Paul was expecting Timothy to come to him in Rome at the time he was writing 2 Timothy (2 Tim 4:9-13, 21). Perhaps Timothy was imprisoned during Nero's campaign against the Christians in 64. The call for perseverance in the face of suffering throughout Hebrews (2:10-18; 4:14–5:10; 10:19–12:13) is certainly quite consistent with a post-64 Roman provenance. On the other hand, and with greater probability, "those from Italy" could refer to expatriate Italians living for the time be-ing in some other place, for example, Jews like Priscilla and Aquila who had been expelled from Rome in ca. 49 by the decree of Claudius (Acts 18:2). They were in Corinth[18] and Ephesus at the same time as Timothy, though we know of no imprisonment for Paul's coworker then.

Who, then, are the readers of this letter? One important clue is that initially the writer was one of their number (2:3). Another is that the writer and the readers are, broadly speaking, sympathetic to Paul; the reference to Timothy supports this suggestion.

In our view, the most likely recipients were Greek-speaking Jews of Palestine, more specifically of Jerusalem, who were the descendants of the original Hellenist believers.[19] Their anti-cult stance sets them apart from the wider community of Jewish Christians in Jerusalem led by James, who

18. The conjunction of Timothy with "those from Italy," if that refers to Priscilla and Aquila, raises the possibility that the letter was written from Corinth (Acts 18:2, 5) or Ephesus (Acts 18:26) in the early fifties. In this case the author may have been Barnabas. In favor of Barnabas it is noted that (1) he was one who heard the original disciples, (2) he had most likely been in Corinth (1 Cor 9:5) in the early 50s, that is, (3) at a time when Timothy and (4) Priscilla and Aquila ("those from Italy") may also have been there. As an early leader who had heard the disciples of the Lord and who is referred to as an "apostle" (Acts 14:4; cf. 1 Cor 9:5), Barnabas had the status and broad acceptability necessary for the writing of this letter. As a teacher in the church (Acts 11:26; 13:1) he would have had the necessary theologi-cal expertise.

19. Alternatively, many hold that the readers were Jewish Christians in Rome who had suffered under the Claudian expulsion of Jews in 49 and the Neronian pogrom of 64 (see, e.g., W. Lane, "Hebrews," R. P. Martin and P. H. Davids, eds., *Dictionary of the Later New Tes-tament and Its Developments* [Downers Grove: InterVarsity, 1997], 444-49). "Those from It-aly" (13:24) who send greetings are, on this interpretation, expatriate Italians. Against this we note that the readers are believers on account of the preaching of the original disciples of Je-sus (2:3) and that the many references to cultic activity are difficult to explain on the Rome hypothesis but readily explicable on the Jerusalem hypothesis.

were quite closely associated with mainstream Jewish life (Acts 21:20). Reference to Mnason of Cyprus may be an opened window through which to view a continuing Hellenist presence in Jerusalem (Acts 21:16). As "an early disciple" and a Cypriot, Mnason is most probably a Hellenist who dated his conversion to the 30s. Because Paul stayed with Mnason rather than with James during his final visit to Jerusalem we conclude that Mnason was not part of James's community. Mnason may have been a leader of a surviving Hellenist group in Jerusalem.

Several reasons support the hypothesis that the community of the Letter to the Hebrews were a group of continuing Hellenists in Jerusalem. First, the letter is written in superior koine Greek, with an elaborate use of allegory consistent with the Hellenistic Judaism of Alexandria. Presumably the readers were able to grasp the meaning of this author's sophisticated Greek and imagery. We know of a synagogue of Alexandrians in Jerusalem whose members were involved in the ministry of Stephen (Acts 6:9). It is quite possible that there were Alexandrian Jews among the early Hellenist Jewish Christians in Jerusalem.

Second, the writer and readers have become believers through the ministry of the original disciples of Jesus, presumably including Peter (2:3; 13:14). The "signs and wonders and various miracles and . . . gifts of the Holy Spirit" are consistent with the circumstances of the early preaching in Jerusalem at and subsequent to the day of Pentecost, through which the Hellenists became believers (2:4).

Third, this community of readers (they are groups with leaders: 13:7, 24) appear to be located in or near Jerusalem and the Temple. The numerous cultic references in the letter hardly make sense unless the readers were actually able to "go forth to [Christ] outside the camp" as he had done (13:12).

Fourth, the anti-Temple, anti-priest stance in the letter is consistent with the Diaspora-oriented preaching of Stephen recorded in Acts 7. The writer actually declares that "those who serve in the tent" have no right to participate in the blessings of Christ's unique sacrifice (13:10). At a time when some appear to be inclined to return to Judaism and Temple worship this writer urges them not to participate in the Temple cultus (6:6-8; 10:26-31; 13:13).

Fifth, at or near the beginning of their history these readers, like the Hellenists, endured "hard sufferings," public exposure to "abuse and affliction," imprisonment and "plundering of property" (10:32). The writer does not mention death among these sufferings, despite the execution of Stephen the Hellenist leader, though it is possible that it is included in these descriptions.

Whatever their origins this group is facing further imprisonment and sufferings (13:3), in the face of which the readers are dispirited (12:3-13), and their faith is stagnating (5:12). Some are inclined to return to the wider community of Jews from which they originally came (6:4; 10:26-31). They are a church, but they were in danger of ceasing meeting together (10:25). It is doubtful if such a group, whose existence we have suggested and whose character we have described, would have survived the turmoil of the war of 66-70. Their negative attitude to the Temple and cultus must have been a "death sentence" in those days of escalating religious nationalism before and during the war.

Paul in Israel

The earlier chapters of the book of Acts leave the impression that Paul's preaching in Israel was limited to Jerusalem at the time of his first return visit (Acts 9:28-29). We are surprised to hear Paul tell the young Agrippa that he had preached in "Jerusalem *and throughout all the country of Judea*" (Acts 26:20), that is, comprehensively in "city and country." Several factors call this assertion into question. One is the difficulty in locating such mission work within the Acts narrative. The other is Paul's own statement that he was "not known by face to the churches of Judea" (Gal 1:22).

Yet Paul does claim to have "fulfilled the gospel of Christ in an arc *from Jerusalem* to Illyricum" (Rom 15:19), implying a ministry in Palestine. This is strengthened by his questions "How can they hear without a preacher and how can they preach unless they are sent?" (10:14-15). From the context it is clear that Paul the apostle is the one *sent*[20] and those to whom he is sent and who do not *hear* are the people of Israel. While Jews of the Diaspora may have been in Paul's mind, it is chiefly Jews of Palestine to whom he is referring.

We conclude that notwithstanding the silence of the first part of Acts Paul did engage in mission preaching in the land of Israel. The most likely

---

20. J. P. Dickson, *Mission-Commitment in Ancient Judaism and in the Pauline Communities* (WUNT 159; Tübingen: Mohr, 2003), 166-73.

occasions for such preaching were during his journey from Damascus to Jerusalem and while he was in Jerusalem, as noted above (Acts 9:28-29). Presumably such mission work was of limited extent.

Conclusion

Although Acts passes quickly over the spread of Christianity in the land of Israel it is clear that churches were established in the various regions in the years following Saul's persecutions. After the cessation of persecution it seems that many believers returned to Jerusalem (Gal 1:18–2:10) and that the church resumed its pattern of growth.

At the same time the regions outside the city were evangelized, first by Philip, who took the word to the Samaritans and to the towns and cities on the coastal plain. Acts indicates that Philip was not alone, but that many others "went about preaching the word" in Judea and Samaria (8:1, 4; cf. 11:19). This did not include the apostles, who for the time being remained in Jerusalem (Acts 8:1). Acts notes that the scattered Jerusalem members took root as churches in the three constituent regions of the land — Judea, Galilee, and Samaria (9:31).

The resulting growth of Christianity, however, was characterized by diversity. Paul mentions "churches of Judea" that were probably Aramaic-speaking. Churches established by Philip, on the other hand, were likely Greek-speaking. The letter to the Hebrews may point to Greek-speaking Jewish believers in Jerusalem who were subject to ongoing persecution. From Acts 9:31-32 and Gal 2:8-9 it appears that Peter (with John) had special oversight of the churches in the land of Israel of both linguistic groups.

ELEVEN

Between Jesus
and Gospel Text

The oral phase of the Jesus tradition is now forever lost.

Barry Henaut, *Oral Tradition and the Gospel*[1]

Clearly the question of the transmission of Jesus' words through to the written text is critical. Inseparable from this is the matter of the length of time between the two.

That time between the historical Jesus and the earliest Synoptic biography is in fact quite brief. Few would argue that Mark must be dated later than 70. Thus forty years at most separate Mark from Jesus (and about fifty years from Jesus to Luke and Matthew). These dates may be shifted a few years earlier or later, but that scarcely affects the observation that the time was brief.

Furthermore, as we shall see, that time is not altogether blank.[2] About twenty years after Jesus, Paul's letters begin appearing, some of them echoing teachings of Jesus that we encounter in the first Synoptic Gospel twenty years later. In James's letter and 1 Peter, though they are not securely datable, we also find teachings of Jesus that will appear later in the Synoptic Gospels. We may reasonably assume that the task of collecting Jesus' teachings had begun prior to Paul's references to them from around 50.

---

1. Barry Henaut, *Oral Tradition and the Gospel* (Sheffield: JSOT, 1993), 295.

2. J. D. Crossan, *The Birth of Christianity* (San Francisco: HarperCollins, 1998) refers to the 30s and 40s as "lost years," "empty years," and "darkened decades" (ix).

Critical Questions

Given that the space of time between Jesus and the earliest Synoptic Gospel is broadly agreed, the more pressing issues relate to the processes by which Jesus' teachings were transmitted during those forty years. By what means did Jesus' words and deeds become after four decades his *written* words and deeds in the Gospel of Mark? The one firm point is that Mark and the other Gospels were written in Greek. Beyond that, however, we face a number of questions.

First, in what language[3] did Jesus teach? Was it Aramaic or Greek or Aramaic *and* Greek, depending on the audience? Aramaic had been the *lingua franca* of the Persian Empire, which included Palestine. Since the time of Alexander's conquests three hundred years earlier, however, Greek had become the *lingua franca* of the eastern Mediterranean. Was Aramaic or Greek the common language of Palestine in NT times? Some say Aramaic, others Greek,[4] others again that Palestine was bilingual[5] or multilingual.[6]

In favor of Aramaic we note the frequent occurrence of that language in the Gospels.[7] Embedded within these Greek texts are Aramaic place-names (e.g., *Akeldama, Bethzatha, Gabbatha, Golgotha*), Aramaic surnames (e.g., *Cephas, Boanerges*), Aramaic words in common usage (e.g., *korban, messias, cananaean, hosanna, pascha, rabbi, satan*), words spoken by Jesus (e.g., *amen, mammon, raka, talitha cumi, ephphatha, abba, Eloi Eloi*). Based on the frequency of these words in the Gospels it is hard to escape the conclusion that Aramaic remained the basic tongue of Jews in Palestine.[8] Furthermore, the Galilean disciples who came to live in Jerusalem were called "Hebrews" to distinguish them from the "Hellenists"; the former spoke Aramaic, the latter Greek.

---

3. For a review of literature on languages in Palestine in the first century see G. H. R. Horsley, *New Documents Illustrating Early Christianity* 5 (Sydney: Macquarie University, 1989), 19-26.

4. See S. E. Porter, *The Criteria for Authenticity in Historical Jesus Research* (Sheffield: Sheffield Academic, 2000), 126-41.

5. Horsley, *New Documents* 5, 6-19.

6. A. Millard, *Reading and Writing in the Time of Jesus* (Sheffield: Sheffield Academic, 2000), 132-53.

7. See Millard, *Reading and Writing,* 140-41; J. Jeremias, *New Testament Theology* I (London: SCM, 1971), 3-8.

8. Millard, *Reading and Writing,* 85-102.

On the other hand, however, Jesus traveled extensively in Hellenized regions to the north and east of Galilee, where Greek was dominant. The woman of Syria-Phoenicia with whom Jesus conversed is specifically identified as "Greek" (Mark 7:26). Most likely their conversation was in Greek. Three of the disciples, Philip, Simon, and Andrew, had Greek names and were from Bethsaida in Gaulanitis, a Greek-speaking principality. Galilee was ringed with Greek-speaking city-states: Tyre and Sidon to the northwest, Hippos and Gadara to the east, Scythopolis to the south. Sepphoris and Tiberias, the major cities of the tetrarch of Galilee, were culturally Hellenistic. Caesarea, the provincial capital, was predominantly Greek-speaking. Buying and selling in Galilee depended on use of Greek due to the travelers streaming along the Via Maris, which passed through Galilee. Likewise the proximity of nearby city-states to Galilee implied travel to and fro to buy and sell. The degree to which Palestine had been Hellenized is evident in the inscriptions and papyri from that era, including such intensely Jewish centers as Qumran, Masada, Murabba'at, and Jerusalem itself.[9]

On balance, Palestine appears to have been multilingual; both Aramaic and Greek were in common usage, and Latin was not unknown. Nonetheless, it seems likely that Aramaic remained the "first language" of the people and that Jesus taught in that language.[10] At the same time, he and his disciples doubtless knew Greek, and on occasion Jesus conversed and taught in Greek.

A second question relates to the means by which Jesus established his teachings with his disciples. Was it by repetition of aphorisms, proverbs, and parables so that they remembered his teachings? Or, did one or another of the disciples write down what he said and did? Culturally Palestine at that time was characterized by both orality and textuality.

We must allow the probability that orality was significant. Within that culture a rabbi would be "followed" by a disciple who memorized his master's teaching mediated by parables, aphorisms, and poetic forms. Jesus was called "rabbi" and "followed" by "disciples" who "sat at his feet," "learned from him," took his "yoke" upon them. Much of his teaching is cast in poetic form, employing alliteration, paronomasia, assonance, paral-

9. Millard, *Reading and Writing,* 102-17.
10. So Jeremias, *Theology* I, 8-37. S. E. Porter, "Jesus and His Use of Greek," *IBR* 10.1 (2000), 71-87, argues that Jesus taught in Greek and that the Jesus tradition existed in Greek from the outset. Porter quotes H. D. Betz with approval asserting that the Synoptic texts and their underlying sources were not translated from Aramaic.

THE BIRTH OF CHRISTIANITY

lelism, and rhyme. According to R. Riesner, 80 percent of Jesus' teaching is cast in poetic form.

At the same time, there is some evidence that Jews of that era took notes on waxed tablets.[11] There is no reason in principle that literate members of Jesus' group might not have written down his teachings.[12] Attention is drawn to the Teacher of Righteousness, founder of the Qumran sect, whose teachings appear to have been written down during his lifetime, perhaps on waxed tablets.[13] According to S. Lieberman, it was "general rabbinic practice" for disciples to write down the sayings of their masters.[14] Even so emphatic an advocate of oral transmission as B. Gerhardsson allows the possibility of the disciples making written records (private notes) of Jesus' teaching.[15] This may explain the origin and transmission of the longer discourses in the Gospel of John, whose format is unlike the pithier teachings in the Synoptic Gospels and less easy to memorize.

When did the practice of writing down Jesus' teachings begin? Most likely they were committed to writing earlier rather than later within the twenty-year period between Jesus and Paul's westward mission. Why was this done? Several overlapping reasons may be suggested. One is that the creation of congregations in Israel (which were based on synagogue structures) demanded written texts for instruction and church use. Local churches lacked the ongoing presence of a Peter or a John. Texts were needed for the teachings of the Master, along with whatever summaries had been committed to memory at occasions like baptism (as likely with Paul in Damascus). Someone who could read aloud was easier to find than an apostle! A further possible reason may be sought in the immense instability in the late 30s due to Caligula's assaults on the Jews in the eastern Mediterranean. If the original disciples were killed, the teachings of the Lord would die with them.

A third question is: In the time between Jesus and the biographies,[16]

---

11. See Millard, *Reading and Writing*, 26, 27, 28, 63, 67.

12. See H. Schürmann, "Die vorösterlichen Anfänge der Logientradition," *Traditionsgeschichtliche Untersuchungen* (Düsseldorf: Patmos, 1968), 39-45.

13. Millard, *Reading and Writing*, 222-23; S. Talmon, "Oral and Written Tradition in Judaism," in H. Wansbrough, ed., *Jesus and the Oral Gospel Tradition*, JSNTSup 64 (Sheffield: JSOT, 1991), 157-58.

14. S. Lieberman, *Hellenism in Jewish Palestine* (New York: Jewish Theological Society, 1962), 203.

15. B. Gerhardsson, *The Origin of the Gospel Traditions* (London: SCM, 1977), 68.

16. For the argument that the Gospels are "biographies" see R. A. Burridge, *What Are*

how were his actions and teachings remembered? It is widely and correctly held that orality was significant within that culture (cf. Mark 7:3, 9-13; Gal 1:13-14). There are many evidences of oral transmission in the NT.

Paul commends the Corinthians because "you hold to the traditions even as I handed them over to you" (1 Cor 11:2) for example, the "traditions" of the Last Supper/Lord's Supper and the narrative of the death, burial, and resurrection of the Christ (1 Cor 11:23; 15:1-3). Believers are those who have "learned Christ," that is, who have "heard" and "been taught" and who are now "walking" according to Christ (Eph 4:20-21; cf. 1:13; 1 Thess 4:1). This is a new *halakhah*, "received" from Christ, "handed over" by Paul and "received" by believers.

Paul uses this vocabulary also in addressing believers outside his apostolate, for example, the Christians in Rome. Paul is thankful that they "have become obedient from the heart to 'the pattern *(typos)* of teaching'" to which they had been "handed over" (Rom 6:17). Whereas the usual reference is to "handing over" a body of teaching to the people, in this case, interestingly, the *people* are "handed over" to the body of teaching. At the end of the letter Paul warns the Romans to take note of those who oppose "the teaching" which they have "learned" (Rom 16:17).

Luke also uses this technical rabbinic vocabulary for "apostles' teaching" (*didachē*, Acts 2:42; 5:38). The readers of Hebrews, having "heard" the living word of God, the gospel, ought by now to be *teachers* of others (Heb 4:2, 12-13; 5:11-12; 6:1). Prominent also in Hebrews is the notion of a "confession," a body of teaching (*homologia*) which the readers were to "consider" and "hold to" (Heb 3:1; 4:13; 10:23). It is possible that "confession" and its antonym "denial" had roots in the rabbinic language of synagogue culture.[17] 2 John speaks of "the doctrine *(didachē)* of Christ." A person who comes from outside is not to be received, unless he brings that "doctrine" (2 John 9-10). Jude exhorts his readers to struggle for "the faith" which was once "handed over" (by Jesus, as by a rabbi) to the saints, his original followers (Jude 3).

It is almost certain that the pattern of oral teaching begun by Jesus continued after Easter and became a feature of early Christianity for a

---

the Gospels? (Cambridge: Cambridge University Press, 1992); P. Stuhlmacher, "The Genre(s) of the Gospels," in D. L. Dungan, ed., *The Interrelations of the Gospels* (Leuven: University Press, 1990), 484-94, rejects an over-close identification of the Gospels as Hellenistic *vitae*.

17. O. Hofius, *EDNT* II, 514.

century or more. There is the well-known reference by Papias (ca. 130) to his preference for the "living voice" over "books." This orality, however, was not that of the storyteller of Middle Eastern village culture, whose stories were marked by "fixity and flexibility." Of special significance is the observation that the transmission of tradition issues from urban Jerusalem, not rural Galilee.[18] Equally, it was not a communal orality "told by many people to many people" in which "some people hear the account numerous times and fuse various elements of a variety of reports into their own account."[19]

On the contrary, the orality evident in Rabbi Jesus' method as continued by his disciples post-Easter was *didactic,* transmitted authoritatively from teacher to disciple. Oral transmission of the NT era was not the orality of the village raconteur or of a shared community transmission ("by many to many"), but the narrowly focused "traditioning" of instruction from master to disciple. To be sure, Paul (for example) would pastorally expand upon and adapt the "tradition" he had "received," but in a disciplined manner.[20] This is quite unlike current theories of "orality."[21] B. Gerhardsson refers helpfully to "a controlled transmission of Gospel traditions."[22]

At the same time, however, we must assert that the written existed side-by-side with the oral in the world of Jewish Christianity in the four (or less) decades between Jesus and the Gospel of Mark.[23] It is now evident from Qumran studies that written text figured significantly in a wider religious culture (Israel) that was also significantly oral. We may conjecture that, just as written text came to the fore in Qumran, it also began to

18. Talmon, "Oral and Written Tradition," 126.

19. B. W. Henaut quoted in H. W. Hollander, "The Words of Jesus in Jesus and Q," *NovT* 42.3 (2000), 353.

20. See, e.g., 1 Cor 11:23-26, where Paul both cites the Lord's Supper tradition and adapts it pastorally for the situation in Corinth. Cf. P. Borgen, "John and the Synoptics," in Dungan, *Interrelations of the Gospels,* 411-17.

21. See W. Kelber, *The Oral and Written Gospel: The Hermeneutics of Speaking and Writing in the Synoptic Tradition, Mark, Paul, and Q* (Philadelphia: Fortress, 1983), 27; K. Bailey, "Informal Controlled Oral Tradition and the Synoptic Gospels," *Asian Journal of Theology* 5 (1991), 34-54.

22. Gerhardsson, *Origin of the Gospel Traditions,* 68; E. E. Ellis, "Reading the Gospel as History," *Criswell Theological Review* 3.1 (1988), 3-15.

23. On the dynamic relationship between orality and textuality see J. D. Harvey, "Orality and Its Implications for Biblical Studies: Recapturing an Ancient Paradigm," *JETS* 45.1 (2002), 99-109.

emerge within the new sect within Judaism that was Christianity.[24] That new sect, unlike that of the Qumranites, was mission-minded, overseeing the creation of new synagogues ("churches") among Jews.[25] These new assemblies needed instructors who, in turn, needed the wherewithal to teach new members. Here the place of public reading was critical.[26] In our view at quite an early stage the expansion of congregations hastened the evolution of written text from oral version. Not that the written replaced the oral; the two existed side-by-side for many years.[27]

We note with interest that the meeting in Jerusalem ca. 49 issued a *letter* to "the brothers who are of the Gentiles in Antioch, Syria, and Cilicia" (Acts 15:24). Even Paul's early letter 1 Thessalonians, written around 50, is so well formed stylistically that we can reasonably assume

24. So Talmon, "Oral and Written Tradition," 157-58.

25. So E. E. Ellis, "The Making of Narratives in the Synoptic Tradition," in Wansbrough, ed., *Jesus and the Oral Gospel Tradition*, 310-33.

26. Talmon, "Oral and Written Tradition," 148-56.

27. J. D. G. Dunn, *Jesus Remembered* (Grand Rapids: Eerdmans, 2003), 205-54, follows Kenneth Bailey's observations of village storytelling, in which core elements of the story, with many identical words though also with idiosyncratic adaptation and variation, are retained generation by generation. According to Dunn this accounts for similarities and differences among texts in the Synoptics. Dunn is inclined to reject the older text-based adaptations arising from source and redaction criticism in favor of Bailey's more "sociological" approach.

But the culture Bailey observed was post-Islamic Arabic whereas the culture of Jesus' day was Jewish, in the Hellenistic, pre-Islamic era. Who can say with confidence that the villages of Jesus' Galilee had storytellers who gave oracular performances like those described by Bailey? Do we know that the deeds and teachings of Jesus were told as "stories" in the Galilean villages in the years after Jesus?

Rather, based on the evidence of the Gospels and archaeology, the towns and villages of Galilee were synagogue-based. Synagogue culture was liturgical (with repetition of prayers and benedictions) and text-based; the *reading* of the Law and the Prophets with "sermon" (midrash) was central. It is more likely that "the churches of Christ in Judea" (Gal 1:22; cf. 1 Thess 2:14) followed the praxis of the synagogue. Mark's instruction, "Let the lector understand" (Mark 13:14), is but one of many hints that *reading* aloud a written text to a gathered group was the practice in the early churches.

Dunn's rejection of the written in favor of the oral also flies in the face of the opening lines of Luke's Gospel, where those who "handed over" written "narrative[s]" to Luke were "those who from the beginning were eyewitnesses and ministers *(hypēretai)* of the word." In other words, these persons (disciples/apostles) spanned the few decades between Jesus and Luke's text, effectively guaranteeing the probity of the tradition. The point is that Luke's sources were written not oral.

that it was by no means his first written text. It is not difficult to believe Paul wrote earlier letters (back into the early 40s?) that have not been preserved. By the later 50s, it would seem, "eyewitnesses and ministers of the word" "handed over" to Luke "narratives" that many had "compiled" (Luke 1:1-2). It is almost certain that such "narratives" were *written*.[28]

In short, the creation of *written* Gospels from ca. 70 (if not earlier) was a natural development, given the existing use of written texts, which may have gone back to and perhaps into the span of Jesus' ministry.[29] Moreover, it had a parallel in another marginal sect within Judaism, the Qumran covenanters, where oral transmission and written texts existed side-by-side.[30] One writer has observed that in both groups "orality and textuality were both deemed handmaidens of aurality."[31]

A fourth question relates to the Greek language in which each of the Gospels is written. If Jesus taught (mainly) in Aramaic, as seems likely, how do we explain that our Gospels are written in Greek (with embedded Aramaisms)? Critical to this is a subsidiary question. Were the various sources underlying the Gospels and Acts written in Aramaic or Greek?

The "narratives" that came into Luke's hands are of special interest (Luke 1:1-4). Were they in Aramaic or Greek? Texts like the Gospels of Mark and John, which have no identifiable underlying sources, are significant. These Gospels contain Aramaisms (as noted), but do not appear to

28. Cf. L. Alexander, *The Preface to Luke's Gospel* (Cambridge: Cambridge University Press, 1993), 115, who notes that the phrase "compile a narrative" is "splendidly ambiguous" and that Luke does not say that his predecessors had produced written documents. A little earlier, however, Alexander applies the word "text" to *diēgēsis* (111). Much depends whether Luke's words "it seemed good to me also . . . to *write*" are governed by "Inasmuch as many have undertaken to compile a narrative" or "just as they were delivered to us by . . . eyewitnesses." Since the first option is more likely, it follows that "compile a narrative" points to *written* texts that "eyewitnesses and ministers" "handed over" to Luke.

Attention is drawn to a pseudonymous *Letter of Peter to James* in the (second-century?) pseudo-Clementines (*Ante-Nicene Fathers* VIII, 215-16). "Peter" urges that the Gentiles not "receive" the books of Peter's preachings; only to fellow Jews who have been found worthy may these books be "handed over." The provenance of this letter, which is clearly Jewish Christian, is most probably Galilee (so A. I. Baumgarten, "Literary Evidence for Jewish Christianity," in *The Galilee of Late Antiquity*, ed. L. I. Levine [Jerusalem: Harvard University Press, 1992], 50). Its culture of tradition/transmission of texts is evocative of the opening sentences of the Gospel of Luke.

29. See H. Schürmann, "Vorösterlichen Anfänge," 39-65.

30. Talmon, "Oral and Written Tradition," 127-32.

31. Talmon, "Oral and Written Tradition," 150.

be Greek translations of earlier Aramaic versions.[32] Attempts at retroversion into Aramaic have largely been abandoned.

Scholars have identified Aramaisms in the koine of Acts.[33] Most likely these had already been translated into Greek before they came into Luke's hands.[34] According to F. F. Bruce, retroversion from Luke's Greek into Aramaic "must be undertaken with the utmost caution."[35] Furthermore, it appears unlikely that texts "handed over" to Luke were written in Aramaic since this would unreasonably assume that Luke was sufficiently accomplished in both languages to convert them into the superior koine we find in Luke-Acts.

The situation appears to be that fairly soon after the rise of Christianity in Palestine in the 30s its thought world was mainly articulated in Greek, both oral and written. Whether Jesus taught in Aramaic or Greek or both, his teachings survive in Greek. Regardless whether the original "eyewitnesses . . . of the word" spoke Aramaic or Greek as their mother tongue, those "many" who wrote the "narratives" of the events "fulfilled" in Jesus wrote those "narratives" in Greek. Our only significant access to the historical Jesus is through the Greek language, notwithstanding the Aramaisms embedded in the Gospels. The fact that there is only one remaining echo of Aramaic-speaking Christianity (*maran tha* — 1 Cor 16:22; cf. Rev 22:20) supports the proposal that Greek became its linguistic mode from early times.

As to the reason Greek totally eclipsed Aramaic as the medium for the written Gospel, we may only speculate. First, we have noted previously the very significant extent to which Palestine was Hellenized by NT times, encircled by Greek city-states and permeated as it was by Greek influence. Perhaps it was believed then that Aramaic was bound to decline culturally with Greek likely to take its place even at the grassroots level. Second, resistance to the message about Jesus as Messiah among Jews in Palestine may

---

32. So Porter, "Jesus and the Use of Greek," 86-87. For general discussion on "Jewish Greek" see G. H. R. Horsley, *New Documents* 5, 5-19.

33. Appendix A.

34. C. F. D. Moule, *An Idiom Book of New Testament Greek* (Cambridge: Cambridge University Press, 1960), 171-72; D. F. Payne, "Semitisms in the Book of Acts," in *Apostolic History and the Gospel*, ed. W. Gasque and R. P. Martin (Grand Rapids: Eerdmans, 1970), 134-50. For references to Aramaisms in Acts see C. Hemer, *The Book of Acts in the Setting of Hellenistic History* (WUNT; Tübingen: Mohr, 1989), 212-14; Horsley, *New Documents* 5, 26-37.

35. F. F. Bruce, *The Acts of the Apostles: The Greek Text with Introduction and Commentary* (Grand Rapids: Eerdmans, 1990³), 69.

have inclined the apostles to see the future of the faith lying beyond the land of Israel, either with Jews of the Diaspora or even with Gentiles, that is, in the Greek language. Third, this may have coincided with their further reflection on Jesus' words about "sending" them to the nations. If the message was for the nations then its written Gospel must be in the *lingua franca* of the nations, Greek. Perhaps for these reasons the sayings and teachings of Jesus were expressed in Greek from the time they began to be collected.

A.D. 50-57: Echoes of Jesus in Paul's Letters

Finding traces of the teaching of Jesus in Paul's letters has been the subject of considerable research.[36] Opinions vary as to the frequency of these "words" in the letters. In Paul's case, for example, the estimates vary from just a few references to many hundreds.[37] It is not my purpose to engage in precise debate on this matter but merely to observe that we cannot deny that Paul's letters contain echoes of the "instructions" of the Lord, whatever their precise frequency proves to be. The point is simple: the NT letters demonstrably contain traces of such teachings. Echoes of the teaching of Jesus can be heard in at least three letters of Paul, each of which is datable. They are 1 Thessalonians (ca. 50), 1 Corinthians (ca. 54), and Romans (ca. 57).

1 Thessalonians

The meaning of Paul's reference to "the word of the Lord" (1 Thess 4:15) is debated.[38] It seems likely that in 1 Thess 4:13–5:11 Paul is echoing teachings

36. See, e.g., S. Kim, *Paul and the New Perspective* (Grand Rapids: Eerdmans, 2002), 259-92; Hollander, "Words of Jesus," 340-57.

37. See D. C. Allison, "The Pauline Epistles and the Synoptic Gospels: The Pattern of the Parallels," *NTS* 28.1 (1986), 1.

38. See D. Wenham, *The Rediscovery of Jesus' Eschatological Discourse* (Gospel Perspectives 4; Sheffield: JSOT, 1984) for a detailed argument that pre-Synoptic eschatological discourses can be discerned in 1 Thessalonians. For a minimalist view see C. M. Tuckett, "Synoptic Tradition in 1 Thessalonians?" in J. Collins, ed., *The Thessalonian Correspondence* (Leuven: Peeters, 2000), 174-75.

of Jesus drawn from various sources that ultimately formed part of the Synoptic tradition.[39]

First Thessalonians	The Jesus Tradition
4:15-16	**Matt 24:31**
For this we declare to you by the word of the Lord, that we who are alive, who are left until the appearing *(parousia)* of the Lord, will not precede those who have fallen asleep.	. . . he will send out his angels with a loud *trumpet* call, and they will gather his elect from the four winds.
For the Lord himself will descend from heaven with a cry of command, with archangel's call, and with the sound of the *trumpet* of God. And the dead in Christ shall rise first.	
4:17	**Matt 25:5-7**
then we who are alive, who are left, will be caught up together with them in the clouds to *meet* the Lord in the air; and so we will always be with the Lord.	As the bridegroom was delayed, they all slumbered and slept. But at midnight there was a cry, "Behold the bridegroom! Come, let us *meet* him." Then all those maidens arose and trimmed their lamps.
5:3-7	**Matt 24:42-43**
For you yourselves know well that the day of the Lord will come like a *thief* in the night. When people say, "There is peace and security," then sudden destruction will come upon them as travail comes upon a woman with child, and there will be	Watch, therefore, for you do not know on what day your Lord is coming. But know this, that if the householder had known what part of the night the *thief* was coming, he would have watched and not let his house be broken into.

39. See S. Kim, "The Jesus Tradition in 1 Thess 4:13–5:11," *NTS* 48 (2002), 225-42 for the argument that Paul must write these words because the Thessalonians misunderstood his original transmission of words of the Lord about the parousia.

no escape. But you are not in the darkness, brothers, for the day to surprise you like a *thief.* For you are all sons of light and sons of the day; we are not of the night or of the darkness. So then let us not sleep, as others do, but let us keep awake and be sober.

Luke 21:34-36
But take heed to yourselves lest your hearts be weighed down with dissipation and drunkenness . . . and that day come upon you suddenly like a snare . . . but watch at all times, praying that you may have strength to escape all these things that will take place, and to stand before the Son of man.

In common here are: the sudden appearance of the Lord, as in the parable of the thief; the trumpet call signaling the gathering of the elect; the warning for watchfulness, as in the parable of sleeping and waking; and the promise that the godly ones will "meet" the Lord, as in the parable of the virgins. The connections, though evocative, are real. Nonetheless, despite the likelihood that Paul is citing the "words" of Jesus it is not possible to draw any conclusion about the stage of development of the sources Paul cites.

It also seems likely that Paul's appeal to sexual holiness springs from Jesus' injunction about the permanence of marriage (1 Thess 4:1-8; Mark 10:9). Paul calls this "an instruction" *(paraggelia)* he "gave through the Lord Jesus" (1 Thess 4:2). It is much more likely to have been a reminder of a Jesus tradition "given" by Paul to Gentile churches in general than a specific injunction about male sexual self-control in relationship to local Thessalonian cult prostitution.[40] There are also likely allusions to Jesus' teachings elsewhere in the letter (5:13: "be at peace among yourselves" [cf. Mark 9:50]; 5:15: "See that none repays evil for evil . . ." [cf. Matt 5:38-48]).

1 Corinthians

As noted earlier[41] Paul's mission to Corinth followed immediately upon his mission to Macedonia. His reminders of face-to-face teachings in

---

40. Contra Riesner, *Paul's Early Period: Chronology, Mission Strategy, Theology* (Grand Rapids: Eerdmans, 1998), 374-75.
41. See pp. 50-53.

1 Thessalonians and 1 Corinthians likely point to a commonality of oral instruction given in the cities of his Greek mission. There is one reference to
a "word of the Lord" in 1 Thessalonians (4:15-17: the coming of the Lord),
but three occasions in 1 Corinthians where Paul refers explicitly to a
"charge" or command of "the Lord."

Paul in First Corinthians	The Jesus Tradition
7:10-11 To the married I give charge, not I but the Lord, that the wife should not separate from her husband (but if she does, let her remain single or else be reconciled to her husband) and that the husband should not divorce his wife.	**Mark 10:9, 11-12 (cf. Luke 16:18; Matt 5:32)** What therefore God has joined together, let not man put asunder. . . . Whoever divorces his wife and marries another commits adultery against her; and if she divorces her husband and marries another, she commits adultery.
9:14 In the same way, the Lord commanded that those who proclaim the gospel should get their living by the gospel.	**Luke 10:7/Matt 10:10 ("Q")** . . . for the laborer deserves to be paid / for laborers deserve their food
11:24-25 . . . the Lord Jesus on the night he was betrayed took bread and, when he had given thanks, he broke it and said, "This is my body which is for you. Do this in remembrance of me." . . .	**Luke 22:19-20** And he took bread and, when he had given thanks, he broke it and gave it to them, saying, "This is my body which is given to you. Do this in remembrance of me." . . .

Furthermore, there are fleeting allusions to Jesus' teaching in 1 Corinthians 13. "Faith . . . so as to remove mountains" (v. 2) echoes Mark 11:23,
and "if I give away all I have" (v. 3) echoes Mark 10:21.

Clearly, then, by the time Paul wrote 1 Corinthians in the mid-50s
various teachings of the Lord were current, most likely in written form and
in the Greek language.

Romans

The "ethical" section of Romans (chs. 12–14) has a number of allusions to teachings of Jesus as found in the common source Matthew and Luke employ ("Q"). Paul also cites teachings of Jesus found only in Mark.

Paul in Romans	Jesus in the Gospels
12:14 Bless those who persecute you; bless and do not curse them.	Luke 6:28/Matt 5:44 ("Q") Bless those who curse you; pray for those who abuse you.
12:17 Repay no one evil for evil.	Luke 6:27/Matt 5:38-48 ("Q") Love your enemies; do good to those who hate you.
13:7 Pay *(apodote)* all of them their dues.	Mark 12:17 Render *(apodote)* to Caesar the things that are Caesar's.
13:8 . . . he who loves neighbor has fulfilled the law	Mark 12:31 Love your neighbor as yourself. There is no other commandment greater than these.
14:13 . . . never put a . . . stumblingblock *(skandalon)* . . . in the way of a brother	Mark 9:42 Whoever causes one of these little one to stumble *(skandalizein)*. . . .
14:14 . . . nothing is unclean of itself	Mark 7:15 . . . nothing outside a man can defile him
14:20 . . . everything is . . . clean *(panta . . . kathara)*	Mark 7:19 Thus [Jesus] declared all foods clean *(katharizon panta ta bromata)*

The dating of Romans is secure (ca. 57), and the teachings Paul echoes must have been current when he wrote. This means that the traditions that found their way into Mark, Matthew, and Luke were in circulation by the mid-50s and, most likely, earlier.

Were they in oral or written form? There is a good argument that they circulated in written form, and in Greek. This is based on the opening sentences of the Gospel of Luke, which imply that written texts were "handed over" to Luke, whether in Palestine during his sojourn there (as implied by the "we" passages in Acts) or in Rome (as implied by 2 Tim 4:11, 13).

Paul and the Jesus Traditions

D. C. Allison, who has closely examined traces of Jesus' teachings in Paul's letters,[42] notes that such allusions are not scattered uniformly throughout Paul's letters but confined to a "handful of distinct portions of the correspondence: Romans 12–14; 1 Thessalonians 4–5; [Col 3–4; and] 1 Corinthians." In a table setting out likely "sources" of these dominical echoes Allison concludes that Paul knew material from Mark, material common to Luke and Matthew ("Q"), material unique to Luke ("L"), and perhaps material unique to Matthew ("M").[43] Consistent with our observations above we must qualify this: Paul echoes *sources* that may have existed or evolved as "Q," "L," and "M."

As noted, Paul seldom quotes Jesus verbatim but appeals allusively to teachings already known in the churches. Equally, we do not certainly have the defined finished texts of these sources in their final forms but in as yet incomplete versions. Their exact contents and contours remain elusive, despite years of concentrated research.

Notwithstanding these limitations, we are able to make this radical conclusion: by the time Paul's earliest surviving letters appear in ca. 50, collections of Jesus' teachings were in circulation. Furthermore, these collections were (most probably) in *Greek* and they were (most probably) already in *written* form. Of course, such collections had not been assembled the night before Paul set out for his Greek mission. Clearly, the teachings of the Lord had begun to be assembled sometime beforehand, even though we do not know precisely when or from whom Paul received them. Nonetheless,

---

42. Allison, "Pauline Epistles and the Synoptic Gospels," 1-32.
43. Allison, "Pauline Epistles and the Synoptic Gospels," 20.

Paul's several visits to Jerusalem in the 40s would have provided opportunity to obtain this material (Gal 2:1/Acts 11:29-30; 15:2).[44]

The point to be made is that collections of Jesus' teachings had been made in the twenty-year period between Jesus and Paul's Greek mission. In other words, the forty-year space between Jesus and the earliest Gospel is by no means a blank space. Paul's letters between 50 and 57 (to the Thessalonians, the Corinthians, and the Romans) contain direct references to bodies of Jesus' teaching that had by then been collected. While the precise contents of those collections is not known, their existence is certain. By the time the Gospels came to be written there was an established tradition of collecting and passing on the teachings of the Lord. Echoes of Jesus' teachings found in Paul's letters are historically secure evidence of this.

The Wisdom of Jesus in the Letter of James

The Letter of James presents the historian with problems. It is undated, its place of origin is unstated, its text is (apparently) disjointed, and — most important — the author identifies himself merely as "James, a servant of God and of the Lord Jesus Christ." The superior quality of the Greek is seen as an argument against authorship by James the brother of Jesus, a Galilean Jew of working-class background. The letter is not cited by name before Origen (d. 253).

Nonetheless, P. Davids has pointed to elements that would support the traditional authorship.[45] The letter fits into a known genre, the Jewish Diaspora letter. Early Palestinian Christianity, in which James was a leader, was bilingual; in any case the letter has numerous Aramaisms. The linguistic difficulty would be overcome if it were allowed that an editor or amanuensis assembled and wrote out the teaching of a revered teacher. Further, incidental references to a Jewish Christian synagogue meeting, to "early and latter rain," and to the wickedness of the rich point to a Palestinian milieu.

Although the letter raises difficulties, the traditional author himself is well known. James the brother of Jesus was, indeed, a revered figure

44. For general discussion of oral and written traditions within the mother culture of Israel see B. Gerhardsson, "The Gospel Tradition," in Dungan, ed., *Interrelations of the Gospels*, 497-545.

45. P. Davids, "Palestinian Traditions in the Epistle of James," in B. Chilton and C. A. Evans, eds., *James the Just and Christian Origins* (Leiden: Brill, 1999), 33-57.

abundantly qualified to write a Diaspora letter. A witness to the resurrection (1 Cor 15:7), James was a member of the Jerusalem church from the beginning.[46] Within three years of Paul's "call," that is, by the mid-30s James was regarded as an "apostle" and as someone important enough for Paul to meet.[47] When Peter was forced to flee from King Herod Agrippa I in ca. 41, James was able to remain in Jerusalem.[48] From that time James was the prime "pillar" of the Jerusalem church and "president" at the council that met regarding the inclusion of the Gentiles (Acts 15).[49] James's embassy to Antioch indicates that he exercised a kind of primacy within and beyond the borders of the land of Israel.[50] His eminence as leader of the Jerusalem church in the 50s is noted by Acts and in the 60s by Josephus, who writes at length about the death of James, "brother of the so-called Christ."[51] The ossuary epitaph published in 2002 also identifies him as "brother of Yeshua." This, above all, was his qualification to lead the Judean churches and to send a Diaspora letter.

In short, then, there is good reason to believe the letter came from James (or an amanuensis) in Jerusalem to Christian Jews of the Diaspora. But when? Most likely it is an early letter written from the time of James's primacy (beginning in 41) and before the great controversies about the inclusion of the Gentiles (the late 40s). The letter's absence of appeal to "apostle" or "brother of the Lord" and the likely silence about specific issues raised by Paul's mission[52] point to an early rather than a later date.

The critical point about the Letter of James is its many allusions to the Jesus tradition. First, there are a number of "content links" between Matthew and James, for example, "perfect" (Jas 1:4; Matt 5:48; 19:21), "righteousness" (Jas 1:20; 3:18; Matt 3:15; 5:6, 10, 20; 6:1, 33), "church" (Jas 5:7; Matt 16:18; 18:17), "parousia" (Jas 5:7; Matt 24:3, 27, 37, 39), and "oaths" (Jas 5:12; Matt 5:33-37).[53]

---

46. 1 Cor 15:7; Acts 1:14.

47. Gal 1:18-20.

48. Acts 12:17.

49. Gal 2:9; Acts 15:13.

50. Gal 2:12. See M. Bockmuehl, "Antioch and James the Just," in Chilton and Evans, eds. *James the Just,* 155-97. 1 Cor 15:7; Acts 1:14.

51. Acts 21:18; Josephus, *Antiquities* 20.200-201.

52. Davids, "Palestinian Traditions," 53, quoting K. Haacker.

53. For a complete list see J. B. Adamson, *The Epistle of James* (NICNT; Grand Rapids: Eerdmans, 1976), 188.

Second, there are textual allusions, though there is some difficulty in precise identification. According to P. Davids there are up to thirty-five such echoes, mostly from the Matthew/Luke material underlying the Sermon on the Mount/Plain.[54] J. Painter has combined the lists of R. P. Martin and P. J. Hartin to get thirty-three in all.[55] Rather more conservatively, I have identified twenty likely textual links:

James	Matthew	Luke
1:2 Count it all joy . . . when you meet various trials	5:10, 12 Blessed are those who are persecuted. . . . Rejoice and be glad. . . .	
1:12 Blessed is the man who endures trial		
1:5 If any of you lacks wisdom, let him ask God, who gives to all generously. . . .	7:7 Ask and it will be given you	11:9 Ask, and it will be given you
1:17 Every good gift . . . coming down from the Father	7:11 . . . how much more will your Father . . . give good gifts to those who ask him.	11:13 how much more will the heavenly Father give the Holy Spirit to those who ask. . . .
1:20 . . . the anger of man does not work the righteousness of God	5:22 . . . everyone who is angry with his brother shall be liable to judgment	
1:22 . . . be doers of the word, not hearers only	7:24 . . . everyone who hears these words . . . and does them	

54. Davids, "Palestinian Traditions," 33-57.
55. J. Painter, *Just James* (Columbia: University of South Carolina Press, 1997), 261-62.

James	Matthew	Luke
2:5 . . . has not God chosen the poor to be . . . heirs of the kingdom	5:3 Blessed are the poor in spirit, for theirs is the kingdom of heaven.	6:20 Blessed are you poor, for yours is the kingdom of God.
2:8 . . . the royal law . . . "You shall love your neighbor as yourself. . . ."	Mark 12:31 The second is this, "You shall love your neighbor as yourself" = Matt 22:39	Luke 10:27-28 You shall love . . . your neighbor as yourself
2:10 Whoever keeps the whole law but fails in one point has become guilty of all of it.	5:19 . . . whoever relaxes one of the least of these commandments . . . shall be . . . least in the kingdom, but he who . . . does them . . . shall be called great in the kingdom	
2:13 For judgment is without mercy to one who has shown no mercy, yet mercy triumphs over judgment.	5:7 Blessed are the merciful, for they shall obtain mercy	6:37 forgive and you will be forgiven;
2:14 What does it profit . . . if a man says he has faith, but has no works . . . ?	7:21 Not everyone who says to me, "Lord, Lord," shall enter the kingdom of heaven, but he who does the will of my Father. . . .	6:46 Why do you call me "Lord, Lord" and not do what I tell you?
3:12 Can a fig tree . . . yield olives or a grapevine figs?	7:17 Are grapes gathered from thorns, or figs from thistles?	6:44 Figs are not gathered from thorns, nor grapes picked from a bramble bush.

James	Matthew	Luke
3:13 Who is wise and understanding among you? By his good life let him show his works in the meekness of wisdom.	5:5 Blessed are the meek	
4:4 Do you not know that friendship with the world is enmity with God? Therefore whoever wishes to be a friend of the world makes himself an enemy of God.	6:24 No one can serve two masters; for either he will hate the one and love the other or he will be devoted to the one and despise the other. You cannot serve God and mammon.	16:13 No servant can serve two masters; for either he will hate the one and love the other, or he will be devoted to the one and despise the other. You cannot serve God and mammon.
4:8 Cleanse your hands you sinners and purify your hearts, you men of double mind.	5:8 Blessed are the pure in heart, for they shall see God.	
4:9 Be wretched and mourn and weep. Let your laughter be turned to mourning and your joy to dejection.		6:25 Woe to you that laugh now, for you shall mourn and weep.
4:10 Humble yourselves before the Lord and he will exalt you.	23:12 . . . whoever exalts himself will be humbled and whoever humbles himself will be exalted.	14:11 Everyone who exalts himself will be humbled and he who humbles himself will be exalted.

James	Matthew	Luke
4:11 Do not speak evil against one another, brothers. He that speaks evil against a brother or judges a brother, speaks evil against the law and judges the law.	5:22 . . . everyone who is angry with his brother shall be liable to judgment. 7:1 Judge not that you be not judged.	
5:1 Come now, you rich, weep and howl for the miseries that are coming upon you.	19:23 It will be hard for a rich man to enter the kingdom of heaven.	6:24-25 Woe to you that are rich, for you have received your consolation. Woe to you who are full now, for you shall hunger.
5:2 Your riches have rotted and your garments are moth eaten.	6:20 Lay up for yourselves treasures in heaven, where neither moth nor rust consumes	
5:12 Do not swear, either by heaven or by earth, or with any other oath, but let your yes be yes and your no be no, that you may not fall under condemnation.	5:34-35 Do not swear at all, either by heaven for it is the throne of God, or by the earth for it is his footstool. . . .	

James	Matthew
5:19-20 My brothers, if anyone among you wanders from the truth and someone brings him back let him know that whoever brings a sinner from the error of his way will save his own soul from death and will cover a multitude of sins.	18:15 If your brother sins against you, go tell him his fault, between you and him alone. If he listens to you, you have gained your brother.

Of the twenty instances listed above seven are identifiable citations from existing collections of Jesus' teachings (1:22; 2:8; 3:12; 4:9; 4:10; 5:1; 5:12) and thirteen are likely echoes (1:2, 12; 1:5, 17; 1:20; 2:5; 2:10; 2:13; 2:14; 3:13; 4:4; 4:8; 4:11; 5:2; 5:19-20).

These instances appear to be drawn from the following text traditions:

Special Matthew ("M")	10
Special Luke ("L")	1
Shared Luke and Matthew ("Q")	8
Mark	1

The Markan example is uncertain since Matthew and Luke also have this teaching; perhaps it existed independently in Mark and "Q." The sole "L" case, however, is striking. Clearly, though, the overwhelming examples are drawn from "M" and "Q."

Two further comments can be made, both stated as "probable." One is that most likely the sayings collections already existed in Greek. While the cultural setting of James's teaching is identifiably Palestinian it would be difficult to retrovert his koine into Aramaic, despite some evidence of underlying Aramaisms. Secondly, it is more likely than not that the sources from which James drew were already in written form.

Care must be taken as to the claims we are able to make. We do not know the prehistory of the sources from which James drew his teaching.

Equally, we cannot plot the course of such traditions between James's use of them and their incorporation into the Synoptic Gospels.[56] The one thing to be said, which is important to say, is that by the time James wrote his letter there were three or four collections of Jesus' teaching that were then in circulation, that is, "M," "Q," "L," and Mark (or a precursor).

The amount of James's teaching that is cross-referenced in the sources of Matthew and Luke is impressive. It is noteworthy, however, that James does not attribute this teaching to Jesus. Jesus' teaching has become James's teaching. The same holds true for allusions in 1 Peter that can be traced to the Synoptic sources.[57]

Words of Christ in the First Letter of Peter

As with the letter of James this letter of Peter is undated. The reference to "Babylon," however, most likely locates the author in Rome. Like James's letter this letter is marked by a quality of Greek writing that raises problems for Petrine authorship. Following Selwyn's suggestions, however, the "Silvanus" amanuensis hypothesis may accommodate *indirect* Petrine authorship.[58]

It is clear that numbers of *verba Christi* lie embedded within this letter. Here our difficulty is to know whether these "words" come directly from a Jesus tradition or indirectly through other epistolary filters. For example, this "Silvanus" was previously (most likely) a fellow worker with Paul in his Greek mission. Thereafter he disappears from view. Did these "words" of Jesus come to 1 Peter from a Jesus tradition through Paul via Silvanus into 1 Peter? Alternatively, did they come by a more direct route from the Jesus traditions to 1 Peter? It is not possible to be sure either way, though the nature of the sayings points to the latter explanation.

The point being made, however, is unaffected by this. That point is the appearance in 1 Peter of "words of Jesus."[59] These include the following.

---

56. See Painter, *Just James*, 262-64.

57. See E. G. Selwyn, *The First Epistle of Peter* (London: Macmillan, 1961), 23-24.

58. *First Epistle of Peter*, 9-17.

59. See R. H. Gundry, "'Verba Christi' in 1 Peter: Their Implications concerning the Authorship of 1 Peter and the Authorship of the Gospel Tradition," *NTS* 13 (1966-67), 336-59; "Further Verba on the Verba Christi in First Peter," *Biblica* 55 (1974), 211-32. For a contrary view see E. Best, *1 Peter* (NCB; Grand Rapids: Eerdmans, 1971).

Peter in 1 Peter	Jesus in the Gospels
2:12 . . . seeing your good works they will glorify *(doxasōsin)* God. . . .	Matt 5:16 Let your light so shine before men that they may see your good works and give glory *(doxasōsin)* to your Father who is in heaven.
2:19 [context of non-vengeance] . . . for this is thankworthy . . . *(touto gar charis)*	Luke 6:32-34 [context of non-vengeance] . . . what credit is it to you *(poia charis estin hymin)* x 3
2:20 . . . when you are beaten for it . . .	Matt 5:39 If any one strikes you on the right cheek . . .
3:9 Not returning *(apodidontes)* evil for evil	Luke 6:27 Do good to those who hate you
3:14 . . . if you should suffer for righteousness, blessed.	Matt 5:10 Blessed are those who are persecuted for righteousness' sake
4:14 . . . if you are reproached *(oneidizesthe)* for the name of Christ, blessed.	Matt 5:11 Blessed are you when men revile *(oneidisōsin)* you

This list is fairly conservative; Gundry, for example, finds more echoes of words of Jesus, including some from Johannine traditions.[60] Whatever the precise extent of the traces, their fact is undeniable.

It is immediately clear that the tradition underlying the Sermon on the Mount is prominent, though it is from a pre-Synoptic tradition later traceable in Matthew and Luke. Whether that tradition was written or oral cannot be determined from 1 Peter. Nonetheless, as with the Jesus traditions alluded to in the letters of Paul and James it is more likely that Peter drew from traditions that were *written*, written in *Greek*.

60. Gundry, "Verba Christi," 366.

The lack of secure dating prevents firm conclusions being drawn. At the very least, however, the *verba Christi* in 1 Peter confirm the usage of such words by leaders in the NT and demand that such material had been assembled and was in circulation prior to their inclusion in the letters in which they appear.

The Nature of the Jesus Tradition

One striking characteristic of the "words of the Lord" in 1 Peter, James, 1 Corinthians, and Romans must be noted. It is that these logia, apart from the eucharistic tradition (in 1 Cor 11), are universally parenetic. Without taking other evidence into account we might think that Jesus was first and foremost a moral teacher. Echoes of the Lord's eschatological teachings in 1 Thessalonians, however, prevent us from too easily drawing this conclusion. When we add the eucharistic tradition to the dominical eschatology from 1 Thessalonians the picture changes and we see Jesus not only as a teacher and apocalyptic prophet but also as a messianic deliverer. This latter element is reinforced as we recall that the messianic traditions arose immediately after the first Easter, as echoed explicitly in 1 Cor 15:3-7 and implicitly in Rom 1:1-4.

The attempts of those who portray Jesus only as a moral instructor and reformer[61] do not address the totality of the evidence. Contrary to the assertion that only the parenetic tradition was true to Jesus, the evidence points equally to the kerygmatic tradition, centered as it was on christology. In fact, both go back to the historical Jesus. This is no less true in the "Q" tradition (see chapter 12 below). Those who reject the christological tradition, preferring the parenetic alone, do not share the vision of the Christians in the 30s, 40s, and 50s of the first century. Theirs was not a perverse vision, however, since the kerygmatic and christological existed alongside the parenetic from earliest times, going back to Jesus himself.

Authentic or Corrupted?

Because Christ and Christianity are both important and controversial there has been much debate whether the Gospels are trustworthy biogra-

---

61. For example, Crossan, *Birth of Christianity*, 110-11.

phies of Jesus. Does the Jesus we see and hear in those texts in any way correspond with Jesus as he was? Was the tradition corrupted — whether innocently or deliberately — during that forty-year period between Jesus the man and Jesus as written Gospel?

There has been a widespread assumption that the Gospel records reflect the post-Easter church setting rather than the pre-Easter words and works of the historical Jesus. The classic form critics, notably Bultmann, argued that the pericopes of the Gospels had undergone major adaptation and that they bore little relationship to the now lost sequence of events. More recent studies based on the culture of orality and communal storytelling have effectively closed off any pathway to the actual teaching of Jesus. Either way, the "real" Jesus and his teaching are seen as obscured by developments in the era after him.

Several factors speak in favor of the integrity of the process. First, we have in the letters of Paul, James, and Peter windows into living tradition streams that would soon empty into the Gospel pools. It is significant that we have not one set of windows, but several independent ones.

Second, Luke's prologue states that the "eyewitnesses" of Jesus who became "ministers of the word" "handed over" the *written* traditions to the author (as noted earlier). In other words, the traditioning was a *guided* process, and the guardians of its integrity were those who were the original disciples of the Master himself. Source criticism has identified the traditions Luke received, namely Mark, "Q," and "L." These prove to be the source streams from which Paul, James, and Peter draw as those streams made their way to their final destinations.

Third, the widespread assumption that orality was only overtaken by textuality late in the day must be rejected. If a non-mission movement such as Qumran was marked by the practice of writing in tandem with orality, then the messianic missionary movement was even more likely to have employed written texts for dissemination among the rapidly emerging house congregations in Israel. Given the relatively high levels of literacy among Jews of the era it should come as no surprise that written texts were part of nascent Christianity from the beginning.[62]

In other words, the various theories that erode confidence in the process of transmission must be questioned, whether those of the classical form critics who assumed a fundamental corruption in transmission of

62. See E. E. Ellis, "Gospels as History," 3-11.

the pericopes or recent hypotheses relating to oral transmission which also assume partial corruption in transmission. Regarding the latter, we repeat that evidence for orality in the NT points to a controlled *didactic* orality, not a communal orality ("by many for many").

Conclusion

Once we have established from these letters the fact and earliness of collections of Jesus' teachings, the critical question, then, is who assembled these teachings. The letters themselves are silent as to the identity of the "many who undertook to compile a narrative of the things accomplished among us" (Luke 1:1). More important by far is the assurance that these were "handed over" by the original disciples as guardians of the traditions.

The significance of Paul's letters is that they lie about midway between the historical Jesus and the written Gospels. In other words, the forty-year span between Jesus and Mark is not a blank space. By the early 50s, that is, twenty years after Jesus, various letters of Paul point to collections of Jesus' teaching which, most likely, were already written, and most likely in Greek. This is corroborated by Jesus traditions evident in the letters of James and Peter, notwithstanding the difficulties in dating those letters.

The point needs to be made, however, that these collections most likely predated Paul's Greek mission in ca. 50. It appears that Jesus' teachings began to be assembled from earliest times and that they were transmitted in both oral and written form.

Thus the letters provide windows through which we can see "work in progress" only twenty years after Jesus. In comparison with the many years involved in the evolution of the Apostles' and Nicene Creeds, for example, a twenty-year span in which the "formation" had well and truly begun and a forty-year span by which it had been completed is relatively brief.

TWELVE

A Collection Called "Q"

One of the attractions of Q in some quarters today is that it seems to say nothing about Jesus' death and resurrection, thus providing evidence of a flourishing type of early Christianity for which those . . . emphases, so strikingly evident in the canonical gospels, were unimportant.

N. T. Wright, "Resurrection in Q?" (2000).[1]

"Q," a source used by both Matthew and Luke, has been hypothesized for several centuries by that dry as dust discipline known as Source Criticism.[2] In recent times, however, "Q" has become electrifyingly important to the study of Christian origins.

Members of the Jesus Seminar and others have proposed that "Q" represents the beliefs of the original post-Easter disciples of Jesus in Galilee, which authentically reflect the mind of the pre-Easter Jesus. They argue that "Q," unlike the canonical Gospels, has no Passion narrative (or atonement theology), no resurrection appearances, and no confession of Jesus as the Son of God. Accordingly, they contend that the agenda of the "real" Jesus was reformist and ethical and that the redemptive and messi-

---

1. N. T. Wright, "Resurrection in Q?" in D. R. H. Horrell and C. M. Tuckett (eds.), *Christology, Controversy and Community* (Leiden: Brill, 2000), 87.

2. The existence of Q has always been doubted. See, for example, M. Goodacre, "A Monopoly on Markan Priority? Fallacies at the heart of Q," *SBL Seminar Papers 2000* (Atlanta: Society of Biblical Literature, 2000), 583-622.

anic elements in the canonical Gospels were distortions attributable to the influence of Paul and Mark.

This proposal assumes that "Q" and the "Q" community were somehow walled off, quarantined from other currents of thought among the early Christians.

Despite the recent reconstructions of "Q" with attendant claims about its real but different Jesus, this view is not altogether new. Kloppenborg quotes Bultmann with approval for his assertion that "Q" was "a transitional stage between the unmessianic preaching of Jesus and the fully self-conscious kerygma of the Hellenistic churches."[3]

It may be agreed immediately that "Q" was indeed an early compilation that reflected the mind of Jesus of Nazareth. A matter of strong disagreement, however, is the contention that "Q" represents a merely ethical/reformist Jesus. To the contrary, I will argue that in "Q" Jesus is the Messiah, and his coming death and resurrection are presupposed.

In that case — and provided "Q" really did exist in a discrete form — the Jesus Seminar members and others who have raised the importance of "Q" to redefine Jesus may have succeeded only in reinforcing the historical redemptive view of him as Messiah. Their "Q" strategy may yet prove self-defeating, having an outcome opposite to their intentions.

But first, how good is the case for "Q"?

The Case for "Q"

First, a description of "Q" is in order. In broad terms it is material found in both Matthew and Luke but not in Mark.[4] "Q" is the abbreviation of *Quelle,* German for "source." It consists in about 235 verses that are mostly, but not entirely, sayings of Jesus. While some scholars use the term merely for this material, others, with greater probability, are thinking of a body of teaching. In this latter case, such a corpus is more likely to have existed in written rather than in an oral form.

3. J. Kloppenborg, *The Formation of Q* (Harrisburg: Trinity Press International, 1987), 21.

4. See the sharp critique by D. H. Akenson, *Saint Saul* (Oxford: Oxford University Press, 2000), 324, of Koester and Kloppenborg, who introduce into their "Q" material texts from Mark.

Many have argued in detail and at length for the existence of "Q."[5] Put simply the case for a common source used by Matthew and Luke is called for because of the significant number of critical texts that have identical or almost identical wording, because this material follows the same sequence in both Matthew and Luke, because neither Gospel always gives the earliest likely form of the tradition, suggesting that both rely on a common source, and because "Q" as reconstructed has a historical and theological coherence.

Due to the perceived superiority of Luke's version the Lukan reference is given before the Matthean, or alternatively cited as, e.g., Q 11:3 (= Luke 11:3).

The "Q" hypothesis has always had critics not least since it depends on *both* Markan priority *and* the independence of Matthew from Luke. And other hypotheses have been advanced. Some have argued that Matthew has incorporated Luke in his Gospel, thus explaining the "double tradition" (i.e., the common source, "Q").[6] Others follow the so-called Griesbach or "double-Gospel" hypothesis that Luke made direct use of Matthew and that Mark then reduced both Matthew and Luke to his more or less bare narrative.[7]

Nonetheless, although the "Q" hypothesis and its close relative, Markan priority, are not without deficiencies most scholars remain unmoved by the criticisms or persuaded by the alternative explanations for the origin of and relationship between the Synoptic Gospels. The case for "Q," though beyond proof, remains quite strong and, for this author at least, is the most likely explanation of the relationships among the Synoptic Gospels.

The Content of "Q"

It seems wise to consult the cooler heads of the older source critics for their understanding of the contours and character of "Q" rather than the

5. For example, J. A. Fitzmyer, "The Priority of Mark and the 'Q' Source in Luke," in *To Advance the Gospel: New Testament Studies* (Grand Rapids: Eerdmans, 1998), 3-39.

6. E.g., M. Hengel, *The Four Gospels and the One Gospel of Jesus Christ* (London: SCM, 2000), 169-207.

7. E.g., A. J. McNicol, D. B. Peabody, and D. L. Dungan (eds.) *Beyond the Q Impasse: Luke's Use of Matthew* (Valley Forge: Trinity Press International, 1996).

emotionally involved exponents and opponents of the Jesus Seminar. One such source critic from an earlier era was T. W. Manson, who (based on the Lukan version) analyzed the contents of "Q" as follows[8]:

A. John the Baptist and Jesus
   The preaching of John
   The temptations of Jesus
   The preaching of Jesus
   The centurion of Capernaum
   John and Jesus
B. Jesus and his disciples
   Candidates for discipleship
   The mission charge
   The privileges of discipleship
C. Jesus and his opponents
   The Beelzebul controversy
   Flattery rebuked
   Against sign-seekers
   Against Pharisaism
   Disciples under persecution
D. The future
   The time of crisis
   The fate of the unrepentant
   Discipleship in a time of crisis
   The day of the Son of Man

Based on this arrangement of the contents Manson comments,

> It is in fact possible on this order to establish a rough parallelism be-
> tween Mark and Q — at least at the beginning and end of the docu-
> ments.

This opinion, however, depends on the view that "Q," as we are able to re-construct it, is the authentic original compilation. This is precisely the problem the members of the Jesus Seminar and others have with the "Q" source.

---

8. *The Sayings of Jesus* (London: SCM, 1961), 39-148.

Is "Q" an Archaeological "Tell"?

The most prominent "Q" scholar among the Jesus Seminar members is John Kloppenborg (now Kloppenborg Verbin). His first major text, *The Formation of Q*, was written in 1987.[9] His later text, *Excavating Q*,[10] invites the pursuit of the archaeological metaphor. Kloppenborg Verbin assumes a degree of stratification in the present "Q" document, whose "layers," he says, can be isolated and identified. He argues that "Q" began as a sapiential ("wisdom") document (Q1), was then revised with the addition of prophetic/judgment/apocalyptic passages (Q2), and was finally revised by the addition of narrative passages (Q3). By this method Kloppenborg Verbin effectively reduces the "Q" Jesus to a speaker of "wise" sayings and has removed any messianic, atonement, or resurrection associations from Jesus.

There are several problems with this approach. First, the assumption that texts of that era were monocultural must be questioned. Contrary to various attempts to tease apart and analyse separately language strands we must insist that Second Temple texts routinely intermix wisdom, prophecy, eschatology and apocalyptic vernacular, especially in passages that prophesy a coming messianic deliverer. According to Edward Meadors,

> . . . clearly defined "compartmentalized" stratification of "Q" classified as "sapiential," "prophetic," "apocalyptic," "polemical," "paraenetic," etc. accord poorly with the diversity of First Century Palestinian life.[11]

Jesus' seamless use of these categories is no basis for identifying earlier and later strands but is rather gratuitous evidence of his messianic consciousness in the context of those times.

Second, Kloppenborg Verbin's analytical "tools" are problematic. The first, "the determination of compositional principles" assumes at the outset that the sayings of "Q" were originally separate, the work of one or more editors. The second, working from the assumption that "compositional activity may be seen as insertions or glosses" is entirely

9. Kloppenborg, *Formation of Q*.

10. J. Kloppenborg Verbin, *Excavating Q: The History and Setting of the Sayings Gospel* (Minneapolis: Fortress, 2000).

11. "The 'Messianic' Implications of the Q Material," *JBL* 118.2 (1999), 261.

subjective. In other words, these "tools" are arbitrary and will offer differ-ent verdicts on texts depending on the assumptions of the critics.[12]

The following criticism is well made:

> Let me repeat: Q is a source that *we don't have.* To reconstruct what we think was in it is hypothetical enough. But at least in doing so we have some hard evidence, since we do have traditions that are verbatim the same in Matthew and Luke (but not found in Mark), and we do have to account for them in *some* way. But to go further and insist that we know what was *not* in the source, for example, a Passion Narrative, what its multiple editions were like, and which of these editions was the earliest, and so on goes beyond what we can know. . . .[13]

N. T. Wright's comment, though briefer, is no less trenchant:

> I find it impossible to believe that we can now discern developmental layers within [documentary Q] which involve significant theological shifts and transformations.[14]

The most prudent position to adopt is to take "Q" more or less at face value and analyze it for any signs of messiahship and other critical indica-tors regarding Jesus of Nazareth. Our results as summarized below prove quite surprising and do not at all correspond with the Jesus the Jesus Semi-nar finds in "Q."

Christology in "Q"

Meadors[15] has established that there is a deep-rooted messianism in "Q," notwithstanding the absence of the word "Christ" or the lack of "organis-ing faith statements." Within Second Temple Judaism there was wide-spread conviction of a coming, anointed deliverer from the line of David

---

12. For a critical assessment of Kloppenborg Verbin's judgments on specific texts see D. Ingolfsland, "Kloppenborg's Stratification of Q and Its Significance for Historical Jesus Studies," *JETS* 46.2 (June 2003), 227-31.

13. B. Ehrman, *Jesus: Apocalyptic Prophet of the New Millennium* (New York: Oxford University Press, 2002), 133.

14. "Resurrection in Q," 86.

15. "'Messianic' Implications," 253-77.

who would reign within a kingdom blessed by God. The Jesus of "Q" fulfills this expectation:

First, Jesus is implicitly this "Messiah":

1. In his response to John in Luke 7:22/Matt 11:4-6 Jesus says

   > Go and tell John what you have seen and heard: The blind receive their sight, the lame walk, lepers are cleansed, and the deaf hear, the dead are raised up, the poor have good news preached to them. And blessed is he who takes no offense at me.

   Here Jesus combines Isa 61:1-3 (the herald of the Lord) with Isa 29:18; 35:5-6; 42:19 (the end-time Day of the Lord), a conflation already implicit in the Qumran fragment 4Q521 (7-14). Jesus concludes, "Blessed is he who takes no offence at *me.*" Having established the significant role of John at the beginning of "Q" this exchange between the imprisoned prophet and Jesus' revelation that he is the "one who was to come" is critical.

2. A further connection between John the forerunner and "the one who was to come" is found in their respective references to the Spirit. John declared that the Coming One was to "baptize with the Holy Spirit and fire" (Luke 3:16-17/Matt 3:11-12), and Jesus declares that "if I by the finger/Spirit of God cast out demons, then the kingdom of God has come upon you" (Luke 11:20/Matt 12:28).

When these key texts are considered together it becomes clear that the Jesus of "Q" regarded himself as the Spirit-anointed one to come, in short, the Messiah, regardless of the absence of the latter title.

Second, Jesus exercises "messianic" authority. This authority is seen in various sayings:

1. His "I say to you" form of speech occurs fourteen times in "Q" texts and implies a messianic status as opposed to the prophetic status of "thus says the Lord."

2. The "woes" Jesus pronounces against religious leaders (Luke 11:43/ Matt 23:6) and the villages of Galilee (Luke 10:13/Matt 11:21) indicate God's judgment against the messianic rule of Jesus that has now begun.

Third, Jesus promises a "messianic" banquet:

And you are those who have stood by *me* in my trials;
And just as *my* Father has granted *me* a kingdom,
I grant that you may eat and drink at *my* table in my kingdom,
And you will sit on thrones judging the twelve tribes of Israel.

(Luke 22:28-30/Matt 19:28)

In another "Q" passage he refers to "my banquet" (Luke 15:24/Matt 22:1-10). Given the background in Second Temple Judaism of the messianic banquet, the claims of Jesus to messiahship could hardly be more explicit.[16]

And fourth, Jesus identifies himself messianically in "Q":

1. In Luke 10:21-22/Matt 11:25-27 he is "the Son" who calls God "my Father" an expression of messianic-filial self-awareness that arises from 2 Sam 7:14; Ps 2:7 (cf. 4QFlor).
2. Throughout "Q" he is "the Son of Man," a Danielic title that is unquestionably messianic (*1 Enoch* 48:2-10; Mark 14:61-62).
3. Jesus is also the "blessed one" that "comes in the name of the Lord" (Luke 13:34, 35/Matt 23:37-39).

The Death and Resurrection of Jesus in "Q"

According to Kloppenborg Verbin "Q seems curiously indifferent to both Jesus' death and a divine rescue of Jesus from death."[17]

But while "Q" has no narrative of Jesus' last days in Jerusalem and his death there (nor any theology of atonement) it does not follow that this source has no reference to the Passion of Jesus. In fact, numbers of texts only make sense in the light of the death of Jesus the Messiah:

1. Jesus' word that one must "take up" one's "cross" and "follow" Jesus in order to be a disciple (Luke 14:27/Matt 10:38) presupposes awareness that Jesus himself carried his cross (cf. John 19:17; Mark 15:21).

---

16. See *1 Enoch* 62:12-16; *2 Baruch* 29:1-8; 1QSa 2:11-21.

17. Quoted in A. J. Hultgren, *The Rise of Normative Christianity* (Minneapolis: Fortress, 1994), 35.

2. In Jesus' lament over Jerusalem (Luke 13:34-35/Matt 23:37-39) Ps 117:27 (LXX) is cited ("Blessed is he who comes in the name of the Lord"). In the Markan and Johannine traditions, however, this text is inextricably connected with the Passion of Jesus (Mark 11:9; John 12:13).

3. In the parable of the pounds/talents (Luke 19:12-17/Matt 25:14-20) the central figure ("the Lord") departs to a far country and then returns to hold his servants accountable. The telling of this parable in the "Q" context would have necessitated some reference to the death and parousia of the Messiah.

4. Likewise, the narration of the sufferings of the messengers of God (Luke 13:34/Matt 23:37) and the homelessness of the Son of Man (Luke 9:58/Matt 8:20) would have demanded some mention of the fact and meaning of the death of that Son of Man.

The theme of future resurrection in "Q" is found in both implicit and explicit references:[18]

1. Resurrection as a present fact is seen in "Q" in, for example, the words "the dead are raised" (Luke 7:22/Matt 11:5), referring to Jesus' raising of the widow's son at Nain and Jairus's daughter.

2. Jesus' words about the patriarchs and believers seated at table in the kingdom (Luke 13:28-29/Matt 8:11-12) while those watching gnash their teeth imply the notion of a coming resurrection and final judgment. Likewise, the "Q" saying of John the Baptist about Abraham makes sense only in a setting where the coming general resurrection is expected (Luke 3:8/Matt 3:7-10). Again, Jesus' promise that his followers will sit upon thrones judging the twelve tribes (Luke 22:30/ Matt 19:28) presupposes future resurrection and final judgment.

3. Jesus explicitly speaks of his own coming resurrection as the "sign" of the prophet Jonah. As Jonah was a "sign" to the people of Nineveh, so one greater than Jonah, the Son of Man, will be in his generation. That "sign" — explicit in Matt 12:40, implicit in Luke 11:31-32 — can only mean Jonah's "extraordinary escape from the sea monster,"[19] which pointed to the resurrection of Jesus.

18. See Wright, "Resurrection in Q," 85-97; *The Resurrection of the Son of God* (London: SPCK, 2003) 429-34.
19. So Wright, "Resurrection in Q," 94.

"Q" — Collection or Kerygma?

From the foregoing items it is evident that those who formulated "Q" believed that Jesus was the long-awaited Messiah of God, rejected by the people of Israel and put to death only to be vindicated in resurrection by God. It is equally clear that they held the new, final era had come, blessed with the gift of the Spirit of God (Luke 12:10/Matt 12:32). The Messianic epoch had dawned and they were part of it.

If these were the convictions of the formulators of "Q" it does not follow, however, that this "collection" was formulated to be "published" as a "Gospel" in the way that Mark's book would be. Rather, "Q" is better regarded as a proto-Gospel, an early draft, so to speak.

It is a collection of texts for catechetical use rather than a finalized and coherent document for winning the outsider's obedience to Christ. References in "Q" to Jesus as Messiah, his death, resurrection, and parousia strongly imply that such tenets undergirded the convictions of those who compiled these texts. The fact of the kerygma currently being proclaimed is implied by the contents of "Q." Such was its evident value that within several decades Matthew and Luke embodied it as a major source within their own larger works.

The Origin of "Q"

As noted above the texts of Matthew and Luke written (we suppose) by A.D. 80 testify to the existence of "Q" by that time (cf. Luke 1:1-2), that is, within a half-century of the pre-Easter Jesus. As noted earlier, however, "Q" texts are cited or echoed in letters of Paul written in the mid-fifties. We conclude, therefore, that "Q" was formulated in the two decades between the historical Jesus and Paul's missions in Greece and Asia.

How did "Q" come to be written? Most likely the disciples of the pre-Easter Jesus memorized his words as he spoke them, with one or more of their number copying them down.[20] In the post-Easter period when these disciples won converts for Jesus the Messiah the original disciples assembled the words and works of the pre-Easter Jesus for catechetical purposes in the newly formed messianic synagogues. While most likely written orig-

20. See pp. 113-18 above.

inally in Aramaic, the text of "Q" we encounter in Matthew, Luke and the letters is written in Koine Greek.[21]

"Q" is marked by an immediacy and freshness suggestive of closeness to the mind of the Teacher of the disciple or disciples who compiled this text. It calls for a radical unhypocritical attitude to the Torah as befitting the new age, a readiness to confess Jesus as the Son of Man and an attitude of implicit trust in the goodness of the Father, free of anxiety. Those who follow Jesus are to be not judgmental of others but loving and generous toward them.

Conclusion

More than one observer has noted an ideological agenda driving the Jesus Seminar. The members appear determined to find an ethically motivated, non-redemptive, non-Pauline Jesus. To them "Q," with its absence of reference to "Messiah" or to Jesus' death (whether as an event or in an atonement theology) or to Jesus' resurrection, might easily have appeared an ideal place in which to find a non-messianic, reformist Jesus. Yet to find this Jesus it has been necessary to go to extraordinarily reductionist lengths in editorial deletions.

The day may come, or maybe has come already, when the Seminar regrets having hitched its wagon to the "Q" star. The members are likely right in identifying "Q" as a discrete document and possibly right in concluding that it always lacked a Passion narrative and resurrection appearances. Yet, as it stands, this likely early document testifies to Jesus, the Messiah, who fulfills the Law and the Prophets and who calls upon men and women to follow him in sacrificial discipleship. Indeed, Q may be the earliest document of Christianity, one moreover that exhibits not a low christology but one that is exalted and entirely consistent with the christology set out in "the teaching of the apostles" or, as Paul calls it, "the faith."

In short, "Q" witnesses to the same Jesus as found in other traditions

---

21. M. Casey, *An Aramaic Approach to Q: Sources for the Gospels of Matthew and Luke* (NSNTSMS 122; Cambridge: Cambridge University Press, 2002) argues that there was no single source "Q" but rather sources used by Matthew and Luke and that these sources were written in Aramaic. P. M. Head and P. J. Williams, "Q Review," *Tyndale Bulletin* 54 (2003), 131-44 have critically and negatively reviewed Casey's attempts to retrovert various Greek Q passages into Aramaic.

within the New Testament. If it had been "walled off" from other traditions, as some claim, that may only point to its earliness and its influence on other writings, including the letters of Paul and Peter, Hebrews, and the Gospels of Matthew and Luke. The Jesus of "Q" is therefore most likely the earliest Jesus we encounter, but he is not different in principle from the Jesus we meet elsewhere in the New Testament.

THIRTEEN

Primary Gospel 1: Mark

. . . Mark created a new literary genre, though one of an unprecedented kind . . . a "kerygmatic" biography. . . .

M. Hengel, *The Four Gospels and the One Gospel of Jesus Christ*[1]

Sometime in the 60s of the first century Mark acquired a papyrus scroll and began to write his "Gospel of Jesus Christ." The forty years between that moment and the historical figure Jesus had been full of mission activity, much of it in Israel. Mark's literary opus was not different from the prior mission activity, however, but its climax. If that activity could be characterized by the word "gospel" then his choice of title for his scroll was singularly appropriate.

A Primary Gospel

Mark's is a "primary" document[2] in the sense that no known earlier discrete text upon which it depended has been located. In this regard, Mark is

---

1. M. Hengel, *The Four Gospels and the One Gospel of Jesus Christ* (London: SCM, 2000), 91.
2. We will argue that the Gospel of John is likewise a "primary" text, that is, that it is not identifiably derived from an earlier source or sources.

to be distinguished from Matthew and Luke, both of which incorporated Mark (Matthew has 80 percent; Luke has 50 percent). Matthew and Luke also depended on a common logia source (called "Q"). The dependence of Matthew and Luke upon Mark and "Q" logia is referred to as the two-source theory.[3]

What Happened between Jesus and Mark?

To state the obvious, Mark's Gospel is a written text and is written in the Greek language (with a number of embedded Aramaisms). Jesus, however, taught by known oral forms in the Aramaic language.[4] In the forty years between Jesus and this Gospel several important developments occurred. Jesus' oral teaching was now written, and it was written in Greek.

The NT historian faces several questions. By what means did Jesus' teaching and life come to be written down? When and why were they written? Why was the language changed from Aramaic to Greek? Scholars agonize over these questions, struggling to understand the origins of the traditions underlying the Gospels, whether they existed in both oral and written form, how they were transmitted and developed and the means by which finally they were incorporated into this early Gospel.

Some items can be confirmed. First, the time frame is finite and known. Jesus was crucified in 33 (or 30) and Mark completed his Gospel about forty years later. Second, we know the broad circumstances of people like Mark within that time frame. They were involved in the mission to Israel to win adherents to Jesus the Messiah (Acts 9:31, 32; cf. Gal 1:22; 1 Thess 2:14).[5] In other words, the memory of Jesus had been kept "alive" throughout that period. Mark was not like Suetonius, for example, writing a cold "life" of a Caesar from surviving scraps of information, gossip, and rumors. Third, we know where the greater part of the "living" tradition of Jesus was forged. It was in Jerusalem and the land of Israel. In short, we know the time frame (about forty years), the circumstances of the evi-

---

3. For a convenient survey of the various theories explaining the origins of and relationship among Matthew, Mark, and Luke see B. Reicke, "The History of the Synoptic Discussion," in D. L. Dungan, ed., *The Interrelations of the Gospels* (Leuven: University Press, 1990), 291-316.

4. See pp. 112-13 above.

5. See pp. 95-105 above.

dence Mark used (mission work), and the circumscribed location (Israel). Fourth, we know that vital information was early formulated and transmitted in memorized oral format (1 Cor 11:23-26; 15:1-7). Fifth, we know that within this finite era "many" had "compiled" a "narrative" (Luke 1:1-2), which almost certainly means *written* narrative.

Peter, Apostle to the Circumcised

It is evident both from Paul's letters and the book of Acts that Peter was the leader of the mission to the Jews in Jerusalem and in the land of Israel during the first decade and a half following Jesus (Gal 2:7-8; Acts 1–9 passim).[6] Acts refers many times to the "teaching of the apostles" and summarizes Peter's "teaching" on several occasions in Jerusalem and once outside the city, to the God-fearer Cornelius in Caesarea Maritima (10:34-43).

Peter's "teaching" in Jerusalem recorded in Acts chiefly sought to vindicate Jesus as the Messiah resurrected and exalted by God despite the Jews' shameful rejection of him. By contrast, in Caesarea Peter emphasized the biography of Jesus, beginning with John's preaching of baptism and ending with the appearances of the resurrected Christ in Jerusalem.

The latter section of Peter's teaching (summarized in Acts) is similar to the preformed summary Paul received and "handed over" to the churches:

Acts 10	1 Corinthians 15
39 . . . they put him to *death* . . .	3 Christ *died* for our *sins*
	4 he was buried
40 but God *raised* him	he was *raised*
on the third day	on the third day . . .
and made him *manifest* . . . to *us*	5 he appeared to Cephas
43 everyone who believes in him	
receives forgiveness of *sins*	

The wording is identical at one point ("raised on the third day") and quite close elsewhere. It is likely that Paul merely rehearses the end points of the apostolic "teaching" in 1 Cor 15:3-5 and that, had he chosen to, he could

---

6. See chapter 10.

have reminded the Corinthians of a gospel outline similar to Peter's as summarized in the earlier part of his sermon in Caesarea.

From Acts, a reliable guide to Paul's teaching,[7] we know that he was in possession of extensive biographical information concerning Jesus. Paul's teaching in Pisidian Antioch, summarized in Acts 13:23-38, bears close connection with Peter's teaching about Jesus in Acts 10:34-43. Both mention John's preaching of baptism, Jesus' death in Jerusalem, from which God raised him, and his subsequent appearances there to those who had come from Galilee with him. As noted earlier, Paul would have derived this "teaching" at his baptism ultimately from Peter. Yet each summary has details not found in the other, suggesting that there was extensive knowledge of Jesus current in Israel in that early period.

This "teaching" of Peter in Acts 10:34-43 (and of Peter through Paul in Acts 13:23-38) bears a striking similarity to the biography of Jesus in the Gospel of Mark.

Acts 10	Mark
43 prophetic fulfillment	Mark 1:1-15
37 John's baptismal teaching	sets these out
38 Spirit's anointing of Jesus	in narrative
36 Jesus' gospeling	form
37 Jesus' doing good,	Mark 1:14–8:30
38 beginning in Galilee,	expands on
healing all oppressed	Acts 10:37-38
by the devil	
39 Jesus' activity in	Mark 8:31–16:8
40 Judea and Jerusalem	expands on
climaxed in his death	Acts 10:39-40
and resurrection	

It was C. H. Dodd who is noted for seeing the connection between Peter's teaching in Caesarea and the Gospel of Mark.

> . . . we can trace in the Gospel according to Mark a connecting thread running through much of the narrative, which has some similarity to

7. See Appendix A.

the brief summary of the story of Jesus in Acts x and xiii, and may be regarded as an expanded form of what we may call the historical section of the kerygma. . . .

Mark therefore conceived himself as writing a form of the kerygma, and that his Gospel is in fact a rendering of the apostolic preaching will become clear from an analysis of the book itself.[8]

More recently R. A. Guelich commented along similar lines.

. . . [the] tradition underlying Acts 10:34-43 anticipates the literary genre of gospel, since Mark's Gospel directly corresponds formally and materially with this tradition.[9]

In brief, then, our argument is that textual analysis shows a close connection between the summarized teaching of Peter in Acts 10 (and Peter through Paul in Acts 13) and the written Gospel according to Mark. The former developed into the latter, without hiatus.

Orality and Textuality in Early Christianity

It is widely held that in this early era of Christianity oral transmission was the initial mode of communication, with written texts entering in rather later. Oral transmission cannot be doubted given the evidence of its use within early Christianity as well as its significant place within the Jewish culture in which "the faith" was born. Yet it is likely that the early Christians began to employ written texts rather earlier than is often assumed. By the late 40s the meeting in Jerusalem had written a decree to churches in Syria and Cilicia (Acts 15:23). Within a year or so Paul, who had been educated in Jerusalem, was writing letters to instruct the churches of the Greek mission.

Furthermore, Paul echoes teachings of Jesus in 1 Thessalonians, 1 Corinthians, and Romans.[10] Similar echoes can be heard in James's letter,

---

8. C. H. Dodd, *The Apostolic Preaching and Its Development* (London: Hodder and Stoughton, 1936), 46-52 passim.

9. R. A. Guelich, "The Gospel Genre," in P. Stuhlmacher, ed., *The Gospel and the Gospels* (Grand Rapids: Eerdmans, 1991), 201.

10. See pp. 120-26 above.

though the dating is uncertain. Who can assert with confidence that such teachings of Jesus were not derived from written collections?

Equally, who can say that mission activity in Israel after Jesus was exercised by oral means alone and that written texts were not employed? What cannot be disputed is that written texts came to be used. When that moment came is a matter of judgment.

As noted earlier, there is a likely parallel with the Qumran covenanters, who, like the disciples, were also a marginalized sect within Judaism.[11] The teachings of their founder, the Teacher of Righteousness, were written down more or less at the time he spoke.

Let me propose a likely situation. We know that by the mid-30s churches arose in Jerusalem, Judea, Galilee, and Samaria (Gal 1:22; 1 Thess 2:14; Acts 8:25; 15:3). These would have been based in houses (as many synagogues were). Further, we know that original disciples like Peter and John traveled throughout ministering to these churches (cf. Acts 9:31-32). Just as the "teaching of the apostles" (that is, oral instruction) was critical in Jerusalem (2:42; 5:28; cf. 4:2, 18; 5:21, 25, 42), so we reasonably assume that the apostles orally instructed these nascent churches and that key beliefs were committed to memory. Then, however, the apostle or evangelist moved elsewhere, leaving the new assembly with relatively few resources for their Messiah's "synagogue." Just as the traditional synagogue was a place of reading and hearing texts so it would become necessary for the Jewish churches to have texts for literate members to read to the gathered members.

According to this hypothesis oral tradition and written text, both mediated by "eye-witness" preachers, existed side-by-side from early times in the mission churches in Jerusalem and the land of Israel.

Markan "Blocks"

Although Mark's is a "primary" text, various preexisting "blocks" have been discerned within this Gospel. These include Jesus' dramatic first "day" in Capernaum (1:21-34; cf. 1:35), the conflict stories in Capernaum (2:1–3:6), Jesus' "kingdom" parables (4:1-34), his lake-centered miracles (4:35–5:43), various miscellaneous teachings (9:42-50), the eschatological

---

11. See p. 114 above.

discourse (13:1-37), and, above all, the events of the last "three days" (14:1–16:6). There is no external means of certainly identifying these blocks or determining whether there may have been more or less than those mentioned. Nonetheless, many scholars hold that passages like those above existed (for teaching purposes) before Mark incorporated them within his text. Since there is no discernible Aramaic original underlying Mark (apart from isolated words),[12] we assume that these earlier constituent parts existed in Greek from their beginnings.

Creation of Markan "Blocks"

There are several possible pointers to the time several of these blocks were formulated. In the final "three days" narrative it has been noted that the absence of Caiaphas's name in Mark's account could point to earliness of composition; Caiaphas was deposed as high priest in 37. Matthew's and Luke's accounts, which depend on Mark's, mention Caiaphas by name, suggesting a date later than Mark's.

A further possible indication of the earliness of this block is its inclusion of the Last Supper. The reading of this passage in its wider context provided a natural setting for the liturgical reenactment of the Lord's Supper in the newly formed Jewish house churches.

There is a good case that the eschatological discourse (Mark 13) was written soon after 40, when Caligula had decided to install a statue of himself in the Temple, provoking a crisis that brought Jews and Romans to the brink of war.[13] Jesus' words, ". . . when you see the desolating sacrilege set up where *he*[14] ought not to be (let the reader understand), then let those in Judea flee to the mountains" (13:14), likely point to its writing soon after the event. Perhaps, too, it inspired Paul to write a few years later about "the man of lawlessness . . . [who] sets himself up in God's Temple, proclaiming himself to be God" (2 Thess 2:3-4).

This reconstruction is more likely than one that is said to reflect the Roman assault on the Temple in A.D. 70, demanding a later date for the

12. See pp. 112-13 above.

13. See earlier, pp. 33-37.

14. Because the antecedent of the pronoun is neuter we must assume Mark has deliberately violated the grammar to make a point that the lector must explain to the assembled believers.

writing of this narrative. First, according to Josephus's eyewitness account, the desecration of the Temple came *after* its substantial destruction, not beforehand[15] as implied in Mark 13:7, 14. Second, the flight of Judeans occurred prior to the Romans' final assault, not subsequent to it. The desecration of the Temple was the climax, not the prelude, to the sufferings of the people of Judea. Third, if, as seems likely, Mark wrote from Rome, we must ask how he knew these details from such a distance in an era lacking rapid and detailed news communication.

Paul's letter to the Romans, written ca. 57, also bears on the dating of possible "blocks" of teaching in Mark's Gospel. Paul exhorts the Romans to "render" to authorities what is their due (Rom 13:7, echoing Mark 12:17) and not to cause others to "stumble" (Rom 14:13, echoing Mark 9:42) and teaches that all foods are "clean" (Rom 14:14, echoing Mark 7:19). Most likely these echoes point to Markan teaching blocks circulating by the 50s, which, like those mentioned above, found their way into the final version of the Gospel of Mark.

Gospel — Activity and Text

We must distinguish between the four-decade-long prehistory of Mark, during which its constituent parts were "formed," and that moment when the author began to write his scroll for its release for the churches in the wider world.

Although the Gospels as finished works are broadly identifiable as biographies of that era, the means by which they were written was unlike other "lives" of famous men of those times.[16] Josephus wrote biographically about Herod the Great and his grandson Herod Agrippa I within his larger works, *Jewish War* and *Jewish Antiquities*. Josephus made extensive use of readymade sources. He incorporated the work of Herod's court historian Nicolaus of Damascus, who had already written extensively. His sources for Agrippa are not known.[17]

The sources Mark used for Jesus had been created and used through-

---

15. *War* 6.260, 316.

16. See D. Capes, "Imitatio Christi and the Gospel Genre," *IBR* 13.1 (2003), 1-3.

17. See P. W. Barnett, "Agrippa the Elder and Early Christianity," in P. T. O'Brien and D. G. Peterson, eds., *God Who Is Rich in Mercy* (Sydney: Anzea, 1986), 130-31.

out the period between Jesus and the moment this "biographer" began to write his Gospel. Unlike Josephus's "dead" sources, those employed by Mark and John were "living" sources used in "mission" in Israel (and beyond) in the decades after Jesus. As noted above it is likely that those "living" sources were both written and oral.[18]

Mark appears to have pioneered a new genre, "the kerygmatic biography," as one authority calls it.[19] Mark himself calls it "the Gospel of Jesus Christ" (1:1).[20] This Gospel was not merely theological assertion but a linear biographical narrative filled out by numerous brief episodes each directing attention to Jesus (except the episode about the death of John the Baptist). Mark envisaged an individual story like the anointing in Bethany becoming known worldwide, wherever the gospel is preached (14:9). The "Gospel" was in the whole work, but it was equally in each part. And it was written to be read aloud in the churches (13:14: "Let the lector understand") throughout the world.

Yet what Mark writes in his completed scroll is nothing more or less than the mission activity for which its constituent parts as mentioned above were formulated. The idea of "gospel" did not begin with Mark sometime in the sixties. The letters of Paul in the 50s indicate that the term "gospel" was used for the spoken message centered on the Messiah Jesus, his death, burial, resurrection, and appearances (1 Cor 15:1-7). Clearly the term "gospel" predated Paul's letters and went back into the earliest period and beyond that — most likely — to Jesus himself.

Mark's Gospel according to "the Presbyter"

We are fortunate to have an early account of the processes in the forty years that issued in the publication of the Gospel according to Mark. Its source is Papias, bishop of Hierapolis, a Roman city in the Lycus Valley in the province of Asia. While it was previously thought these words were

18. See pp. 113-20 above.

19. So M. Hengel, *The Four Gospels and the One Gospel of Jesus Christ* (London: SCM, 2000), 91.

20. Matthew and Luke replicated this new genre, though their more expansive contents have effectively diluted the kerygmatic impact of the prototype, Mark. John, which in my view was written in isolation from other Gospels, is neither kerygma nor biography, though it contains elements of both.

written in ca. 130, it is now held to have been written twenty or thirty years earlier.[21] This means that Papias was only one generation removed from the writing of the Gospel of Mark. Irenaeus, who belonged to the next generation beyond Papias, confirmed that Papias was a "hearer" of the pupils of the apostles.

> And the Presbyter was saying this:
> On the one hand,
> Mark, having become Peter's interpreter
> wrote accurately, as many things as he remembered.
> On the other hand,
> [he did not write] in order the things said and done by the Lord.
> For he neither heard the Lord, nor did he follow him,
> but later, as I said, [he followed] Peter.
> [Peter] arranged his teachings as anecdotes,
> but not as a collection of the Lord's teachings.
> So Mark did nothing wrong
> in writing some things as he remembered them.
> His single intention
> was not to omit anything he had heard
> or to falsify anything in them.[22]

It is critical to note that this presents not Papias's words but those of "the Presbyter," reporting what *he* "was saying." Who was this Presbyter? Was he John, "the disciple of the Lord," or that other John, who heard the first John? Most likely it was the second, though his identity is less important to establish than to note his relative closeness to the time the Gospel of Mark was written.

This "Presbyter" is in two minds about the Gospel of Mark. We detect a certain defensiveness. True, Mark wrote "accurately," the word Luke employs to describe the research underlying his own work (Luke 1:3). This is a point in his favor. Yet Mark was not a hearer of the Lord, a significant deficiency. The Presbyter's observation that Mark wrote "not in order" and "as many things as he remembered" and "did nothing wrong" sounds quite

---

21. So R. H. Gundry, *Mark: A Commentary on His Apology for the Cross* (Grand Rapids: Eerdmans, 1993), 1027, who notes that, according to Eusebius, Papias wrote in the time of Ignatius, who died ca. 107 (Eusebius, *Historia Ecclesiastica* 3.36.1-2; 3.39.1).

22. Eusebius, *Historia Ecclesiastica* 3.39.15, quoting Irenaeus.

defensive, as if this Gospel did not at the time enjoy the same good reputation as the other Gospels. Indeed, Mark was to fall into relative obscurity, where it would lie until modern times.

Clearly, though, the Presbyter seeks to establish the genuineness of Mark since its real source was none other than Peter, the leading disciple of the Lord. And whatever his shortcomings as a follower of Peter and not the Lord, Mark did the best he could. At the very least he did not falsify anything but wrote down everything he could remember.

The Presbyter's comments are the more valuable since they are not fulsome, but qualified. His information about the prehistory of this Gospel in the forty years between Jesus and that moment when Mark began to write (sometime in the 60s), in particular the earliest decades after Jesus, is of critical importance. He directs attention to Peter, though again with some defensiveness. Peter arranged his oral teaching as "anecdotes" and not as a "collection of the Lord's teachings." This appears to set Peter's and Mark's version of Jesus' teaching in a defensive contrast with the Gospel of Matthew, which contains precisely what Mark/Peter lack — a "collection" like the Sermon on the Mount. "Anecdotes," however, typifies the Gospel of Mark and likely captures the Petrine method of teaching about the Lord.

The Presbyter describes Mark as the "interpreter" of Peter, presumably meaning that he was Peter's companion explaining the apostle's Aramaic and inferior Greek to Greek-speaking audiences. Did Mark assist Peter in this way during Peter's fifteen-year "apostolate" in the land of Israel (Gal 2:7-9; Acts 9:31-32) or in the 60s in Babylon/Rome (1 Pet 5:13)? Between those two periods of time Mark engaged in mission work in Cyprus and Roman Asia (Acts 13:5; 15:39; Col 4:10; 2 Tim 4:11). Acts hints at an earlier association between Mark and Peter; Peter led the Jerusalem group that met in the house of Mark's mother (Acts 12:12). That may have been the Peter-Mark nexus in the mind of the Presbyter. Presumably Mark had some missionary experience prior to mission work with Barnabas and Paul in the late 40s. This mission experience would have been with Peter in the land of Israel.

Mark is of interest due to his two names, one Jewish ("John") and the other Roman ("Mark"), suggestive of both affluence and education. His suitability to accompany Barnabas and Paul to Cyprus and Anatolia implies fluency in Greek. His precise citation of Aramaisms and his accurate translation of them indicates easy fluency in both languages.[23] This man is

23. Hengel, *Four Gospels,* 79.

often described in relation to other, more senior leaders. He is "cousin" of Barnabas (Col 4:10), "follower" and "interpreter" of Peter (so, the Presbyter), "assistant" of Barnabas and Paul (Acts 13:5) and "of use" to Paul (2 Tim 4:11). These give us a glimpse of a literate and capable associate of the first leaders of early Christianity.

In short, then, the Presbyter's words that he "was saying" to Papias open an interesting window into the otherwise darkened tunnel period of the first decade and a half of earliest Christianity. Through that window we see a young bilingual Jerusalemite accompanying an older, less well educated man who was, however, the prime missionary and church planter in Judea, Galilee, and Samaria. Peter would tell the global Jesus story from the baptism of John through to the discovery of the empty tomb, filling it out here and there with "anecdotes" of the things said and done by the Lord (as in the teaching blocks, noted above). Years later, so it seems, the two men came together again, not in Palestine but in faraway Rome. Once again they collaborated in ministry until the martyrdom of the old man in the mid-60s. Soon afterward Mark acquired papyrus scroll, pen, and ink and began work on what would become, with John's "book," one of the two prime Gospels.

In his brief chronicle the Presbyter revealed how the oral word (of Peter) became the written word of Mark.

The Significance of Peter in the Gospel of Mark[24]

The universal view of the second century, which saw Petrine authority undergirding Mark, is implicit within the Gospel itself. Peter is the first disciple called and the last one mentioned in this Gospel. In Mark he is referred to more frequently by name relative to the other disciples than in any other Gospel. Peter was a Galilean and this Gospel is of predominantly Galilean character, though seen through the eyes of a Jerusalemite with an imprecise knowledge of the northern tetrarchy. Above all, Peter is the great confessor of Jesus' Messiahship at Caesarea Philippi. At the same time, Mark is not afraid to point out Cephas's shortcomings in arguing with Christ and, above all, in his public denial of Jesus at the time of the trial.

In brief, the actual contents of the Gospel of Mark confirm the verdict of the Presbyter that the authority of Peter undergirded this Gospel.

24. See Hengel, *Four Gospels,* 81-84.

The Publication of Mark

It is not possible precisely to determine the place and date Mark wrote his Gospel. Second-century writers point to Rome as the place and modern scholars suggest the middle to late 60s as the date.[25]

Related to its dating is the fact that Mark's text was extant when Luke came to write (cf. Luke 1:1-2). Luke had opportunity to write ca. 57-60, during Paul's imprisonment in Palestine (Acts 21:17–27:1) as well as during his imprisonments in Rome ca. 60-62 (Acts 28:16, 30) and ca. 64-65 (2 Tim 4:11, 13; 1 Pet 5:11).

The remarkably numerous Latinisms embedded in Mark,[26] along with its Roman "flavor" in its opening lines and the prominence in it of the centurion's confession are consistent with Rome as the provenance of this early Gospel. True, Palestine was quite "Romanized" in the first century, as is made evident by Latin inscriptions and the presence of Roman troops. There is no reason in principle that Mark could not have been written in Caesarea Maritima sometime in the 50s. Yet the second-century authorities consistently point to Rome as the place where Mark wrote. Passing references in 2 Tim 4:11 ("Get Mark . . . bring him with you . . . also the scrolls, above all the parchments") and 1 Pet 5:11 ("Mark my son [sends you greetings]") locate Mark in Rome, possibly with Paul and certainly with Peter.

Yet our concern here is not with the final phase of "gospeling" in the writing of this "Gospel of Jesus Christ" forty years after Jesus. Rather, our interest is in the two-decade-long mission period that immediately followed Jesus. In Galatians and Acts we see Peter (and John) leading a mission to the Jews in Israel and establishing congregations. From Papias's account of the words of the Presbyter we see Mark "following" Peter and "interpreting" the "anecdotes" of the apostle, most likely for Greek-speaking Jews of Palestine.

As scholars increasingly realize, Mark's Gospel is a subtle and skillful work, despite its appearance of naiveté. Yet there is no hiatus, no invisible barrier between this written Gospel and its four-decade-long prehistory in oral and written forms in the "gospeling" activities of Peter and his colleague Mark.

25. For example, Hengel, *Four Gospels,* 78, thinks the Gospel was written between the murder of Nero and the siege of Jerusalem, and J. A. Donahue, "Windows and Mirrors: The Setting of Mark's Gospel," *CBQ* 57 (1995), 1-26, suggests a date between the Neronian persecution in the middle 60s and the fall of Jerusalem in 70.

26. See Gundry, *Mark,* 1044.

FOURTEEN

Primary Gospel 2: John

The Gospel according to John has so different a character in comparison to the other three and is to such a degree the product of a developed theological reflection, that we can only treat it as a secondary source.

G. Bornkamm, *Jesus of Nazareth*[1]

Bornkamm's observation about John's *distinctiveness* may be correct, but his explanation based on its "developed reflection" is conjectural. A "product" of "developed . . . reflection" implies temporal lateness relative to "the other three." Bornkamm's view, which many scholars hold, effectively relegates the Gospel of John to the historical dustbin. A merely "secondary source" is of little use to the historian since every detail must be qualified.

That "old look" on the Fourth Gospel, as J. A. T. Robinson called it, expressed in the epigraph (1960), was soon to change.[2] For the next quar-

---

1. G. Bornkamm, *Jesus of Nazareth* (New York: Harper and Row, 1960), 14.

2. J. A. T. Robinson, *Twelve New Testament Studies* (Cambridge: Cambridge University Press, 1959), 94-106. Robinson, Dodd, and others who argued for Johannine independence were powerfully influenced by P. Gardner-Smith, *Saint John and the Synoptic Gospels* (Cambridge: Cambridge University Press, 1938). For a survey of the great effects of this small book see J. Verheyden, "P. Gardner-Smith and 'the Turn of the Tide,'" in A. Denaux, ed., *John and the Synoptics* (Leuven: University Press, 1992), 424-65. Verheyden observes that Gardner-Smith's *Saint John* is a symbol for the independence model and that others were articulating similar views at the time he wrote.

ter century the pendulum swung toward a more positive evaluation of this Gospel's literary independence. Since the mid-1980s, however, opinion has swung back toward the "old" viewpoint. The "old look" — which could be symbolized by the word "posteriority" — is tenacious, and it is likely that it will continue to be very influential.[3]

Does this issue bear on the "birth" of Christianity in its first decades? In fact, it does so to a significant degree. If this Gospel is later than the other Gospels and derived from them, with little identifiable distinctive data of its own, it might tell us about the era in which it was written but not much about that era that immediately followed Jesus.

In this chapter I argue for the independence of the Gospel of John from the Synoptics and for its likely earliness. If that case proves convincing it would mean that the Gospel of John provides a window into Christianity in its earliest decades.

Unfashionable Assertions about the Gospel of John

Let me make four radical assertions about the Gospel of John.

---

3. See, e.g., F. Neirynck, "John and the Synoptics: 1975-1990," in Denaux, ed., *John and the Synoptics*, 3-62. Neirynck supports the hypothesis that John was dependent on the Synoptic texts, but as a redactor (though not of their originating sources). Although Neirynck provides detailed comparisons from which he indicates verbal parallels, he is not able to establish dependence. The differences require some theory of Johannine redaction of the Synoptics, which is conjectural. Scattered verbal coincidence does not necessitate dependence, and even less does sustained coincidence. Equally likely, if not more so, is the explanation that the various tradition streams "crossed over" before reaching their destinations as the published Gospels.

See also M. Sabbe, "The Trial of Jesus before Pilate in John and Its Relation to the Synoptic Gospels," in *John and the Synoptics*, 341-85, who argues against Johannine dependence on a pre-Johannine source in favor of the Synoptic Gospels as "the sole literary source of John" (341).

Voices raised in support of the independence view include P. Borgen, "John and the Synoptics," in D. L. Dungan, ed., *The Interrelationship of the Gospels* (Leuven: University Press, 1990), 408-37, and J. D. G. Dunn, "Jesus and the Oral Tradition," in H. Wansbrough, ed., *Jesus and the Oral Tradition* (JSNT Supplement series 64; Sheffield: Sheffield University Press, 1991), 351-79.

1. The Fourth Gospel Was Written Independently of the Literary Influence of Existing Gospels.

Few words about the Gospel of John have proved so influential as those attributed to Clement of Alexandria: "But that John, last of all, conscious that the outward facts had been set forth in the Gospels . . . composed a spiritual Gospel" (Eusebius, *Historia Ecclesiastica* 6.14.7). According to this opinion John wrote "last of all," and his Gospel was a "spiritual" version of earlier "factual" Gospels.

Basic to historical evidence is the value of primary, underived information. Data that a later document merely repeats with embellishment from an earlier one is of little use to the historian. This is a fundamental rule of evidence applying to both the legal and the historical process.

One interesting example relates to Velleius Paterculus's biographical references to Tiberius written mid first century. Tacitus (ca. 120) and Suetonius (ca. 140) copied the earlier version, and Dio Cassius (ca. 200) copied from all three, using the former two more radically than they had used Paterculus. Since Tacitus, Suetonius, and Dio offer no new information but only prejudiced versions of the earliest text, their information about Tiberius is read with caution.

The "old look" regarded John in similar terms. According to this view Mark (written ca. 70) was the prime Gospel witness to Jesus. In turn Matthew and Luke (written later) used, but reinterpreted Mark. In turn, again, the Gospel of John (written later still) used and embellished all three, and in such a manner as to make it as distinct as it is — and at the same time — historically problematic.

Classical scholars have a low opinion of Dio for their reconstructions about Tiberius. Biblical scholars (in general) have a low or qualified view of the Gospel of John for their reconstructions about Jesus. If for them the Gospel of John was written about Jesus along similar lines to Dio's account of Tiberius, then the skepticism of the biblical scholars would be justified. But is the Gospel of John for Jesus what Dio was for Tiberius?

The processes by which scholars judge a text's dependence or independence are relatively straightforward, requiring patience, common sense, and a competent clerk's eye for detail. First, the documents need to be dated. Second, they must be submitted to painstaking comparison, word by word, line by line. The analyst will ask questions of these texts. Does the later text follow the same sequence globally? Does it use the same vocabulary of the former? Does it provide new information? Is the new information credible? Does it embellish or reinterpret the former? In the grand scheme of things this may be a lengthy process but it is not an intellectually taxing one. Classical historians reach their judgments and biblical scholars reach theirs by the same mundane competencies.

For the biblical historian this will mean examining the Gospel of John and the Synoptic Gospels side by side. First, the historian will compare these texts *globally*. Mark (for example) tells the Jesus story from Jesus' baptism until the discovery of the empty tomb. At the same time, from first to last, Mark is gospel, kerygmatic, pressing the claims of Jesus upon the reader (hearer). When the scholar sets Matthew and Luke alongside Mark he quickly recognizes that they follow Mark's sequence, attaching their own beginnings and endings and adding here and subtracting there along the way.

It is different with the Gospel of John. This Gospel is not a purposeful A to Z Jesus story like Mark, but a narrative of Jesus' seemingly meaningless meanderings between Judea and Galilee. It focuses on a small group of his actions expanded in lengthy discourses and debates. True, Mark and John have an overall common sequence (John's baptism, Jesus' ministry in Galilee after John's arrest, the feeding of the 5000, the final journey to Judea, Jesus' arrest and execution). Yet one must look hard and long to identify this overall sequence; it is not apparent.

Furthermore, the literary objectives of Mark (for example) and John are different. Whereas Mark intends to secure a commitment to Jesus from (Roman) outsiders, John appears to be more defensive, seeking to secure existing commitment from (Jewish) insiders.

Our difficulty is that biblical scholars' judgments are so familiar with John and the Synoptics that they easily lose sight of their fundamental dissimilarity. Place them before a trained classicist innocent of any knowledge of Christianity, however, and he may conclude these texts to be unconnected and unrelated, in a word, independent.[4]

Secondly, the scholar will identify those incidents that both the Synoptics and John report, in particular the clearing of the Temple, the feeding of the 5000, the anointing of Jesus, the entry to Jerusalem, Peter's denial, and Jesus' trial. Next, he will make detailed comparisons between the

---

4. As a lecturer in Ancient History in a "secular" university I have set assignments calling for close comparison of Johannine with Synoptic texts. The students, mostly from non-church backgrounds, innocently concluded that the texts were independent.

corresponding texts, John's and the Synoptics'. It will become apparent that in each case the storyline is divergent and the wording so different so that the "dependence" hypothesis does not seem to work.

True, there are instances of verbal coincidence between John and the Synoptics, for example:

> John 5:8   Rise, take up your pallet and walk.
>
> Mark 2:9   Rise, take up your pallet and walk.

Despite identical wording the stories in which these texts appear are quite different. How does the dependence model apply in this case? An example of verbal agreement in the same story is found in the respective accounts of Peter's denial.

> John 18:25   Simon Peter was standing there *warming* himself.
>
> Mark 14:54   Peter . . . was sitting there with the guards and *warming* himself at the fire.

How are we to account for the similarities and differences? Is John depending on but shortening Mark or is Mark depending on but embellishing John? Or is each articulating his respective tradition of a vividly remembered detail ("warming") in a notorious incident? Taken in isolation it is not possible to say which option is right.

C. K. Barrett, long associated with a theory of a definite relationship between John and Mark (also Luke), concedes that it is "certain that John did not 'use' Mark, as Matthew did."[5] Then, however, he adds that "in Mark are the stories that John repeats." Granted the incidents reported are the same incidents, why must Barrett assert that John *repeats* Mark? Is it not equally likely that Mark and John each expresses the memory for these incidents found in their respective tradition streams? Is it possible that those streams crossed earlier, the one informing the other? Yet the text analyst looking at one incident report, then the other, and noting the differences of both story and vocabulary is driven to conclude that neither writer wrote his text in precise awareness of the other. That Mark and John report certain incidents, yet so differently, is broad evidence of their underlying factuality.

Is Mark the Gospel John has most in common with? Many would say

---

5. C. K. Barrett, *The Gospel according to St. John* (Philadelphia: Westminster, 1978[2]), 45.

Yes and be wrong. To our surprise the Gospel that shares most with the Fourth Gospel is the Third Gospel.[6] John's and Luke's commonalities are most evident in the following:

> the anointing of Jesus (John 12:1-11; Luke 7:36-50),
> the arrest of Jesus (John 18:1-14/Luke 22:39-53),
> the trial before Pilate (John 18:28-40/Luke 23:1-4, 13-25), and
> the post-resurrection appearances (John 20:3-10, 19-20/Luke 24:12, 36-43).

Other commonalities with John have been noted in Luke 3 (John the Baptist), 5 (the miraculous catch of fish), and 7 (the healing of the centurion's slave).[7]

There is nothing new in these observations. The novel element is the question: who depended on whom? The scholarly assumption of John's "posteriority" means that most say that John depended on Luke (or a precursor).[8] While only a few proposed the radically opposite view, that Luke depended on John,[9] there is a growing number who are raising it as a serious possibility[10] or even arguing for it as the most likely hypothesis.[11] After exhaustive analysis of Luke's and John's commonalities Mark Matson makes the following observations:

---

6. Pierson Parker, "Luke and the Fourth Evangelist," *NTS* 9 (1963), 331, indicates that John and Matthew have similarities in 26 cases, John and Mark 29 times, and John and Luke 124 times. See also F. L. Cribbs, "The Agreements That Exist between Luke and John," *SBL 1979 Seminar Papers* (Missoula: Scholars, 1979); R. Maddox, *The Purpose of Luke-Acts* (Edinburgh: Clark, 1982), 158-79.

7. See M. A. Matson, *In Dialogue with Another Gospel* (Society of Biblical Literature Dissertation Series 178; Atlanta: Society of Biblical Literature, 2001), 163.

8. For distinguished advocacy of Johannine posteriority see Neirynck, "John and the Synoptics," 35-41.

9. Notably F. L. Cribbs, "A Study of the Contacts That Exist between St. Luke and St. John," *Society of Biblical Literature 1973 Seminar Papers* (Missoula: Scholars, 1973), 1-93. Cribbs notes that strong similarities between Luke and John coincide with Luke's departures from Mark and Matthew and conversely that Luke's modifications of Mark/Matthew appear to be influenced by the tradition found in John.

10. P. N. Anderson, *The Christology of the Fourth Gospel* (WUNT; Tübingen: Mohr, 1996), 274-76. Anderson notes that Peter's and John's words "we cannot help speaking about what we have *seen* and *heard*" reported in Acts 4:20 have a "Johannine ring."

11. Matson, *Dialogue*, 91-163; B. Shellard, "The Relationship of Luke and John: A Fresh Look at an Old Problem," *JTS* 46 (1995), 71-98.

... it is hard to see their common occurrences as having arisen simply from common use of a source or sources. It would appear that one of the writers has had deep influence on the other.[12]

Ultimately Matson reaches this cautious but important conclusion:

> What has been shown in this study is an extensive pattern of similarities between Luke and John that lend credence to a *literary relationship*.[13]

In short, Matson's analysis reveals extensive commonalities between Luke and John whose pattern points not to oral but to literary dependence, and that by Luke upon John. This is a truly radical assertion that would mean Luke included John (or a precursor) among the texts "handed over" to him, from which he wrote his own Gospel (Luke 1:1-4).

This first (radical) assertion does not depend on any theory of apostolic authorship. It supports the opinion of J. A. T. Robinson, who spoke of the "priority of John." This is not necessarily a temporal priority but a priority of *independent* authorship.[14] By "priority" Robinson was arguing against the scholarly presumption of the "posteriority" of John as reflected in opinions as diverse as those of Clement of Alexandria and Günter Bornkamm.

2. The Gospel of John Reached Literary Fixity in Palestine prior to the Roman Invasion of Israel (A.D. 66).

This proposal also swims against mainstream opinion. Most scholars ascribe a post-80s date to this Gospel, whether its writing is placed in Roman Asia, for Gentiles (e.g., M. Hengel),[15] or in post-Jamnian Judea, for Jews (e.g., W. D. Davies).[16]

Hengel's argument rests on a raft of overlapping conjectures and must be excluded. His assertions that the Presbyter of 2 and 3 John is John

---

12. Matson, *Dialogue,* 162.

13. Matson, *Dialogue,* 443, italics added.

14. J. A. T. Robinson, *The Priority of John* (London: SCM, 1985), 1-23.

15. M. Hengel, *The Johannine Question* (London: SCM, 1989), 109-35.

16. W. D. Davies, "Aspects of the Jewish Background," in R. A. Culpepper and C. C. Black, eds., *Exploring the Gospel of John* (Louisville: Westminster/John Knox, 1996), 43-64.

the Presbyter of Papias's account is as speculative as his proposal that this Presbyter was a Palestinian Jew who migrated to Ephesus to create a school. References to "feast[s] of the Jews" are not explanations for a later Gentile readership but polemical against continuing rejection of the "word" about Jesus by Pharisees and Temple hierarchs in Jerusalem. Likewise, a text written in Greek with Aramaic terms explained need not suppose Gentile readers from the Diaspora and a late dating; there were many Greek-speaking Jews in Palestine. Evidence of this is the "Hellenists" (Acts 6:1–7:53; 8:4-24, 26-40; 9:29; 11:19) as well as numerous Greek funerary and other inscriptions and surviving Greek texts, from Qumran, Masada, and Muraba'at.[17]

Davies's view is influenced by Martyn's famous reconstruction based on the synagogue-exclusion texts (John 9:22; 12:42; 16:2) as explained by the *Birkath ha-Minim* ruling of Jamnia.[18] Very serious doubts have been raised about this explanation, and in the eyes of many it has been overturned.[19] There is no reason that synagogue exclusion might not have been practiced in Jesus' own day, continuing into the immediate post-Easter era; it was practiced in and before the NT era by Pharisees and at Qumran.[20] Doubtless the Jamnian anathema upon Minim (and Nazarenes?) grew out of earlier exclusion practices, but to identify anathema with exclusion may be anachronistic.

While John's reference to Peter's death (21:19) supports the proposition of a post-65 dating, it is quite possible that the author added this detail to his own epilogue later. One possible reason for this insertion would have been to ensure a continuing "good" name for Peter the denier after his death. Had the Gospel of John been allowed to end with ch. 20 the

17. See generally A. Millard, *Reading and Writing in the Time of Jesus* (Sheffield: Sheffield University Press, 2000).

18. Davies acknowledges the influence of the seminal work by J. L. Martyn, *History and Theology in the Fourth Gospel* (Nashville: Abingdon, 1979), 37-62.

19. See R. Kimelman, "The Birkath Ha-Minim and the Lack of Evidence for an Anti-Christian Prayer in Late Antiquity," *Jewish and Christian Self-Definition* II: *Aspects of Judaism in the Greco-Roman Period*, ed. E. P. Sanders with A. L. Baumgarten and A. Mendelsohn (Philadelphia: Fortress, 1981), 226-44; T. Katz, "Issues in the Separation of Judaism and Christianity after 70 C.E.: A Reconsideration," *JBL* 103 (1984), 69-74; A. Reinhartz, "The Johannine Community and Its Jewish Neighbours: A Reappraisal," in F. F. Segovia, ed., *"What Is John?" Literary and Social Readings of the Fourth Gospel* (Society of Biblical Literature Seminar Series 7; Atlanta: Society of Biblical Literature, 1998), 111-38.

20. E. E. Ellis, "Dating the New Testament," *NTS* 26 (1980), 491 n. 22.

readers would have been left with a quite negative impression of Peter, one moreover that would have encouraged apostasy under persecution.

Positively speaking, there are several pointers to a pre-70 dating. First, the farewell discourses and prayer (chs. 13–17) on the eve of the crucifixion envisage a situation that will soon occur, beginning with the betrayal (13:18-30), denial (13:37-38), and oblique references to Jesus' death and resurrection (13:33, 36; 14:1-3, 5, 18, 28-31; 16:16-24). Looking beyond his death and resurrection, Jesus speaks of his "going" or "departing," which will be matched by the "coming" of the Paraclete to "teach" and "remind" the disciples of everything he told them (14:25-26; 15:26; 16:7-15). This "remembering" points to the disciples' Spirit-led reflections on Jesus' pre-Easter works and words as fulfillment of OT prophecy (2:17, 22; 12:16). At the same time, the Paraclete will "witness" to Jesus as the disciples — who have been "with" Jesus "from the beginning" (15:26) — will "witness" to him.

One way of reading these prospective acts of the "Paraclete" is that they were fulfilled soon after his coming, that is, soon after the first Easter as the original disciples were engaged in their mission in the land of Israel. That mission would attract severe persecution (15:20; 16:1), including synagogue exclusion and death (16:2). Against this expected onslaught Jesus admonished his disciples to "remain" in him, the "true vine," that is, the true Israel (15:4, 9). The point is that the disciples' post-Easter circumstances are directly continuous with Jesus' pre- and post-Easter circumstances. There is no hiatus between his circumstances and theirs. In terms of an early (Israel) or late (Israel or Roman Asia) historical setting, the former is the more likely.

Second, the ministry of Jesus is entirely circumscribed within the land of Israel; Jesus does not go outside those borders, as he does in the Gospel of Mark. In the Gospel of John there are mission frontiers to the land which will be breached in the future. There is "the Diaspora among the Greeks" (7:32-36), the "other sheep" (10:16), the "dispersed children of God" (11:49) and the (God-fearing) Greeks who came to "see Jesus" in Jerusalem (12:20-24).[21]

---

21. There is no agreement among scholars whether John's texts refer to Gentiles, Diaspora Jews, or God-fearers (see J. L. Martyn, "A Gentile Mission That Replaced an Earlier Jewish Mission," in Culpepper and Black, *Exploring the Gospel of John*, 127-28). Be that as it may, the point is that as "Greeks" they lay beyond the borders of Israel. They are the "mission frontier" of John and his circle of believing Judeans, Galileans, and Samaritans *inside* Israel.

This gives a "primitive" feel to the Gospel of John that would not represent contemporary reality after the westward missions of Paul, when the land of Israel was beginning to belong to the past. Until the meeting between the Jerusalem "pillars" James, Cephas, and John and the Antioch delegates Barnabas and Paul in ca. 47, Paul's "going" to the uncircumcised had not really begun. To that point Cephas had been apostle to the circumcised (in Israel) and Paul had preached on the fringes of the land (Damascus, Arabia, Syria). Serious mission work beyond the land had not yet begun in ca. 47 (Gal 2:1), and this coincides with the limited horizons of the land in the Gospel of John.

The world in which the missionaries in Israel preached was a bilingual world in which Greek was highly significant. It is no longer held that a Gospel written in Greek demands a non-Palestinian origin. Furthermore, philologists refer to the Greek of the Gospel of John as a form of koine that is at once "Semitic" but also "correct."[22] In short, the assumption that a Greek text demanded a Diaspora origin is not sustainable.

Third, as many scholars now recognize, the Gospel of John provides extensive and intricate detail of life in Israel in the period of Jesus' ministry.[23] The war of 66-70 cut a broad swathe through the cultural landscape so that life post-70 became less and less recognizable in contrast to life in Israel beforehand. Since this Gospel reflects the life and times of the pre-70 era, it is more likely that John wrote during the earlier period and not afterward. This view rests on several considerations.

Historical   The subject matter in the Gospel of John "fits" the known circumstances of Israel A.D. 30-60. First, the primacy of the "witness" of John the Baptizer in the structure of the Gospel (1:6-8, 15, 19-36; 3:27-36; cf. 5:33; 10:40-41) supports an early date. The memory of the martyred prophet was revered in the aftermath of his death,[24] but doubtless less so as time passed. The author's appeal to John's "testimony" to Jesus belongs

---

22. Hengel, *Johannine Question*, 110.

23. So Hengel, *Johannine Question*, 110-13; J. Charlesworth, "The Dead Sea Scrolls and the Gospel according to John," in Culpepper and Black, ed., *Exploring the Gospel of John*, 67-68.

24. According to Josephus, some Jews believed Aretas's destruction of Herod Antipas's army was divine retribution for the tetrarch's murder of John the Baptizer six years earlier (*Antiquities* 18.116-17).

to an earlier mission period in Israel but less plausibly to the post-Jamnian era.[25]

Second, the threefold reference to "the Prophet" (1:21; 6:14; 7:40) resonates with the appearance of various "prophets" in the decades after Jesus. During Fadus's years as Procurator (A.D. 44-48) the self-professed prophet Theudas led a large crowd to the Jordan promising to make the waters part, affording dry passage to the wilderness (*Antiquities* 20.97-99). Under Felix (A.D. 52-60) unnamed leaders called many to the wilderness promising them "signs of freedom" (*Antiquities* 20.167-68; *War* 2.259). An Egyptian "prophet" led his followers from the Mount of Olives promising that the walls of Jerusalem would collapse (*Antiquities* 20.168-72; *War* 2.261-63; Acts 21:38). These "sign" prophets arose in the era A.D. 30-70, but not afterward.

Here we see a pattern in which a prophet, accompanied by a crowd, attempted to perform miracle-signs. This is evocative of Moses and Joshua in years of the exodus and conquest and suggests a current expectation of a Moses-Prophet to lead the people in times of difficulty, as those pre-war times were.[26] Is it mere coincidence that the Gospel of John reveals a contemporary interest in the Moses-Prophet?

To the common mind John the Baptizer or Jesus might have been "the Prophet," as the references above indicate. At the Feeding of the 5000 the Galileans were certain that Jesus was "the Prophet" and would have forced (Mosaic) messiahship on him (6:14-15). In short, "the Prophet" references in the Gospel of John (and in Acts 3:22; 7:37) are consistent with the appearance of Moses-prophets in the years A.D. 30-70. After A.D. 70, however, when war with Rome had been fought and lost, expectations of "the Prophet" disappear from the records.

Third, as Dodd pointed out, John's trial narrative belongs authentically and distinctively to the pre-66 period when the Roman governor ruled the province of Judea as surrogate of the distant Caesar in an uneasy partnership with the high priest.[27] This was to change forever after the Roman invasion in 66-70, when there would be no more Temple or high priest.

---

25. Of course the Baptist's influence continued for many years, including beyond Israel, as evidenced in Acts 18:25. That influence, however, was embodied in "sectarian" form, whereas in this Gospel John is a major figure to the people within the land of Israel.

26. See P. W. Barnett, "The Jewish Sign Prophets," *NTS* 27 (1981), 679-97.

27. So C. H. Dodd, *Historical Tradition in the Fourth Gospel* (Cambridge: Cambridge University Press, 1963), 120.

There were other changes following the invasion of the Romans and their depredations.[28] The physical appearance of the land was now different. From that time Jerusalem lay in ruins and its Temple destroyed to be replaced by a pagan shrine. The hillsides surrounding Jerusalem were denuded of vegetation used for the siege of the city. According to Josephus, "those who visited the city could not believe it had ever been inhabited" (*War* 7.3). Other cities and towns throughout Israel were ruined. Likewise longstanding institutions and prominent groups were no more. No longer would the Romans govern Judea through intermediary "client" kings or by a Sanhedrin led by a high priest. Roman rule now would be direct and unmediated in a "full" military province, renamed "Colonia prima Flavia Augusta Caesarensis." Various factions that figured significantly before the war disappeared, such as Sadducees, Zealots, and Essenes. The synagogue became the center of Jewish life, with Pharisaism now becoming "rabbinic" Judaism.

The point is that the Gospel of John portrays an earlier and different time. While memory can recapture things as they were, with the passage of time it is increasingly difficult to do so, especially in an age before photography.

Geographical This author effortlessly reveals an awareness of the "ups" and "downs" of the topography of the land (e.g., 2:13; 4:47, 49, 51). He knows the names of villages and their distinguishing qualifiers (e.g., Bethany beyond Jordan, Cana in Galilee, Aenon near Salim, a pool called Bethzatha with five porches, a town called Ephraim in the wilderness).[29]

Cultural There are numerous examples of this author's awareness of the religious culture of Palestinian Jews of this era. These include the refusal of Jews to share drinking vessels with Samaritans (John 4:9),[30] the debate over circumcising on the Sabbath (7:22),[31] and the use of stone vessels for purifying (2:6).[32]

---

28. See E. Schürer, *The History of the Jewish People in the Age of Jesus Christ*, revised and ed. G. Vermes and F. Millar, I (Edinburgh: Clark, 1973), 514-28.

29. See E. M. Meyers and J. Strange, *Archaeology, the Rabbis and Early Christianity* (London: SCM, 1981), 160-61.

30. J. P. Meier, "The Historical Jesus and the Historical Samaritans," *Biblica* 81.2 (2000), 229.

31. Hengel, *Johannine Question*, 111.

32. Charlesworth, "Dead Sea Scrolls and the Gospel according to John," 68.

In sum, our argument for this second assertion is that there is such a closeness of text to the soil from which it grew that a plausible explanation is that John wrote from Israel in the pre-war period.[33] It is less plausible, in our view, that the author wrote several decades after the war, based on recollections of life that were by then dramatically different.

3. *The* Sitz im Leben *of the Gospel of John Is Mission to Jews in the Land of Israel.*

Jesus' dialogue with Nicodemus reflects a post-Easter setting. At a critical point in the dialogue Jesus says, "*We* speak of what *we* know and *we* bear witness of what *we* have seen but you [plural] do not receive *our* witness" (3:11). This contrasts pointedly with Jesus' earlier "*I* say to you [singular]" in vv. 3, 5, and 11a and the sharp "*I* say to you [plural], 'you [plural] must be born from above'" (v. 7). In other words, John *simultaneously* reports the historic words of Jesus to this distinguished leader of "the Jews" while also reporting the "witness" of the apostolic community to "the Jews" and the failure of "the Jews" to accept their "witness" to Jesus in Judea.[34]

In this Gospel Jesus goes to each of the regions of the land of Israel, but with contrasting responses. In Judea "the Jews" (the Jerusalem-based leaders) reject him, whereas the Samaritans acclaim him and the Galileans "welcome" him. In Acts the apostolic mission of Peter (and John) occurs in the same regions: "the [Jerusalem] church [scattered] throughout all *Judea* and *Galilee* and *Samaria* . . . was built up. Now Peter went here and there *among them all* . . ." (Acts 9:31-32). The progress of the incarnate "Word" is matched (inexactly) by the apostolic "word." And just as there was opposition to Jesus' ministry in Judea in the Gospel of John (as noted above) so there was opposition to the apostles' ministry of the word in Judea (Acts 3–5; cf. 1 Thess 2:14-16; Acts 9:29; 26:20).

---

33. See B. F. Westcott, *Gospel of John* (London: Murray, 1903), who noted that the author of John was "a Jew of Palestine . . . an eye-witness of what he describes" (x, xviii).

34. One senses that R. Bauckham is correct in principle in seeing the Gospels as published for readers outside the communities in which they arose. See S. Motyer, "The Fourth Gospel and the Salvation of Israel: An Appeal for a New Start," in *Anti-Judaism*, 92-110, who applies Bauckham's insights to the Gospel of John. Yet we must not overlook the fact that the Gospels arose out of local mission work and so inevitably reflect the "culture" of the original communities in their mission interface with unbelievers.

By the mid-50s Paul speaks of the failure of the mission to Israel because the people "stumbled" over the "stone," Christ (Rom 9:30–10:4, 18-21). The rejection and opposition to the "word" in Israel in the years 30 to 50 more or less coincides with the opposition to Jesus in Judea from the "rulers," Pharisees, and chief priests noted in the Gospel of John (chs. 5, 7–19).

Yet not all the leaders among "the Jews" reject Jesus. The Nicodemus "story" runs like a thread through this Gospel modifying the impression of a total rejection of Jesus by "the Jews." This "ruler" and "teacher" who initially came *secretly* to see Jesus later defends him *publicly* in the face of scorn and finally identifies *openly* with "Christ crucified" (3:2; 7:50; 19:39). Nicodemus stands in contrast with "rulers" who do not believe (7:48) or who believe but fearfully stay in the "night" of secrecy fearing "synagogue exclusion" (12:42). Nicodemus's burial of the crucified Jesus, unlike the shrinking withdrawal of secretive "rulers," brings him into the "light" of public exposure as a disciple.

In the "double vision" of this Gospel that simultaneously narrates the progress of Jesus the incarnate "Word" with the progress of the apostolic "word," John intends us to understand that some of "the Jews" did inquire positively about Jesus, both during Jesus' ministry and during the apostles' ministry. Acts hints that some Jewish leaders responded either neutrally or agreeably in the post-Easter mission era in Israel, for example, the open-minded Gamaliel and the "many" priests who became "obedient to the faith" (Acts 5:33-39; 6:7).

The Acts account of mission work in Samaria (Acts 8:4-25) corresponds with the major references in John to Jesus' ministry in that region. Jesus "must pass through Samaria" (4:4) to speak to and be confessed by a woman there as Messiah (4:29) and be acclaimed as "Savior of the world" by the Samaritans (4:42). The salvation of such people is Jesus' "food," his obedience to the will of God, and the future mission field of his followers (4:34). Acts mentions "brothers" in Samaria visited by Paul, Barnabas, and others in the late 40s (Acts 15:3), probably intending the reader to assume that these were converts from the missions of Philip and then of Peter and John. The point is that John's narrative of Jesus' mission in Samaria is written out of an awareness of a subsequent apostolic mission in Samaria, as many have noted.

What, then, of Galilee? Unlike Judea and Samaria there is only one reference to "the church [of Jerusalem] multiplied" in Galilee, through which Peter traveled (Acts 9:31-32). There is no reference in Acts to John accompanying Peter in Galilee. Yet various specific references to Galilean towns in the Gospel of John may be deliberate, giving hints of current mission work there. The twofold references to Cana (2:1; 4:46) and the reference to Capernaum (2:12; cf. 6:17, 59) may point to churches in these places in Galilee, as well as others.

Our third assertion, then, is that the Gospel of John was written out of the perspectives and experiences of the apostles in Israel in the pre-war mission era. It would be going too far, however, to suggest that John mechanically squeezed his account into the mold of the apostles' missionary experience in the regions of the land of Israel, namely Judea, Galilee, and Samaria. Nonetheless, it is likely that the mission of Peter and John to the circumcised in the land and the varying reactions — negative in Judea, but positive in Galilee and Samaria — influenced the "shape" of the Gospel of John and helped determine its narrative in regard to Jesus' ministry in those regions.

4. The Gospel of John Was Written for Jews While There Was Still Hope.

This fourth assertion is based on the meaning of the term "the Jews" in this Gospel. Clearly, "the Jews" in this Gospel are the religious authorities in Jerusalem, broadly called "rulers" (7:26) and more specifically "Pharisees and chief priests" (7:32, 45).[35]

"The Jews" in the Gospel of John are Jesus' "own people" (1:11), in "his own country" (4:44). Instead of "welcome" as in Galilee and acclamation as in Samaria, these "rulers" in Jerusalem reject him altogether and bring about his death. In this respect they embody the "darkness" of "the world" subject to its murderous "father" and "ruler" (8:44; 12:31).

Contrary to much popular opinion this Gospel is not ultimately hostile to "the Jews." There are various positive references to "the Jews," as for example in the very passage where Samaritans acclaim Jesus as "Savior of

---

35. Various broadly understood explanations have been offered. "The Jews" are: (1) symbolic representatives of the unbelieving "world" (Bultmann), (2) the Jewish religious authorities (von Wahlde), (3) the people of Judea (Lowe). The approach taken here sees little merit in the proposal that *hoi Ioudaioi* are the Judeans (3). John does not portray the people of Judea/Jerusalem negatively (e.g., John 12:3), but does consistently portray the leaders ("Pharisees," "chief priests," "rulers") negatively. Option (2) is correct historically, while option (1) captures the theological insight of the Gospel of John.

the world" (4:42) Jesus insists that "salvation is *from* the Jews" (4:22). John makes much of the confessions of Jewish men that Jesus is "the Messiah," "him of whom Moses in the Law and also the prophets wrote," and "the Son of God, the King of Israel" (1:41, 45, 49). The confessor Nathanael, though a Galilean, is a "true Israelite" (1:49). The Galileans' attempt to make him "king" (6:15), though misguided, is well meant. At the end of the Gospel John intends the reader to see Jesus as "king of the Jews" (18:33–19:22 passim) and to believe on him as "the Christ" (20:31).

Furthermore, John takes no pleasure in the Jews' rejection of Jesus. The whole Gospel is tinged with irony and not a little regret, as 1:11-13 and 4:44 make clear, and appears saddened by the unfolding story. Here we sense a parallel with Paul's deep regret that his people have not (yet) claimed Jesus as the Messiah (Rom 9:1-5).

Significantly, however, there are positive and hopeful signs for "the Jews" in the Gospel of John. The encouraging if gradual response of Nicodemus significantly mitigates an otherwise negative impression of Jerusalem-based "rulers." Unlike Luke-Acts, where no positive future for Israel is entertained, the Gospel of John still looks for a good response from "the Jews." This is why Nicodemus a "ruler of the Jews" is so important in this Gospel. He begins as an inquirer and finishes as a confessor, at least passively. In this regard, John shares with Paul in Romans 9–11 a broad optimism for a good future response from "the Jews." This is reason enough to date the Gospel to the years 30-60, rather than in later decades when hopes seem to have faded.

Conclusion: The Prehistory of the Gospel of John

John has stubbornly resisted the various attempts at finding underlying sources. Identification of the strands identifiable in Matthew and Luke (Mark, "Q," "M," and "L") understandably inspired hopes that source criticism would locate preexisting traditions that John wove together as his text. Despite the efforts of Bultmann, Fortna, and others, this Gospel remains a "seamless robe." In the absence of other texts related to the Gospel of John like those that tie together the Synoptics, this situation is likely to remain.[36]

---

36. See D. A. Carson, "Current Source Criticism of the Fourth Gospel: Some Methodological Questions," *JBL* 97 (1978), 411-29; E. Ruckstuhl, "Johannine Language and Style: The

Similarly, theories of stages of development prior to the publication of this Gospel must be questioned, in particular that of R. E. Brown, who envisaged five such stages.[37] While not implausible, such theories always sit beyond reach of confirmation, as more than one scholar has noted.[38] There may have been such sources or stages of development of the text of the Gospel. The problem is that we have no objective markers to identify these sources or stages.

Our simple if radical assertions are that the Gospel of John arose within Palestine in the period between the crucifixion and the Roman invasion in the late 60s and that it was written in literary independence of the Synoptics. Beyond that there is no scientific means by which its dating can be established.

One thing that may be assumed is that the prehistory of this text did not begin a few days before the writer opened his scroll and began to write. On the contrary, the tradition stream began with the earliest community in Jerusalem as its leaders proclaimed Jesus as the Christ, suffered persecution, and reflected on the words and deeds of Jesus, led by the Spirit. Whatever course that stream took before the critical moment came to begin writing, its origins are to be sought in the shadow of the crucifixion of Jesus, his resurrection, and the coming of the Paraclete.

Question of Their Unity," in M. de Jonge, ed., *L'Evangile de Jean* (Leuven: University Press, 1977), 125-48.

37. R. E. Brown, *The Community of the Beloved Disciple* (New York: Paulist, 1979).

38. See, e.g., R. Kysar, *The Fourth Evangelist and His Gospel: An Examination of Contemporary Scholarship* (Minneapolis: Augsburg, 1975), 53.

FIFTEEN

Final Reflection:
What Cannot Be Denied

Christian Origins and History

Is a "faith" that is transcendent susceptible to historical investigation? Although many have answered in the negative, whether explicitly or implicitly, the answer must be Yes. Since early Christianity makes truth claims in a world of myth and legend, it is reasonable to apply historical tests to those claims. N. T. Wright has demonstrated the importance and sustainability of arguments for the historical truth of the resurrection.[1]

The same holds true for those who propose idiosyncratic explanations for the rise of Christianity, idiosyncratic, that is, as alternatives to "historic" interpretations about such matters as Jesus' claimed identity, his resurrection, and the core beliefs of the first disciples. Negative reconstructions must submit to the same canons of historical inquiry as positive ones.

The "rules of evidence" that apply to the study of the Greeks and the Romans must apply with equal rigor to the study of Christian origins. These include "Momigliano's Rule," mentioned earlier,[2] which looks for the "primary" evidence as opposed to evidence in "secondary" or "derived" sources. Conjecture must be identified appropriately, qualified, and limited. It may cast light on an unresolved issue, yet it remains conjecture apart from some means of lateral verification. Imaginative history writing

---

1. N. T. Wright, *The Resurrection of the Son of God* (London: SPCK, 2003), 3-10.
2. See pp. 17-18 above.

may prove stimulating to further investigation, but, again, may not be helpful if it strays too far from the evidence. The imaginative historian, like a flighty poodle on a retractable lead, must be reeled in by that mundane and boring reality called evidence, evidence weighed according to criteria and "rules." Otherwise history writing is fiction writing.

Boundaries for the Mind's Focus

Many scholars appear to think the field for their studies of the New Testament is temporally undefined, boundary-less, somehow able to accommodate the most remarkable explanatory hypotheses. The same holds true for various rhetorical and literary theories that have arisen to explain the character of the texts.[3] It is as if the documents of the New Testament evolved over many centuries rather than within just a few decades.

Chronology is a critical boundary. Within seventy years of the first Easter all twenty-seven texts of the NT had been written and were in circulation. More importantly, our broadly agreed earliest Gospel (Mark) had been completed within forty years of the historical Jesus. Paul's earliest letters had been written within twenty years of Jesus, with clear echoes of Jesus' words as they would appear later in the Gospels.

This study has concentrated on that forty-year space, with particular interest in the first twenty years. This space of time is finite and brief, as any person of "mature" age will confirm. The time span between Jesus and Paul's first letter to the Thessalonians is the same as between the end of the "Great" War and the beginning of the Second World War. Not a few soldiers who survived the first war also served in the second.

Another boundary is the activity that characterized the first disciples. Their leaders were missionaries, bent on winning further loyal adherents to "the faith." Furthermore, they were engaged in mission activity from before the time of the first Easter up to and beyond the writing of the earliest Gospel. No glass wall separated the oral from the written Gospel; the former flowed uninterrupted into the latter. Indeed, written precursors were employed alongside the oral, most likely from earliest times after Jesus. The gospel the eyewitness Peter *preached*, assisted by his amanuensis

3. See J. R. Donahue, "Windows and Mirrors: The Setting of Mark's Gospel," *CBQ* 57 (1995), 4-8.

Mark, seamlessly became the Gospel Mark *wrote*. It was one and the same entity. Thus the "space" between Jesus and the early written Gospel was not empty or lifeless space. Rather, it was filled with activity by known persons, who were leading associates of the Master himself.

A third boundary is geography. By the time of Mark's Gospel, ca. 70, assemblies meeting in the name of Jesus the Messiah had been established westward from the Levant through Anatolia and the Greek provinces to the Italian peninsula. Between 30 (or 33) until Paul's first westward mission ca. 48 the disciples' mission work had been limited to the Levant and Syria-Cilicia, but largely focused in the land of Israel (Judea, Galilee, and Samaria). Apart from Syria-Cilicia, where the Hellenists and Paul took refuge, the effective locus for the formation of the gospel tradition was Israel. The critical development of the oral gospel and the written Gospel occurred among Jews in the land of Israel.

In short, we have a finite and brief time frame (two decades) laid over a small country (Israel) where we are told what was going on (mission activity). Chronology, geography, and known activity — these are the stuff of history, all dependent on available and credible sources, which we have in the letters of Paul confirming the broad historicity of the Acts of the Apostles.

The First Twenty Years

In A.D. 50 Paul arrived in Corinth and soon afterward wrote his First Letter to the Thessalonians, that is to say, about twenty years after the historical Jesus.

Within those twenty years Christianity was born. We cannot dismiss those two decades as a "blank space" since it is quite evident that they yield considerable information about the birth years of Christianity. The data following is primarily derived from Paul's own writings (which are not controverted) with minimal confirmation from the book of Acts (which is problematic to many).

> The Jerusalem-based apostolate was in place when Paul made his first return visit to Jerusalem not more than four years after the crucifixion. Cephas (with John) initially led the "apostolate" to the circumcised in the land of Israel. At some point (early 40s?) they yielded the hegemony to James, the brother of the Lord.

Soon after the crucifixion of Jesus of Nazareth, Paul, Pharisee and Zealot, persecuted the church and attempted to destroy both it and "the faith." Having succeeded in Jerusalem, he set out for Damascus, the nearest place of refuge beyond the land of Israel.

Within the brief corridor "between Jesus and Paul" (about one year) the Jerusalem apostles had (a) formulated a christological kerygmatic and catechetical outline (substantiated by OT proof texts), which was (b) matched by a corresponding eucharistic formulation, and which was (c) supported by the beginning of (written?) collections of the teachings of Jesus. Paul had early access to these formulations, whether in Damascus (at his baptism) or at Jerusalem (on his first return visit).

Near Damascus Paul was "called by God" to "proclaim his Son among the Gentiles." From his own writings we are able to trace his mission movements ca. A.D. 34-55 from "Jerusalem in an arc to Illyricum," including in Damascus and Arabia and within the provinces of Judea, Syria-Cilicia, Galatia, Macedonia, Achaia, and Asia.

Through Paul's own writings we meet Jerusalem-based leaders (James, Cephas, and John) and his own traveling associates (Barnabas, Silvanus, Timothy, and Titus).

Again from Paul's writings we are able to recover the kerygmatic outlines of his initial mission preaching to the Gentiles and his follow-up christological and ethical catechesis.

Clearly, therefore, we have extensive firsthand information from those first twenty years that illuminates this critical period.

It is logical to argue that the trajectory evident from the above did not originate with those who immediately preceded Paul but must have received its impetus beforehand from Jesus himself.

Things Difficult to Deny

Two historical phenomena in the first century are not easily denied.

First, in the years following his historical lifespan Jesus was proclaimed as "Messiah" and its Greek equivalent, "Christ."

Within five years of Jesus' crucifixion in Jerusalem the people of Antioch in Syria (or the authorities) identified the disciples in that city as a movement. This is implicit in the name *Christianoi* (Acts 11:26), in which the *-ianoi* suffix points to "followers of a leader."[4] These persons were followers of a leader named Christ. How did they come to be called this, if not because of christology?

In ca. 49 when Paul preached Jesus as *the* Christ in the synagogue in Thessalonica (Acts 17:3), resistant Jews complained to the wider community, leading to the accusation that he was proclaiming "another king" (Acts 17:7). This king's name was "Jesus" and his title was *the* Christos.

Also in ca. 49 Claudius expelled the Jews from Rome who were disputing over "Chrestus," most likely because the preaching of Jesus as the Christ in the synagogues created such disturbances that the emperor dispatched the entire Jewish community.[5]

The Roman authorities and the people at large were doubtless mystified at the identity of a leader called "the smeared one." Presumably they thought of him and his followers as just another oddity within Judaism. Jews, however, harbored no such uncertainty. These disciples of Jesus were insisting that he was the Davidic Messiah, notwithstanding his humiliation at Gentile hands.

The titulus attached to Jesus' stauros bearing the words "king of the Jews," as reported by Matthew, Mark, and John, must be regarded as authentic.[6] Jesus was not stoned by the Jews for a religious breach (as Stephen was) but crucified by the Romans for treason. Pilate the Roman prefect understood that the Jewish charge that Jesus was "Messiah," when translated into Roman terms, meant a claim to be "king of the Jews" (see Mark 14:61; 15:2). Luke's account gives some of the supporting evidence from the Jewish accusers (Luke 23:2). This Jesus was directly repudiating Caesar's empire-wide sovereignty (John 19:12). One who entered Jerusalem mounted as Jesus did might well cause the Romans deep concern, deep enough to accede to the requests of the high priest.[7]

---

4. The faction called "Herodians" (Mark 3:6; 12:13; cf. 8:15), who most likely were supporters of Herod Antipas, provide a parallel.

5. Suetonius, *Claudius* 25.4; Acts 18:2. See further P. W. Barnett, *Jesus and the Rise of Early Christianity* (Downers Grove: InterVarsity, 1999), 29-30.

6. A. E. Harvey, *Jesus and the Constraints of History* (London: Duckworth, 1982), 11-35.

7. Harvey, *Constraints*, 11-35 is most likely correct in regarding Jesus' appearances be-

Thus there is a consistent continuum of evidence from the Palm Sunday entry through Jesus' crucifixion to early evidence in Roman Antioch, Roman Thessalonica, and Rome itself that points to Jesus' claimed messiahship as critical within earliest Christianity.

Based on the Gospel of Mark and our argument that this written text was in seamless continuity with the proclaimed gospel of Peter, we hold that the disciples themselves recognized and confessed Jesus as Messiah during the course of their relationship with him. The incident at Caesarea Philippi occupies such an important place within the Gospel of Mark that we must assume it occupied a comparable place in the preaching of Peter. In turn, we assert that this event is securely historical.

A second and related observation is that the resurrection of Jesus was fundamental to the early preaching of the apostles. "God raised him from the dead . . . ," Peter declared repeatedly, as reported in Acts (2:4, 32; 3:7, 15; 4:10; 5:30; 10:40). This is confirmed by Paul's quotation of the preformed tradition he received years earlier, "He was raised the third day" — that is, raised by God (1 Cor 15:4). Paul's letters, Romans especially, are suffused with belief in the resurrection of Jesus.[8] Clearly, then, the letters of Paul confirm the central place of the resurrection of Jesus in the early preaching of Peter according to Acts.

Indeed, it must be noted that the disciples' assertion of Jesus' messiahship, as outlined above, would have been meaningless had he ended his days as an indicted and crucified criminal, buried somewhere near Jerusalem. If he had, it is safe to say that he would have more or less disappeared from history. The dramatic actions of fellow martyrs like Judas the Galilean and Simon bar Gioras left greater imprints in Josephus's annals than Jesus did. But no ongoing movements succeeded either Judas or Simon, despite large followings during their lifetimes. The assertion of resurrection gave credence to Jesus' messianic claims and must be regarded as basic to the early witness of the disciples.

Furthermore, in his day Jesus would have been but one of the descendants of King David and thereby qualified for messianic recognition. There is evidence that Roman emperors Vespasian, Domitian, and Trajan were aware of the "royal family of David" and the potential threat of a king

---

fore the chief priests as some kind of a hearing to clarify the charges they were to bring to the prefect. There was no formal Sanhedrin trial.

8. So Wright, *Resurrection of the Son of God*, 241-45.

from that dynasty.[9] But of the many who might have been recognized as Messiah, including James the brother of the Lord, there was only one Davidide so honored, Jesus of Nazareth. That recognition arose from and depended on his miracle-signs, above all on his resurrection from the dead on the third day.

Both these convictions — messiahship and resurrection — are expressed in the sonorous creed-like words with which Paul begins Romans. Paul may have expressed himself in this way at the head of the letter to identify the common ground on which he and the Roman readers stood. Paul writes of the gospel "concerning [God's] Son,"

> who was descended from David,
> who was designated Son of God in power,
>   according to the Spirit of holiness
>   by his resurrection from the dead.

Of course, the crucifixion was a saving act; it was "for" others. Yet that depended on Jesus' identity as Messiah and the reality of the resurrection, the absence of either of which would have made saving claims meaningless. Crucifixion was not uncommon and David's descendants numerous, and some had been wrongfully executed. Jesus' resurrection identified him as the Messiah, qualified to save others.

It was this twin conviction, that Jesus was the Christ and that God had raised him alive from the dead, that drove and energized the first disciples and that alone accounts for the rise of Christianity as we encounter it in the historical records.

---

9. Eusebius, *Historia Ecclesiastica* 3.12, 19, 22.

APPENDIX A

History and Geography in Acts

When we examine the whole contents of the narrative its historical value shrinks until it reaches the vanishing point. No single detail is possible.

C. von Weizsächer, *The Apostolic Age
of the Christian Church*[1]

The problem for the historian of earliest Christianity is the disputed nature of our most direct historical narrative, the book of Acts.

First we must state a matter that is not in dispute. The "movement" established by Jesus continued after his historical lifespan. Studies in chronology, whether of Jesus or of Christian origins, agree that there was no hiatus between Jesus and his movement, which rather continued directly after his crucifixion. Consequently, investigations into earliest Christianity cannot be done independently of inquiry about its founder and of the relationship between founder and movement.

---

1. C. von Weizsächer, *The Apostolic Age of the Christian Church* (London and Edinburgh: Williams and Norgate, 1894), I, 106. The quoted passage refers to the Antioch incident but is true of this author's attitude to the book of Acts *in toto*.

The Importance of Luke-Acts

Clearly, then, not only is Acts critical but equally its precursor, the Gospel of Luke. The importance of Luke-Acts is that these two are one work from one pen (as argued below) and that they alone join earliest Christianity to Jesus. Without Luke-Acts there is a two-decade gap in sequential history writing. The other Gospels give us a window into Jesus ca. 28-30 (or 29-33) and Paul's letters a window into Christianity in the late part of his career, ca. 50-64. It is only Acts that sequentially narrates the intervening years and joins the movement back to its founder. Without Luke-Acts the historian would have no *narrative* of earliest Christianity and would not know how earliest Christianity connected with Christ.

One result of rejecting Acts for reconstructing the "gap" years has been the focusing instead on the sources underlying the Synoptic Gospels, in particular "Q."[2] "Q" is the name given to a "source" both Matthew and Luke are believed to have used in writing their Gospels. Studies in the "Q" tradition lead some to conclude that the historical Jesus was different from the person we meet in the Gospels and, furthermore, that earliest Christianity was different from how it is portrayed in (the first part of) the book of Acts.

A brief parallel narrative to Luke-Acts is found in the writings of the historian Tacitus, who was hostile to Christianity. Like Luke-Acts, Tacitus sees the integral connection between a founder who was killed and the movement that continued despite his death.

> Christus, the founder of the name [Christian], had undergone the death penalty in the reign of Tiberius, by sentence of the procurator Pontius Pilatus, and the pernicious superstition was checked for the moment, only to *break out once more* . . . in Judea, the home of the disease. . . . (*Annals* 15.44, LCL)

The *superstitio* ("political sect") begun by "Christus" was not stamped out by Pilate, but "broke out afresh" in Judea and spread to Rome. With these few words Tacitus confirms the broad sequence from the end of Luke (the death of Jesus) into the beginning of Acts (the birth of Christianity in Judea).

---

2. See pp. 138-49 above.

If our only sources were the other Gospels and the letters of Paul, we would have no way of knowing in detail about the twenty-year space between Jesus and the time Paul began writing. The birth of Christianity, its date and circumstances, would be matters of speculation. Luke and Acts, however, are connected windowpanes through which we view in sequence the death and resurrection of Jesus and the immediate birth of the church.

But is the glass in these panels transparent, allowing the reader to see through to true pictures, or is it so flawed that little approximating to the truth can be seen? That Acts is our only source does not by itself make it helpful. We must not attribute historical accuracy to this book merely because there is no other means of knowledge. What if Acts is fundamentally inaccurate, as many think? In this case an untrustworthy narrative would be worse than no narrative. Forming a positive opinion about the book of Acts, therefore, is critical to using this text for the study of earliest Christianity.

In Defense of Luke-Acts

Following are some of the reasons for a positive attitude to Luke-Acts as a historical source for the recovery of earliest Christianity.

Luke-Acts Is One Work by One Author.

Few today question that Luke and Acts are by one author. Acts identifies itself as a continuation of Luke by referring to it as "the former book" (*ton prōton logon*), by again addressing "Theophilus," and by summarizing the "former book" as "all that Jesus began to do and also to teach." Both "books" were written by the one author.

What is the relationship between the "books"? Was the "former" written before and independently of the "second," or did the author write the two as parts of the one work? The latter alternative appears almost certain. "Things" that have "come to fulfillment" among "us," as in the preface (Luke 1:1-4) point toward Jesus "fulfilling" the Law and the Prophets (Luke 24:25-27), but also to the post-Easter outpouring of the Spirit and the spread of the gospel "fulfilling" his own words. Most likely, therefore, the preface introduces both the Gospel and the Acts.

Furthermore, when the end of the Gospel is compared with the beginning of the Acts it is clear that the former anticipates the latter and that the latter is continuous with the former. In the Gospel the risen Jesus declares, "behold, I send the promise of my Father upon you, but stay in the city until you are clothed with power from on high" (24:49). Although the Gospel concludes, "they returned to Jerusalem with great joy and were continually in the temple blessing God," it is clear that the narrative has not reached its terminus. In the first few sentences of the "second book" the author picks up the narrative, ". . . he charged them not to depart from Jerusalem, but to wait for the promise of the Father" (Acts 1:4).

The "former book" narrated the "works and words" of Jesus and the "second book" narrated what he continued to "do and say" — through his Spirit-filled apostles.

We conclude, therefore, that Luke and Acts are respective parts of a two-volume composition that we are justified in hyphenating as Luke-Acts.[3]

The Author of Luke-Acts Was Paul's Companion in the "We" Passages (Acts 16:10-16; 20:5–21:18; 27:1–28:16).

This is a critical point to establish. As long ago as 1901 Plummer pointed out that "It is perhaps no exaggeration to say that nothing in biblical criticism is more important than this statement," namely that "the Author of Acts was a companion of S. Paul."[4] The ability or otherwise to establish *historically* the circumstances of the birth of Christianity depends on it.

When evaluating Paul's information about himself it has become customary to assign priority to his letters over Acts. It is repeatedly asserted that Paul is writing about himself, at first hand, whereas Luke writes at second hand. Further, if, as many scholars argue, Luke was not Paul's companion, it follows that Acts has no inside knowledge about Paul. In effect, therefore, Acts is of no special value in regard to Paul's career.

Much, therefore, is at stake in establishing that the author of Acts was the personal companion of Paul. This, precisely, is our contention: Luke

---

3. This was classically argued by H. J. Cadbury and restated by I. H. Marshall, "Acts and the 'Former Treatise,'" in *BAFCS* 1:163-84.

4. *St. Luke* (ICC; Edinburgh: Clark, 1901), xii.

was Paul's personal companion for many years and therefore had direct personal knowledge of Paul's life and ministry. Furthermore, through Paul Luke also had indirect knowledge about the first leaders of Jerusalem Christianity reaching back to Jesus himself.

The first "we" passage begins in Troas and ends in Philippi in ca. 49 (Acts 16:10-16). This presupposes prior contact between the two men and supports the theory that Luke had been based in Antioch (see below). The second "we" passage begins in Philippi in ca. 57 and encompasses Paul's final journey to Palestine, his imprisonment there, and his journey to and imprisonment in Rome, a period of about five years (20:5–21:18; 27:1–28:16).

When the reader of the prologue (Luke 1:1-4) reaches the "we" passages, he naturally concludes that the author became Paul's companion throughout what is narrated in those passages, that author and companion are one and the same person.[5] Fitzmyer agrees, observing about the "we" sources: ". . . they are drawn from a diary-like record that the author of Acts once kept and give evidence that he was for a time a companion of Paul."[6] Hengel reached the same conclusion:

> . . . the remarks in the first person plural refer to the author himself. They do not go back to an earlier independent source, nor are they merely a literary convention, giving the impression that the author was an eyewitness. . . . "We" therefore appears in the travel narratives because Luke simply wanted to indicate that he was there.[7]

This, surely, is correct. What else could "we" mean in the "we" passages? The alternatives, that the author has employed the second person for stylistic reasons or has reproduced "undigested" a diarist's source, seem farfetched.[8] We cannot overemphasize the importance of establishing this connection between Luke and Paul.

Who, then, was this author-companion? While the text of Luke-Acts

---

5. After detailed examination of the evidence and the alternatives C. J. Hemer states, "As the evidence stands, we are constrained to see [Luke] as present in the 'we-passages'" (*The Book of Acts in the Setting of Hellenistic History* [Winona Lake: Eisenbrauns, 1990], 334).

6. J. Fitzmyer, *Luke the Theologian: Aspects of His Teaching* (London: Geoffrey Chapman, 1989), 22.

7. *Acts and the History of Earliest Christianity* (London: SCM, 1979), 66.

8. Contra N. Hyldahl, *The History of Early Christianity* (New York: Lang, 1997), 137-38.

does not identify him, the second-century authorities the Muratorian Canon (lines 2-8) and Irenaeus (*Against Heresies* 3.1.1; 3.14.1) point to Paul's friend Luke (Col 4:14; 2 Tim 4:11; Phlm 24). Be that as it may, it is likely that the anonymous companion was already a believer and an associate of Paul's when he first appears in a "we" passage in Troas in ca. 49. Given that western Asia was as yet unevangelized, it is reasonable to infer that he had gone there from a more easterly place. Some argue that he was a native of Antioch, capital of Syria, on account of his interest in and knowledge of that city (11:19-20; 13:1-4; 14:26-28; 15:1-3, 13-14; 18:22-23).[9]

Acts Is an Equal Primary Source for Paul.

It has become commonplace to regard Acts as a secondary source for details about Paul. By inference it is less important than Paul's own information. This view must be questioned.

Since (as we have argued) the author of Acts was Paul's "companion" during 57 to 62, he was contemporary with the events he narrates, including those involving Paul. He is not, therefore, *in principle* secondary to or less reliable than the person he writes about. An eyewitness of good memory and judicious perception may be an equal or better source of information than the subject himself. A wife's recollection of events involving her husband often proves more accurate than his! Since Paul's "companion" in the "we" passages is the author of Acts, we must allow the probability that he is a valuable source of information about Paul at that time. We assert that Acts should be regarded as an *equal primary source* with Paul for the events where Luke was part of the narrative.

This has major implications about Luke's information about Paul for the years prior to the first of the "we" passages. As Paul's companion beginning in ca. 49 and more particularly for the five years the two men were together in the later "we" passages (ca. 57-62), the author also had ample opportunity to learn about Paul as he was prior to his conversion and during his early years as a believer. Indeed, we glean more about Paul's early life from Acts than we do from Paul himself.[10] In other words, for events

---

9. Based on early traditions and favored by Fitzmyer, *Gospel according to Luke*, 45-47.

10. For a summary of both see D. Wenham, "Acts and the Pauline Corpus," in *BAFCS* 1:216-17.

concerning Paul (at least) we must not disconnect Acts from Paul as a source for his earlier life.

Not so often noticed, however, is a further consequence of the Paul-Luke nexus. Paul's own writings reveal that he possessed firsthand knowledge about Jerusalem-based Christianity. He knew James the brother of Jesus and the leading disciples Cephas and John (Gal 1:18-19; 2:7-9). Through these men Paul had secondhand knowledge of the historical Jesus.

This means that through Paul Luke knew about James, Cephas, and John and beyond them also about Jesus. Thus this author wrote both his Gospel about Jesus and the Acts narrative of Christianity's early years out of the closeness of personal contact as well as from written sources "handed over" to him (see below). The oft-repeated view that an impenetrable wall separates the author of Luke-Acts from the events he narrates must be rejected.

The implications for recovering the history of early Christianity and its connections with Christ himself are great and should be recognized. Continued skepticism regarding Luke-Acts as a source about Paul and the birth of Christianity is unwarranted.

The Author Wrote on the Basis of "Narratives" That "Eyewitnesses and Ministers" "Delivered" to Him (Luke 1:1-4).

In his preface the author claims to have "followed all things closely from the beginning" (Luke 1:3), that is, to have made a study of Christian "origins." "Follow" (*parakolouthein*) most likely means "be thoroughly familiar with." This familiarity was no mere bookish thing, however, since it sprang from the author's years of ministry first in Philippi (Acts 16:11; 20:6) and then as Paul's companion (Acts 20:6–28:31). Consistent with this, his intent in writing to "Theophilus" is pastoral, that Theophilus may know the "certainty" of the "matters" (*logoi*) in which he has been "catechized."

At the same time the author disclaims the qualification of being a contemporary with the people and events he narrates, except by inference in the "we" passages. He was not present as an "eyewitness" of Jesus or of the events of earliest Christianity. Rather, in all frankness, he discloses his sources of information as "handed over" to him by those who "from the beginning were *eyewitnesses* and *ministers* of the word" (1:2). He refers here to one group which were the "eyewitnesses" of Christ in the "former book" and the "ministers of the word" following Pentecost in the "second book" (Acts 6:4; cf. 2:42; 4:2, 18; 5:21, 25, 28, 42, etc.).[11]

Luke distinguishes these "eyewitnesses and ministers" from the "many" who "compiled a narrative" *(diēgēsis)* of the things that "had been fulfilled among us." That such "narratives" were *written* is scarcely to be doubted. The words "many have undertaken to draw up" *(epecheirēsan anataxasthai)*, followed by the author's "it seemed good to me also . . . *to write*" *(kamoi . . . grapsai)* establish that these "eyewitnesses and ministers" compiled *written* texts.

Since, as we have argued, the preface (Luke 1:1-4) relates to both "books," it follows that the "narrative[s]" written by the "many" were the sources for both the Gospel and Acts. They had been "handed over" *(paredosan)* to Luke. This verb was a technical term in Jewish culture for a rabbi "handing over" a body of teaching or legal opinion to a disciple (cf. Mark 7:3-5). This vocabulary elsewhere points to the transmission of oral tradition within early Christianity.[12] The juxtaposition of "handed over" with *written* texts is striking and surprising in view of the assumptions that early Christianity was solely an oral culture. The preface indicates that it was also a written culture and that the two-"book" work arose out of *written* traditions.[13]

When did the "eyewitnesses and ministers" "hand over" these "narratives" to the author? Although he does not say, it is likely that he means "Theophilus" to understand that this took place during his sojourns in Palestine and Rome while Paul was in prison in those places.

Careful analysis of the Gospel of Luke and comparison of Luke's text with other Gospels conveys some idea of the "narratives" that were "handed over" to Luke. These include the Gospel of Mark (or a precursor), the source documents known as "Q" (the common source), "L" (Luke's special source), and, arguably, the Gospel of John[14] (or a precursor).

---

11. In rather similar words Paul repeats the words of the risen Lord to him to be "a *minister* and *witness* to the things in which you have seen me . . ." (Acts 26:16).

12. 1 Cor 11:12; 15:3; Rom 6:17; Col 2:6-7; 1 Thess 2:2:13; 4:1; 2 Thess 3:6; 2 Tim 2:2.

13. See pp. 117-18 above.

14. See pp. 167-69 above.

The Book of Acts Is Primarily Historical in Character.

Theological elements in the book of Acts prompt some to regard it as *primarily* "theological" in character.[15] A corollary for some is that Acts is unhistorical and factually unreliable. This assumption, too, must be questioned.[16]

In both the Gospel and the Acts the author signals that he is writing *history*. His stated intention in the preface (Luke 1:4) is to "write an orderly account" which, as it unfolds, narrates the time and place of Jesus' birth, his genealogy, and the beginnings of his ministry ("at about thirty years of age"), located historically by elaborate cross-referencing (Luke 2:1-5; 3:1-2, 23-38).

The second volume is also overtly historical in style. There is a driving sequential style to the narrative. We find many elements common to histories of the era — speeches (about 30 percent of the book), passing mention of eminent people (e.g., the Temple hierarchy), and reference to events occurring under Claudius, the emperor of the day (e.g., the famine and the expulsion of Jews from Italy). In other words, by these well-established conventions the author is signaling to the reader of that era that he is writing *history*.

Readers of the period familiar with Thucydides, Polybius, or Josephus would draw just that conclusion. Prefaces, assurances of truthfulness and objectivity, dovetailing of events with wider history, speeches of key people, even a shipwreck were the historian's stock-in-trade. The author has presented his work in the established format, conventions, and style of a Hellenistic history.[17]

The ascription of "theology" to Luke-Acts is a modern construct. Of course, Luke was also a theologian. Everyone who wrote history then was a

15. See I. H. Marshall and D. Peterson, eds., *Witness to the Gospel: The Theology of Acts* (Grand Rapids: Eerdmans, 1998), where the various entries relate to theological and ethical issues and none touch on issues of historiography, giving (unintentionally) an impression that Acts is primarily a work of theology.

16. See F. F. Bruce, *The Acts of the Apostles: The Greek Text with Introduction and Commentary* (Grand Rapids: Eerdmans, 1990³), 27-34; M. Hengel, *Acts and the History of Earliest Christianity* (Philadelphia: Fortress, 1980), 59-68.

17. There is debate as to exactly which genre of history Luke-Acts belongs, whether "historical monograph" (Aune), "succession narrative" (Talbert), or "scientific treatise" (Alexander). See Marshall, "Acts and the 'Former Treatise,'" 178-80; Hemer, *Acts,* 33-43.

"theologian" of sorts, that is, a writer with a religious worldview. True, there were differences; Hengel's reference to Luke as a "theological historian" is apt.[18] Luke wrote for a Christian catechumen about the Son of God who was raised from the dead to heaven as Lord in fulfillment of the Law and the Prophets. In both volumes we sense a connection with OT salvation-history. God himself is at work in both the earthly Jesus and the risen and ascended Jesus. Even in the more overtly historical second volume the author is pressing the reader to confirm his commitment to the risen Lord. Nonetheless, the stated intention of both volumes makes Luke-Acts first and foremost a work of *history*.

The Alleged Theological Disparity between Paul and Luke Is Overstated.

Granted that Acts has a (secondary) theological character, how does the theology measure up against Paul's? Even cursory reading reveals differences of theological emphasis. According to Vielhauer,[19] for example, Luke is more positive toward paganism than Paul; unlike Paul Luke is not anti--*nomos* and betrays little understanding of justification by faith; Luke's christology appears to be earlier than and different from Paul's; and Luke's eschatology, unlike Paul's, sees the church as replacing the parousia.

These concerns have been addressed and answered by C. Hemer,[20] who points out that we are not comparing like with like. Paul wrote letters; Luke wrote biography-history. Paul is an intentional theologian-pastor whose concerns are explicit; Luke's "theology" is implicit and not so easy to identify. Granted there are differences in emphasis and expression, but this is only what we find from author to author in the NT. They do not imply that Luke has no real knowledge of the "historical" Paul.

---

18. Hengel, *Acts,* 59.

19. P. Vielhauer, "On the 'Paulinisms' in Acts," in L. E. Keck and J. L. Martyn, eds., *Studies in Luke-Acts* (Nashville: Abingdon, 1966), 33-50.

20. See Hemer, *Acts,* 245-47.

The Historical Competency of Acts

Are we able to rely on the book of Acts[21] for its history of earliest Christianity? Here we must consider some of the difficulties that have been raised.

The First Disciples in Jerusalem

The use of Acts for historical reconstruction of earliest Christianity is problematic to critical scholarship since it is regarded as colored by the apologetic theological interests of the author.[22] It is true that the early chapters are presented in rather idealized terms. That idealism is represented, for example, in the community of goods within the life of the first disciples. But Acts does not fail to report on the failure of Ananias and Sapphira or the dispute between the Hebrews and the Hellenists over the welfare of widows. The idealistic picture is soon shattered!

Furthermore, the author of Acts supplies many impressive details, which for the greater part are incidental to his narrative and to his apologetic and theological intentions. These are found within the early chapters, as well as throughout the book.

People and Officials   In the early chapters we meet John and Alexander "who were of the high-priestly family" of Annas,[23] the property-owning Joseph the Levite from Cyprus, Ananias and Sapphira,[24] an official referred to as the "captain of the Temple,"[25] and the seven named almoners from the "Hellenist" community.[26] Where the author is part of the narrative in the "we" passages the detail given is more intense than in passages where he is dependent on oral testimony from eyewitnesses or on written

---

21. We pass over discussion of Luke 2:1-5, a notorious crux; our concern is with the usefulness of the book of Acts for the birth of Christianity. In our view it is doubtful that Luke made a mistake. In any case, however, Luke was dependent on earlier source material for an event many years earlier.

22. See Bruce, *Acts,* 21-26, 60-66.

23. Acts 4:6.

24. Acts 4:36—5:1.

25. Acts 4:1; 5:24, 26.

26. Acts 6:5.

sources. In principle, however, the same interest in people and their positions can be traced throughout Acts, including in the early chapters.[27]

Topography and Geography   The early chapters also establish the author's interest in topographical details. Thus Olivet is "near Jerusalem, a Sabbath's journey away."[28] He mentions also "the upper room where they were staying," "the gate of the Temple that is called beautiful," and "the portico called Solomon's."[29] The information is fragmentary, being dependent on the author's notation of oral data combined with visitation of the sites, or on now lost written sources. His interest in such details will be reflected repeatedly throughout his extensive narrative,[30] especially in the "we" passages. Nonetheless, as Hengel has demonstrated, Luke is accurate as to places familiar to him in Palestine (consistent with the final "we" passage), whether the connection between citadel and Temple in Jerusalem, the cities on the coastal plain, or the road from Jerusalem to Caesarea.[31]

1 Peter and the Sermons of Peter   E. G. Selwyn made an exhaustive survey of points of possible contact between 1 Peter and the speeches of Peter in Acts. Selwyn found numerous parallels between the two as "utterances from the same mind." He concluded that "the connexion . . . is not literary, but historical: the common ground lies in the mind of St Peter who gave . . . teaching along these lines. . . ."[32]

Aramaisms[33]   The studies of Torrey and Wilcox detected Aramaisms beneath the Greek text of Acts, particularly in 1:1–5:16; 9:31–11:18 and parts of chs. 12 and 15. These features are consistent with a hypothesis of written Aramaic records of speeches of Peter which subsequently found their way into the Greek text of Acts. There has been debate over the extent of the Aramaisms with recognition of the difficulty in retroverting from Luke's

---

27. See further Hemer, *Acts*, 159-243; Bruce, *Acts*, 27-34.

28. Acts 1:12. A Sabbath journey was less than one kilometer. See Bruce, *Acts*, 105.

29. Acts 1:13; 3:2; 3:11; 5:11.

30. Hemer, *Acts*, 100-220.

31. Hengel, *Acts and the History of Earliest Christianity*, IV, 27-78; "The Geography of Palestine in Acts," *BAFCS* 4:27-78.

32. *The First Epistle of St. Peter* (London: Macmillan, 1946), 36.

33. See Bruce, *Acts*, 69.

Greek to a Semitic original.[34] Most likely, the source used by Luke was already in Greek. Nonetheless, the presence of Aramaic coloring within chs. 1–15 of Acts "is in the last resort undeniable."[35]

In our view, the early chapters focusing on Peter are undergirded by the same fundamental historicity that we find throughout Acts. Moreover, the earliest chapters flow naturally into those that follow, making any division between the "romantic" and the "real" arbitrary.

Theudas

Critics rightly point to problems in the author's account of Gamaliel's speech to the Sanhedrin (Acts 5:33-39). According to Gamaliel, Judas the Galilean "arose . . . after" Theudas. The only Theudas known to us (from Josephus, *Antiquities* 20.97-99), however, was a self-styled prophet who appeared when Cuspius Fadus was procurator of Judea (A.D. 44-46). It appears Luke has made two errors: placing Theudas before Judas, who "arose in the days of the census" which, as Luke well knew, occurred decades earlier (cf. Luke 2:1-5), and putting Theudas in the mouth of Gamaliel ten years earlier than Theudas "arose."

Theudas's march to the Jordan, as narrated by Josephus occurred in the mid-40s, that is, only three or four years before Luke joined Paul in the first of the "we" passages (Acts 16:10). Most likely, Luke would have known about this Theudas since he was a notorious figure (according to Josephus). It seems unlikely that Luke would have made an error about an infamous contemporary.

Furthermore, in the turbulent times after the death of Herod in 4 B.C., that is, before Judas "arose" in A.D. 6, there were many uprisings (so Josephus, *Antiquities* 17.269). It is possible that an otherwise unknown Theudas was among their leaders.[36] "Theudas" was a contraction of "Theodotus," the Greek equivalent of the Hebrew "Jonathan" ("given by God"). Apart from the son of Saul, a more recent Jonathan was the Maccabean warrior king (161-43 B.C.). Many Jewish boys were given the names of Maccabean

---

34. See pp. 118-19 above.

35. D. F. Payne, "Semitisms in the Book of Acts," in W. W. Gasque and R. P. Martin, eds., *Apostolic History and the Gospel* (Grand Rapids: Eerdmans, 1970), 146.

36. So Bruce, *Acts*, 175-77.

heroes.[37] Greek versions of "Jonathon" appear in inscriptions as "Theudion," a contraction of Theodotion, which was a variant of Theodotus.[38] Josephus and Luke coincidentally may have been using the name "Theudas" to refer to different men whose original name was Jonathan.

In short, had Luke confused Theudas with someone closer to the time of Judas, our suspicions of inaccuracy may have been stronger. Confusing him with someone who was a prominent contemporary, however, seems less likely.[39]

Paul's "Unknown" Years

In the course of his apologia to the Galatians Paul provides many details about his movements from the time of his "call" on the Damascus road to his meeting "fourteen years" later with the "pillars" of the Jerusalem church, James, Cephas, and John (Gal 2:1-10). Since the Acts narrative also mentions Paul at a number of points during this period we are able to make some assessment of Luke's competence as a historian (Acts 9:1-31; 11:22-30).

The two sources are in agreement about the broad sweep of Paul's life in these "unknown years":

The christophany occurred before Paul's arrival in Damascus.
After a period in Damascus Paul returned to Jerusalem.
Paul went from Judea to Tarsus/Syria-Cilicia.
Paul arrived in Antioch in partnership with Barnabas.

Not all the pieces fit together, however. Some dislocations are either relatively minor or easily explained. For example, Acts makes no reference to a journey to "Arabia" or to the problems Paul faced from Aretas, king of the Nabateans (Gal 1:17; 2 Cor 11:32-33).

37. See W. R. Farmer, "Judas, Simon and Athronges," *NTS* 4 (1958), 147-55.

38. G. H. R. Horsley, *New Documents Illustrating Early Christianity 4* (Macquarie: Macquarie University, 1987), 183-85; M. H. Williams, "Palestinian Personal Names in Acts," in R. Bauckham, ed., *BAFCS* 4:99-100.

39. We note that the two notorious cruxes regarding Luke's reliability — the date of Jesus' birth (Luke 2:1-5) and the Theudas reference (Acts 5:36-37) — both relate to the census *(apographē)* under Quirinius, which provoked Judas's uprising (Josephus, *Antiquities* 18.1-6). A possible alternative explanation is that Luke was depending on a source or sources that were flawed or misleading.

Most likely the author has deliberately omitted the Arabia/Nabatea detail since in his "program" Paul has not yet begun actively to press the word of God from Jerusalem to Rome. For the moment Peter is his focal figure; Paul's time will come. Paul, however, has a different perspective; even from the Damascus "call" he has begun to "proclaim the Son of God among the Gentiles" and so "fulfill the gospel" among them (Gal 1:16; Rom 15:18-20).

The contradiction between the two in regard to Paul's first return visit to Jerusalem, however, is not so easily resolved. For his part Paul solemnly assures the Galatians that he saw none of the apostles except Cephas and James and that he was not known by sight to the churches of Judea (Gal 1:19-20). Acts, however, states that Barnabas brought Paul first to the apostles and that "he went in and out among them at Jerusalem, preaching boldly . . ." (Acts 9:27-29).

Is this disparity due to the differing apologetic concerns of our authors? It is not always recognized that Paul, in his own way,[40] was as selective in his use of events as Luke. Is Acts romantically seeking to portray Paul and the Jerusalem "apostles" enjoying amicable relationships? Is Paul shoring up his authority with the Gentile churches by playing down any appearance of dependence on the Jerusalem apostles? It is possible that factors like these played their part.

Yet these explanations are not altogether convincing. For his part, Paul dare not lie, since discovery would have bad consequences for his already battered reputation.[41] Many Jews among the believers in his mission

---

40. Various kinds of "historical" information are found in Paul's letters: disclosures explaining his own past actions (e.g., 1 Thess 1:2–3:10; 1 Cor 1:14-17; 2:1-5; 2 Cor 1:8–2:13; 7:5-7; 4:12-15), his dealings with other church leaders (e.g., Gal 1:18–2:14), the Damascus road "call" and Paul's subsequent ministry (e.g., Rom 1:5; 15:17-21; 1 Cor 9:1; 15:8; Gal 1:11-16), and echoes of the historical Jesus, e.g., "I Paul myself entreat you by the meekness and gentleness of Christ," 2 Cor 10:1. In this last example Paul appears to be echoing Matthew's source referring to Jesus' "meekness" (Matt 11:29; 21:4-5 quoting Zech 9:9). On this see L. L. Belleville, "Gospel and Kerygma in 2 Corinthians," in L. A. Jervis and P. Richardson, eds., *Gospel in Paul: Studies on Corinthians, Galatians, and Romans* (Sheffield: Sheffield University Press, 1995), 140-42.

41. In Galatians Paul is at his most informative as to details about himself in regard to *time* (1:18: "after three years"; 2:1: "after fourteen years"), *places* (1:17-18: Arabia, Damascus, Jerusalem; 1:21: "the regions of Syria and Cilicia"; 2:1: Jerusalem; 2:11: Antioch), and *people* (1:18-19: Cephas and James; 2:1-10: Titus, Barnabas, James, Cephas, and John; 2:11-15: Cephas, "certain men from James," and Barnabas). Yet nowhere is he more vulnerable to intellectual counterattack than in his relationships with the Galatians. Most likely, therefore, these details should be regarded as historically secure.

churches retained their connections with the synagogues. Their members traveled to and from Jerusalem for the feasts and to deliver the annual temple dues.[42] On the other hand, the Acts account of the awkwardness of Paul's first contact with the Jerusalem church is quite feasible.

Arguably, therefore, the two accounts can be reconciled, at least to some degree.[43] The Acts version, that Paul needed an intermediary like Barnabas to bring the former persecutor first to the apostles before meeting the wider community, makes good sense, given the ferocity of his assaults. It would follow that only when Paul proved his genuineness by preaching in Jerusalem that Cephas and James felt sufficiently confident to meet Paul in more personal terms, in line with his narrative in Galatians.

In short, Paul and Acts are in agreement about the sequence of locations in the "fourteen" years of Paul's relative obscurity. The accounts of Paul's first return visit to Jerusalem vary, though some reconciliation seems possible. In regard to Paul's "obscurity" for so many years we must allow the possibility that Luke sought to avoid confusion between the roles of Peter and Paul. Luke appears to be concerned to show that Peter, the apostle initially responsible for bringing the gospel to the Jews, was also the first to bring the gospel to the Gentiles. Luke leaves Paul out of his story for the time being so as not to confuse the broad historicity of the events and the significant early role of Peter.

Paul's Visits to Jerusalem

Another problem is the alleged discrepancy between Paul and Acts regarding the number of visits Paul made to Jerusalem. Hyldahl, for example, dismisses Acts for its fivefold visits by Paul, because in Paul's letters we find only three visits.[44] Insisting that Paul is primary and Luke secondary, this author eliminates two of Luke's visits as due to his "editorial adaptation."

---

42. Most likely by means of these networks Paul's opponents in Jerusalem had informed their fellow Jews among the Galatians that Paul was "still preaching circumcision" (Gal 5:11). Likewise, through these same channels reports of Paul's (alleged) de-judaizing activities among the Gentiles would have found their way back to Jerusalem (e.g., Acts 21:21).

43. See M. Hengel and A. M. Schwemer, *Paul between Damascus and Antioch: The Unknown Years* (Louisville: Westminster/John Knox, 1997), 132-50; D. Wenham, "Acts and the Pauline Corpus," in *BAFCS* 1:221-26.

44. Hyldahl, *History,* 136.

Paul, however, only mentions his journeys when there is special reason to do so. His letters do not yield a comprehensive account of his travels. As argued earlier, Acts is with Paul's letters "an equal primary source" for Paul so that the two can be employed to reconstruct an outline of Paul's career.

Verdicts on the Historical Competency of Acts

Is this text useful to the historian? Few would declare Acts to be altogether useless. Many, however, regard it as quite problematic because of perceived historical incompetence or theological fixity or both. This viewpoint was classically stated by Haenchen: "Luke was no professional historian and he was not interested in writing a history of early Christianity. . . ." Rather, he declared, "the book of Acts gives rich history about . . . 'the post-apostolic age.'"[45] Many have followed this opinion, including influential theologians like Conzelmann.[46]

By contrast, various scholars of differing aspects of antiquity have reached quite different conclusions. In regard to historiography the noted scholar Mommsen observed: "The numerous small features — features not really necessary for the actual course of the action and yet which fit so well there — are internal witnesses to his reliability."[47] Meyer, another distinguished historian of classical antiquity, commented that Luke's work, in spite of a more limited content, "bears the same character as those of great historians, of a Polybius, a Livy and many others."[48] More recently Hengel pointed out that the book of Acts "always remains within the limits of what was considered reliable by the standards of antiquity."[49]

Sherwin-White, an authority on Roman law and provincial administration, after reviewing the data in the book of Acts wrote, "any attempt to reject its basic historicity even in matters of detail must now appear absurd. Roman historians have long taken it for granted."[50]

45. Quoted in Hemer, *Acts,* 101 n. 7.

46. See Hyldahl, *History,* 135 n. 2.

47. Quoted in R. Riesner, *Paul's Early Period: Chronology, Mission Strategy, Theology* (Grand Rapids: Eerdmans, 1998), 326.

48. Quoted in Bruce, *Acts,* 27.

49. M. Hengel, *Acts and the History of Earliest Christianity* (Philadelphia: Fortress, 1980), 61.

50. A. N. Sherwin-White, *Roman Society and Roman Law in the New Testament* (Oxford: Clarendon, 1963), 189.

Classical scholar and traveler in Anatolia C. Hemer for many years engaged in painstaking study of what he calls the "trivia of Acts" in place-names, topographical and travel details, and titles of local officials. After exhaustive tabulation of such detail Hemer, a model of caution, notes that he had "discovered a wealth of material suggesting an author familiar with particular locations and at the times in question." After examining these details Hemer concluded that, "By and large these all converged to support the general reliability of the narrative, through details so intricately yet often unintentionally woven into that narrative."[51]

The widespread assumption that the author of Acts was concerned only in matters relating to theology and that he was governed by his apologetic agenda must be questioned. In the light of the marks of his historical interest and competence noted above we conclude that the historian is able, with confidence tempered with critical caution, to make use of the data in Acts in pursuit of the task of historical reconstruction. At the same time we must not expect the author of Acts to have the techniques and standards of modern historiography. Such expectations are unreasonable and impractical.

Few have so clearly stated the importance of Acts for early Christianity as Meyer, who was himself critical of Christianity. Meyer writes that, "for the history of Christianity . . . we have the completely inestimable advantage . . . of having access to the portrayal of the beginning stages of the development directly from the pen of one of its co-participants. That alone ensures for the author an eminent place among the significant historians of world history."[52]

Conclusion

It is not possible to exaggerate the critical significance of Luke-Acts for a history of earliest Christianity and its connection with Jesus. Without these texts no historical reconstruction is possible.

This alone, however, is no basis for endorsing the book of Acts. The "we" passages point to a companion of Paul as the author of Luke-Acts. From Paul he enjoyed direct knowledge of Paul's early life, conversion, and

51. Hemer, *Acts,* 412.
52. Quoted in Riesner, *Paul's Early Period,* 326.

ministry. Through Paul's connections with James, Cephas, and John the author had secondhand contact with early Jerusalem leaders and beyond that, with Jesus himself. Furthermore, the "eyewitnesses" of Jesus who became "ministers of the word" "handed over" to Luke written "narratives" about Jesus and early Christianity which were subsequently incorporated in his two-"book" work. The usual assumption that Luke-Acts is separated from Jesus and the early church by an impenetrable wall must be rejected.

While several matters leave Luke open to criticism with some scholars, overall the book of Acts is a work of serious history and invaluable for our grasp of the birth of Christianity.

Dating Galatians

NT scholars have for many years debated whether Galatians should be dated in the middle 50s as written to "north Galatian" churches or in the late 40s as written to churches of "southern" Galatia.[1] The northern destination has traditionally been connected with the later date and the southern destination with the earlier date. Those connections are not ironclad, however. It is possible also to argue that Galatians was written later (in the mid-50s) to churches in "southern" Galatia. On the other hand, a northern destination would appear to necessitate a date in the mid-50s. I will be arguing that Paul wrote Galatians from Antioch in Syria to churches in southern Galatia in the late 40s, soon after his missionary tour in those regions, which is narrated in Acts 13–14. It will be convenient to consider the destination question first.

The "north Galatian" hypothesis was supported by such eminent scholars as J. B. Lightfoot and J. Moffatt[2] and has been followed by many others. Their main argument is that the migrating "Galatians" (from Gaul) who settled well to the north of the region visited by Paul in Acts 13–14 gave their name to *that* region. The Roman province of Galatia is that northern region; the Pisidian and Lycaonian districts visited by Paul in Acts 13–14 were not then part of "Galatia" or referred to as "Galatian." Acts

---

1. Traditionally a northern destination and a later dating are connected. There is no logical reason, however, that Galatians might not have been written in the mid-50s to churches in southern Galatia. This, however, is not the view taken here.

2. Moffatt's detailed arguments are given and answered in C. J. Hemer, *The Book of Acts in the Setting of Hellenistic History* (Winona Lake: Eisenbrauns, 1990), 294-95.

13–14 nowhere refers to the regions evangelized by Paul as "Galatia." Accordingly, his letter addressed to "Galatians" must be directed to more northerly regions. It was only after Paul had revisited the churches of the earlier mission that he went "through the region of Phrygia and Galatia" (Acts 16:6; cf. 18:23). The "north Galatian" view proposes that Paul evangelized this region at that later time and that the letter to "churches of Galatia" was written some years later.

The primary consideration here is that Acts has a detailed and lengthy account of Paul's visit to these cities of the Anatolian plateau (13:14–14:28), which he later revisited and strengthened (16:1-5). On the other hand, we know of no evangelism by Paul in the northern region, nor of the creation of churches there. Paul appears to have set his sights on Roman colonies and capitals of well-established provinces like those of southern Anatolia. The rather wild northern Galatian region and upper Anatolia generally was not notably Romanized at this time and would have been of little interest to the Pauline strategy.

What, then, of the assertion that the southern region is not the province which takes its name from the ethnic "Galatians" who settled in the more northerly parts two centuries earlier? The matter is settled by writers of the period, Strabo, Pliny, and Ptolemy, who each include Pisidia as part of the province of Galatia.[3] Further, there is an inscription from Pednelissus in southern Pisidia calling it "a city of Galatia."[4] It is clear that by Paul's day "Galatia" extended south of the ethnically defined northerly region and that the cities evangelized by him in his first missionary journey were part of "greater" Galatia.

Moreover, that southern part of Galatia was described as "Phrygian." Geographical extremities within provinces were often described adjectivally in terms of an adjoining province or region.[5] It is evident that the southern parts of Galatia were so described by reference to the adjoining region of Phrygia.[6] Thus the critical statement of Acts 16:6 (cf. Acts 18:23), that Paul and his companions "went through the region of Phrygia and Galatia" is to be understood as their return journey though "Phrygian Galatia."[7]

---

3. Hemer, *Book of Acts*, 294-95.

4. Cited in Hemer, *Book of Acts*, 301.

5. Hemer, *Book of Acts*, 282-85.

6. Hemer, *Book of Acts*, 295.

7. So F. F. Bruce, *The Acts of the Apostles: The Greek Text with Introduction and Commentary* (Grand Rapids: Eerdmans, 1990³), 353-54.

In short, the reasons advanced against a southern destination can be met. Furthermore, there is a lack of evidence for Paul's missionary work in sparsely settled Galatia proper.

With regard to dating, the major argument for the later date relates to the theological tone of the letter, in particular its forensic arguments and use of "justification" language. It is held that the language is so similar to Romans, written ca. 57, that Galatians must have been written at that time. Here an evolutionary model of Paul's theology is implied. The early Paul (1 and 2 Thessalonians and 1 Corinthians) is preoccupied with eschatological issues whereas the more mature Paul (2 Corinthians and Romans) is concerned with reconciliation issues. Galatians, it is argued, belongs to the era of the more mature Paul.

The principle of a maturing author is readily agreed; his great Romans letter written late is clear evidence of this. Yet it is right to recognize that Paul was no novice when he began his westward missions, from which his earliest extant texts flowed. By that time he was already in his forties and an active missionary for a decade and a half. 1 Thessalonians, written ca. 50, is now recognized as a mature piece of literature with an already developed soteriology and christology (1 Thess 1:10; 5:9-10). While the vocabulary of justification is absent, it is conceptually present.

Critical to this discussion is the need to recognize Paul's capacity to respond to the pastoral issues of the moment. The two Thessalonian letters and 1 Corinthians are dominated by eschatological issues because they were concerns in those churches during the early years of Paul's Aegean mission (50-54).

Clearly Galatians was written to address issues of Law and "righteousness" before God. But when? We know of a Judaizing mission in Antioch in the late 40s (Gal 2:11-14; Acts 15:1-2, 5), of an anti-Pauline mission in Corinth in the mid-50s (2 Cor 2:17–3:18; 11:4, 12-15, 22-23), and that Paul wrote Romans (among other reasons) over the question of the works of the Law (Romans 1–7, 9–11).[8] Does Galatians address the crisis of the late 40s or the crisis of the mid-50s? It is not possible to decide based on theological content alone.

---

8. This is not to assert that the Law-based counterarguments against Paul were identical. Doubtless there had been changes during the six or seven intervening years, including the resolution of the circumcision issue by the Jerusalem decree of ca. 49. See P. W. Barnett, "Opposition in Corinth," *JSNT* 22 (1987), 3-17.

By the time Paul began his Antioch-based missions he would have often debated the issues of Law and christology with resistant Jews. It is likely that he had early established his apologetic with exegesis of texts related to Abraham and Moses. My contention is that when "Jewish" and "Judaizing" issues arose Paul's responses were already formulated and readily introduced. Accordingly, the sophistication of argument evident in Galatians does not of itself establish a later date for the letter.

Our decision about the dating turns on our understanding of Paul's rebuke that the Galatians are "so quickly turning from him who called you in the grace of Christ and turning to another gospel" (1:6). Does "so quickly" refer to the brevity of time between Paul's mission and their apostasy, thus supporting the early date? Or does it refer to the speed with which they deserted Paul's gospel under the pressure of the "agitators," which could point equally to an earlier or a later date?

In favor of the former understanding of "so quickly" is that so much of the letter is devoted to a review of past events. After God's "call" to preach to the Gentiles and his visits to Arabia, Damascus, and Jerusalem, his withdrawal to Syria and Cilicia, his second visit to Jerusalem, and the "incident in Antioch," Paul traveled to Galatia to preach the gospel. This is where Paul's geographical review ends, with his initial ministry to the Galatians. Had the letter been written in the mid-50s we would expect some references to subsequent ministry in Macedonia and Achaia, to his return visits to the Galatian churches, and to his sojourn in Ephesus. There are none. That his review ends with his initial mission among the Galatians is evidence of earliness, that the reproachful "so quickly" means "so quickly after *I* was with you." Indeed, the whole tenor of the letter is one of passionate immediacy of personal dealings with them (Gal 4:19-20; 6:17).

Furthermore, Paul's letters of the mid-50s (1 and 2 Corinthians and Romans) are dominated by his concern to finalize the collection from the churches of Galatia, Asia, Macedonia, and Achaia and to make his departure from those regions. In Galatians, however, we find references to the collection that belong to the genesis of the idea in the 40s (2:10; 6:7-10) rather than to its full-blown form in the 50s.

In sum, there is no compelling reason to subscribe to a "north" Galatian hypothesis and, indeed, good reasons not to do so. The northern theory has no clear historical evidence in support. Consistent with Acts 16:6 and 18:23, the southern region was "*Phrygian* Galatia." On the other hand, the earlier construct fits in exactly with both the narrative of Acts and the chronology of Paul's review in Galatians.

Galatians' own reference to the brevity of time ("so quickly") between Paul's mission to the Galatians and the writing of the letter, together with the passion and urgency expressed throughout and the absence of reference to the collection is good reason for accepting the early dating of the letter. Paul would have been reflecting on the issues in Galatians for a decade and a half before he wrote the letter if it had the earlier date. This, along with his undoubted ability to address issues of the moment with high concentration, will account for the "developed" theological emphases found in Galatians.

Although the "northern" hypothesis, with its customary corollary, a later dating, has had widespread support from NT scholarship, the verdict of ancient historians should be heard. T. S. Mitchell, an authority on Galatia, has commented, "the most authoritative champion of the Southern Galatian Theory was the great explorer of Asia Minor, W. M. Ramsay, and although the North Galatian Theory finds many supporters, his work long ago should have put the matter beyond dispute."[9] According to Mitchell, Galatians is "the earliest surviving document of the Christian church."[10] The noted Roman historian, F. Millar, agrees, referring to Galatians as "almost certainly the earliest" of the Pauline letters.[11]

The dating of Galatians bears on the amount of time between Jesus and the first documentary reference to Jesus. If Galatians was written ca. 48, it would shorten the gap to eighteen years. If, further, the crucifixion occurred in 33, as I believe, then the gap is shortened to fifteen years. In terms of the historical reference to noted persons in antiquity, this would represent a brevity without parallel. This observation remains true if the time frame is twenty years, based on 30 as the date of the first Easter and 1 Thessalonians as our earliest Pauline text, written ca. 50.

9. D. N. Freedman, ed., *The Anchor Bible Dictionary* (New York: Doubleday, 1992), II (1992), 871.

10. "Hagar, Ishmael, Josephus, and the Origin of Islam," in *Anatolia: Land, Men, and Gods in Asia Minor* 2 (Oxford: Oxford University Press, 1995), 3.

11. *JJS* 44 (1993), 38.

Reflections on J. D. Crossan's
Birth of Christianity

In many ways Crossan's subtitle, *Discovering What Happened in the Years Immediately after the Execution of Jesus,* is a fair description of what I have attempted in this book.[1] I have to say, though, that it is an odd subtitle for Crossan's book since he tells us very little in it about those "years after . . . the execution of Jesus."

Similarly puzzling is his opening statement that the decades after Jesus are "dark decades . . . cloaked in silence." His biblical indexes do not have a single reference from the book of Acts. It is not true that we have no evidence for those years. Crossan also fails to cite any text relating to post-execution Christianity by Martin Hengel, despite that author's matchless contribution to our understanding of the era.

His center of gravity is located *before* Jesus' execution, in the circumstances and events of Galilee in the 20s. This is an entirely acceptable methodology. What is questionable, however, is his almost complete failure to address or analyze the post-execution movement in Palestine in the 30s and 40s, its mission activities, and the "faith" reflected then. Since there was no wall separating the early disciples (post-execution) from their Master (pre-execution) we might expect their activities and faith to cast light on him and his activities and teaching in Galilee immediately beforehand.

Establishing the dire socio-economic realities in Galilee in the era of Jesus is critical to his reconstruction of Jesus. Under the wider Roman he-

---

1. J. D. Crossan, *The Birth of Christianity: Discovering What Happened in the Years Immediately after the Execution of Jesus* (San Francisco: HarperCollins, 1998).

gemony the tetrarchy of Galilee was subject to significant urbanization during the 20s resulting in the dispossession and marginalization of the formerly landed peasantry. Crossan offers considerable information from history, archaeology, and anthropology pointing to the severe exploitation and hardship of the lower orders and their social dislocation. In the absence of demographic records, however, we do not know the extent and intensity of the problems faced by poorer folk. These reconstructions are of necessity conjectural, yet his argument depends on them.

Crossan thinks that Jesus was an illiterate peasant among numerous illiterate peasants of Galilee (235). This runs against the evidence, which points to Jesus as "rabbi," one who taught in the synagogues. Among his companions were owners of a fishing collective, a toll collector, and women of means like Joanna, wife of a senior official of the tetrarch. In the Gospels we see Jesus eating in the homes of the wealthy and hear of his reputation as one who "came eating and drinking." Jesus does not appear to have been at the bottom of the social pile.

According to Crossan Jesus' words and deeds can be summed up as "ethical eschatology" and as "actualized eschatology." The ultimate End, as in apocalyptic understanding, is replaced altogether by what this Jesus was doing there and then. The Gospels see Jesus intentionally heading to Jerusalem and death that awaited him, expressed soteriologically. Crossan, however, has no theory of Jesus' death that in any way approaches NT understanding.

From the following words we sense that Crossan's Jesus is in no sense unique:

> To say, therefore, that the healings or exorcisms of Jesus are miracles does not mean for me that *only* Jesus could do such things but that in such events I see God at work in Jesus. God, for me, is one who resists discrimination, exploitation and oppression; who is, for example, on the side of a doomed people rather than their imperial masters at the Exodus and on the side of the crucified Jesus rather than his imperial executioners at the resurrection. And, in the reciprocity of open eating and free healing . . . I see that same God at work — in the healing and in the eating as non-violent resistance to systemic evil. (304, italics added)

Crossan's methodology must be mentioned. His book is long and complex. Its major arguments, buried in discursive and digressive text, could be set out in fewer pages. This is the author's technique, preparing the reader to accept the next part of the argument before he actually reaches it. For example, there is a lengthy discourse about "recovered memory" issues that point up the unreliability of memory so as to call into question memory-related information in the NT.

More significant, though, is Crossan's use of sources. He relies heavily on the Q Gospel, as he calls it. Q is a hypothesis, I would say a likely hypothesis. But Crossan has no mandate from evidence to call Q a "Gospel." We do not know what else belonged to Q apart from tentative reconstructions from Luke and Matthew. Did it have a beginning or end of which we have no knowledge? Why is Q never referred to in its own right? Why did Q not survive as a Gospel alongside the others? We do not know the answers and, unless some further discoveries are made, we shall never know. The practice of emending this hypothetical document, removing various layers to recover the original "Q," merely piles conjecture upon conjecture.

As well as Q, Crossan depends on the *Didache* (late first century?), the Gospels of *Thomas* and *Peter* (third century). On the other hand, Crossan makes no reference to Acts and uses the Gospel of Mark and the letters of Paul sparingly. In short, this author fails to observe one of the basic principles of historiography, namely to use the earliest and best sources and to exercise critical caution with historically remote texts.

Another signal failure is his lack of reference to the didactic culture of those times as Jesus used it among his disciples. They were, indeed, "disciples" and he was their "teacher." He instructed them by means identifiable in those times, by parables, similitudes, aphorisms, rhymes, paradoxes, and the like. After his death the didactic and rabbinic style of instruction became the pedagogical medium among the early Christians, continuing along Jesus' trajectory for the next half century. Within the didactic culture he created, his "eyewitnesses," who became "ministers of the word," must have attained some practical level of literacy. The texts of the NT, as we have them, arose out of the scholarship of Jesus and from the first generation of his disciples.

Crossan has failed to acknowledge that the echoes of Jesus heard in the letters of Paul, James, and 1 Peter are mostly *ethical* instructions, some of which find parallels in Q. This is not evidence of the "real Jesus" of rural Galilee as opposed to the "unreal" Christ of urban Jerusalem. Rather, it indicates that Jesus' teachings were early collected to supplement the moral understanding of converts in the newly formed Jewish churches. These strands do not represent the mind of the "true" Jesus, the "life" or "kingdom" messages of his Galilean movement, as opposed to the inauthentic "sin" and "death" messages in Paul and Mark.

In sum, Crossan's Christianity is an idealization based on his vision for social justice expressed in shared table fellowship. But it hardly throbs with the conviction that God's hour has struck in the coming of the Messiah, who died "for" others and whom God raised alive on the third day.

BIBLIOGRAPHY

Akenson, D. H., *Saint Saul: A Skeleton Key to the Historical Jesus* (Oxford: Oxford University Press, 2000)

Alexander, L., *The Preface to Luke's Gospel* (Cambridge: Cambridge University Press, 1993)

Allison, D. C., "The Pauline Epistles and the Synoptic Gospels: The Pattern of the Parallels," *NTS* 28.1 (1986), 1-32

Anderson, P. N., *The Christology of the Fourth Gospel* (WUNT; Tübingen: Mohr, 1996)

Bailey, K., "Informal Controlled Oral Tradition and the Synoptic Gospels," *Asian Journal of Theology* 5 (1991), 34-54

Barnett, P. W., *Jesus and the Logic of History* (Grand Rapids: Eerdmans, 1997)

————, *Jesus and the Rise of Early Christianity* (Downers Grove: InterVarsity, 1999)

Barrett, C. K., *The Gospel according to St. John* (Philadelphia: Westminster, 1978)

Best, E., *1 Peter* (NCB; London: Oliphants, 1971)

Bockmuehl, M., "Antioch and James the Just," in B. Chilton and C. A. Evans, eds., *James the Just and Christian Origins* (Leiden: Brill, 1999)

Borgen, P., "John and the Synoptics," in D. L. Dungan, ed., *The Interrelationship of the Gospels* (Leuven: University Press, 1990), 408-37

Bornkamm, G., *Jesus of Nazareth* (New York: Harper and Row, 1960)

Bruce, F. F., *The Acts of the Apostles: Greek Text with Introduction and Commentary* (Grand Rapids: Eerdmans, 1990³)

————, *Paul: Apostle of the Free Spirit* (Exeter: Paternoster, 1977) = *Paul: Apostle of the Heart Set Free* (Grand Rapids: Eerdmans, 1977)

Burridge, R. A., *What Are the Gospels?* (Cambridge: Cambridge University Press, 1992)

Casey, M., *An Aramaic Approach to Q: Sources for the Gospels of Matthew and Luke* (Cambridge: Cambridge University Press, 2002)

Chan, M. L. Y., *Christology from Within and Ahead* (Leiden: Brill, 2001)

Chilton, B., and Evans, C. A., eds. *James the Just and Christian Origins* (Leiden: Brill, 1999)

Collins, J., ed., *The Thessalonian Correspondence* (Leuven: Peeters, 2000)

Crossan, J. D., *The Birth of Christianity* (San Francisco: Harper, 1998)

Culpepper, R. A., and Black, C. C., *Exploring the Gospel of John* (Louisville: Westminster/John Knox, 1996)

Davids, P., "Palestinian Traditions in the Epistle of James," in B. Chilton and C. A. Evans, eds., *James the Just and Christian Origins* (Leiden: Brill, 1999), 33-57

Denaux, A., ed., *John and the Synoptics* (Leuven: University Press, 1992)

Dodd, C. H., *The Apostolic Preaching and Its Developments* (London: Hodder and Stoughton, 1936)

———, *Historical Tradition in the Fourth Gospel* (Cambridge: Cambridge University Press, 1963)

Donahue, J. A., "Windows and Mirrors: The Setting of Mark's Gospel," *CBQ* 57 (1995), 1-26

Donfried, K. P., and Beutler, J., *The Thessalonians Debate* (Grand Rapids: Eerdmans, 2000)

Donfried, K. P., and Marshall, I. H., *The Theology of the Shorter Pauline Letters* (Cambridge: Cambridge University Press, 1993)

Dunn, J. D. G., "Jesus and Oral Memory," SBL Seminar Papers 2000 (Atlanta: SBL, 2000), 287-326

———, *Jesus Remembered* (Grand Rapids: Eerdmans, 2003)

Ehrman, B., *Jesus, Apocalyptic Prophet of the New Millennium* (New York: Oxford University Press, 2002)

Ellis, E. E., "The Making of Narratives in the Synoptic Tradition," in H. Wansbrough, ed., *Jesus and the Oral Gospel Tradition* (JSNT 64; Sheffield: JSOT, 1991), 310-33

———, *The Making of the New Testament Documents* (Leiden: Brill, 2002), 228-47

———, "Reading the Gospel as History," *Criswell Theological Review* 3.1 (1988), 3-15

———, "Traditions in 1 Corinthians," *NTS* 32 (1986), 481-502

Evans, R. J, *In Defence of History* (London: Granta, 1997)

Fitzmyer, J., *To Advance the Gospel* (Grand Rapids: Eerdmans, 1998)

———, *Luke the Theologian: Aspects of His Teaching* (London: Chapman, 1989)

Gardner-Smith, P., *Saint John and the Synoptic Gospels* (Cambridge: Cambridge University Press, 1938)

Gerhardsson, B., *The Origin of the Gospel Traditions* (London: SCM, 1977)

Goodacre, M., "A Monopoly on Markan Priority? Fallacies at the Heart of Q," *SBL Seminar Papers 2000* (Atlanta: SBL, 2000), 583-622

Gundry, R. H., *Mark* (Grand Rapids: Eerdmans, 1993)

———, "'Verba Christi' in 1 Peter: Their Implications concerning the Authorship of 1 Peter and the Authorship of the Gospel Tradition," *NTS* 13 (1966-67), 336-59

Harrison, J. R., "Paul and the Imperial Gospel in Thessaloniki," *JSNT* 25.1 (2002), 71-96

Harvey, A. E., *Jesus and the Constraints of History* (London: Duckworth, 1982)

Harvey, J. D., "Orality and Its Implications for Biblical Studies: Recapturing an Ancient Paradigm," *JETS* 45.1 (2002), 99-109

Head, P. M., and Williams P. J., "Q Review," *TB* 54.1 (2003), 131-44

Hemer, C., *The Book of Acts in the Setting of Hellenistic History* (WUNT; Tübingen: Mohr, 1989)

Henaut, B. W., *Oral Tradition and the Gospels: The Problem of Mark 4* (Sheffield: JSOT, 1993)

Hengel, M., *Acts and the History of Earliest Christianity* (London: SCM, 1979)

———, *The Atonement* (London: SCM, 1981)

———, *The Four Gospels and the One Gospel of Jesus Christ* (London: SCM, 2000)

———, *The Johannine Question* (London: SCM, 1989)

———, *The Pre-Christian Paul* (London: SCM, 1991)

———, *The Son of God* (London: SCM, 1976)

Hengel, M., and Schwemer, A. M., *Paul between Damascus and Antioch: The Unknown Years* (Louisville: Westminster/John Knox, 1997)

Hoehner, H., *Chronological Aspects of the Life of Christ* (Grand Rapids: Zondervan, 1977)

Horsley, G. H. R., *New Documents Illustrating Early Christianity* 5 (Sydney: Macquarie University, 1989), 19-26

Hurtado, L., *At the Origins of Christian Worship* (Grand Rapids: Eerdmans, 1999)

———, *One God, One Lord* (Philadelphia: Fortress, 1988)

Ingolfsland, D., "Kloppenborg's Stratification of Q and Its Significance," *JETS* 46.2 (2003), 227-31

Jeremias, J., *New Testament Theology* 1 (London: SCM, 1971)

Kelber, W., *The Oral and Written Gospel: The Hermeneutics of Speaking and Writing in the Synoptic Tradition, Mark, Paul and Q* (Philadelphia: Fortress, 1983)

Kim, S., "The Jesus Tradition in 1 Thess 4:13–5:11," *NTS* 48 (2002), 225-42

———, *Paul and the New Perspective* (Grand Rapids: Eerdmans, 2002)

Kloppenborg, J., *The Formation of Q* (Harrisburg: Trinity Press International, 1987)

Kloppenborg Verbin J., *Excavating Q: The History and Setting of the Sayings Gospel* (Minneapolis: Fortress, 2000)

Lieberman, S., *Hellenism in Jewish Palestine* (New York: Jewish Theological Society, 1962)

Lührmann, D., *Galatians* (Minneapolis: Fortress, 1992)

Manson, T. W., *The Sayings of Jesus* (London: SCM, 1961)

Martyn, J. L., *History and Theology in the Fourth Gospel* (Nashville: Abingdon, 1979, revised and enlarged)

Matson, M. A., *In Dialogue with Another Gospel* (SBL Dissertation Series, 178; Atlanta: SBL, 2001)

McNicol, A. J., Peabody, D. B., and Dungan, D. L., eds., *Beyond the Q Impasse: Luke's Use of Matthew* (Valley Forge: Trinity Press International, 1996)

Meadors, E., "The 'Messianic' Implications of the Q Material," *JBL* 118.2 (1999), 253-77

Meyers, E. M., and Strange, J., *Archaeology, the Rabbis and Early Christianity* (London: SCM, 1981)

Millard, A., *Reading and Writing in the Time of Jesus* (Sheffield: Sheffield Academic Press, 2000)

Moule, C. F. D., *The Origin of Christology* (Cambridge: Cambridge University Press, 1977)

Neirynck, F., "John and the Synoptics: 1975-1990," in *John and the Synoptics* (Leuven: University Press, 1992), 3-62

Painter, J., *Just James: The Brother of Jesus in History and Tradition* (Columbia: University of South Carolina, 2004)

Payne, D. F., "Semitisms in the Book of Acts," in W. Gasque and R. P. Martin, eds., *Apostolic History and the Gospel* (Exeter: Paternoster/ Grand Rapids: Eerdmans, 1970), 134-50

Plummer, A., *St Luke* (ICC; Edinburgh: Clark, 1901)

Porter, S. E., *The Criteria for Authenticity in Historical Jesus Research* (Sheffield: Sheffield Academic, 2000)

Reicke, B., "The History of the Synoptic Discussion," in D. L. Dungan, ed., *The Interrelations of the Gospels* (Leuven: University Press, 1990), 291-316

Riesner, R., "Jesus as Preacher and Teacher," in H. Wansbrough, ed., *Jesus and the Oral Gospel Traditions* (Sheffield: JSOT, 1991)

————, *Paul's Early Period* (Grand Rapids: Eerdmans, 1998)

Robinson, D. W. B, "The Distinction between Jewish and Gentile Believers in Galatians," *Australian Biblical Review* 13 (1965), 29-48

Robinson, J. A. T., *The Priority of John* (London: SCM, 1985)

————, *Redating the New Testament* (London: SCM, 1976)

————, *Twelve New Testament Studies* (Cambridge: Cambridge University Press, 1959), 94-106

Sabbe, M., "The Trial of Jesus before Pilate in John and Its Relation to the Synoptic Gospels," in *John and the Synoptics* (Leuven: University Press, 1992), 341-85

Selwyn, E. G., *The First Epistle of Peter* (London: Macmillan, 1961)

Slingerland, H. D., *Claudian Policymaking and the Early Imperial Repression of Judaism in Rome* (Atlanta: Scholars, 1997)

Schürer, E., *The History of the Jewish People in the Age of Jesus Christ*, rev. and ed. G. Vermes and F. Millar (Edinburgh: Clark, 1981-)

Stuhlmacher, P., "The Genre(s) of the Gospels," in D. L. Dungan, ed., *The Interrelations of the Gospels* (Leuven: University Press, 1990), 484-94

Talmon, S., "Oral and Written Tradition in Judaism," in H. Wansbrough, ed., *Gospel Traditions* (Sheffield: JSOT, 1991)

Theissen, G., *The Gospels in Context* (Minneapolis: Fortress, 1991)

Verheyden, J., "P. Gardner-Smith and 'the Turn of the Tide,'" in A. Denaux, ed., *John and the Synoptics* (Leuven: University Press, 1992), 424-65

Vielhauer, P., "On the 'Paulinisms' in Acts," in L. E. Keck and J. L. Martyn, eds., *Studies in Luke-Acts* (Nashville/New York: Abingdon, 1966), 33-50

Wansbrough, H., ed., *Jesus and the Oral Tradition* (*JSNT* Supplement 64; Sheffield: Sheffield Academic, 1991)

Wenham, D., *The Rediscovery of Jesus' Eschatological Discourse* (Sheffield: JSOT, 1984), 295-96

Wrede, W., *The Messianic Secret* (Cambridge: Clarke, 1971)

————, *Paul* (Boston: American Unitarian Association, 1908)

Wright, N. T., "Resurrection in Q?" in D. R. H. Horrell and C. M. Tuckett, eds., *Christology, Controversy and Community* (Leiden: Brill, 2000), 85-97

————, *The Resurrection of the Son of God* (London: SPCK, 2003)

INDEX OF MODERN AUTHORS

Adamson, J. B., 127n.53
Akenson, D. H., 5-7, 139n.4
Alexander, L., 118n.28
Allison, D. C., 120n.37, 125nn.42, 43
Anderson, P. N., 168n.10

Barrett, C. K., 12n.6, 167
Barnett, P. W., 9n.2, 55n.1, 56n.5, 68n.9, 157n.17, 173n.26, 184n.5
Bailey, K., 116n.21, 208
Bauckham, R., 175n.34
Baumgarten, A. I., 118n.28
Belleville, L. L., 201n.40
Best, E., 133n.59, 134n.60
Betz, H. D., 56n.3
Bockmuehl, M., 40n.30, 80n.1, 127n.50
Borgen, P., 116n.20, 164n.3
Bornkamm, G., 163
Bousset, W., 4, 49, 86
Brown, R. E., 179n.37
Bruce, F. F., 40n.33, 67n.5, 76n.23, 100n.12, 119n.35, 195n.16, 198n.33, 199n.36, 203n.48
Bultmann, R., 50
Burridge, R. A., 114n.16, 197n.22, 207n.7
Burton, E. de W., 98n.6

Campbell, D. A., 26n.9

Capes, D., 157n.16
Carson, D. A., 178n.36
Casey, M., 3, 4, 5, 86, 148
Chan, L. Y., 61n.9
Charlesworth, J. H., 174n.32
Collins, R. F., 44n.3, 46n.8
Cribbs, F. L., 168nn.6, 9
Crossan, J. D., 1, 3, 11n.5, 86, 111n.2, 135n.61, 211

Davids, P., 107n.19, 126nn.45, 52, 128n.54
Davies, W. D., 16n.16, 170n.18
de Jonge, M., 49n.13
Dickson, J. P., 109n.20
Dodd, C. H., 153, 173
Donahue, J. A., 162, 181
Donfried, K. P., 45n.6, 48n.11
Dunn, J. D. G., 117, 164n.3

Ehrman, B., 143n.13
Ellis, E. E., 116n.22, 117n.25, 136n.62, 170n.20
Evans, R. J., 10nn.3, 4

Farmer, W. R., 200n.37
Fiensy, D. A., 19n.14, 77n.26
Fitzmyer, J., 52n.20, 140n.5, 191
France, R. T., 2

Gardner-Smith, P., 163n.2
Gaventa, B. R., 56n.6
Gerhardsson, B., 114n.15, 116n.22, 126n.44
Goodacre, M., 138
Guelich, R. A., 154n.9
Gundry, R. H., 159n.21, 162n.26

Hansen, G. W., 56n.3
Harrison, J. R., 47n.9
Harvey, A. E., 185
Harvey, J. D., 116n.23
Hungerford, B. H., 56n.3
Head, P. M., 148n.21
Hemer, C., 9, 25n.13, 119n.34, 191n.5, 198nn.27, 30, 203n.45, 204n.51, 206n.2, 207nn.3, 4, 5, 6
Hengel, M., 4, 22n.1, 23nn.3,4, 50n.14, 55n.2, 59n.8, 68n.6, 70n.15, 71n.15, 73nn.16, 18, 75nn.20, 21, 22, 77n.25, 90n.9, 91n.10, 95n.1, 140n.5, 150n.1, 158n.19, 160n.23, 161n.24, 162n.25, 169n.15, 172nn.24, 25, 174n.31, 191, 196n.18, 198n.31, 203n.49
Hengel, M., and Schwemer, A. M., 34nn.15, 21, 62n.12, 202n.43
Henaut, B., 111n.1, 116n.19
Hoehner, H., 24nn.6, 7, 8
Hofius, O., 115n.17
Horsley, G. H. R., 112nn.3, 5, 119nn.32, 35, 200n.38
Hultgren, A. J., 145
Humphreys, C. J., 25n.9
Hurtado, L., 4
Hyldahl, N., 191n.8, 202n.44, 203n.46

Ingolfsland, D., 143n.12

Jeremias, J., 113n.10

Katz, T., 170n.19
Kelber, W., 116n.21
Kim, S., 44n.2, 50n.16, 120n.36, 121n.39
Kimelman, B., 170n.19

Kloppenborg (Verbin), J., 139n.3, 142nn.9, 10
Kysar, R., 179n.38

Lewis, N., and Reinhold, M., 38n.27
Lieberman, S., 114n.14
Lüdemann, G., 61n.10
Lührmann, D., 56n.5

Maddox, R., 168n.6
Maier, P. L., 24n.9
Manson, T. W., 141n.8
Marshall, I. H., 190n.3, 195n.15
Martin, R. P., 107n.19
Martyn, J. L., 170, 171n.21
Matson, M. A., 168n.7
McLean, B., 61n.10
Meadors, E., 142n.11, 143, 168nn.7, 11, 169nn.12, 13
Meier, J. P., 174n.30
Millar, F., 210
Millard, A., 112nn.6, 7, 8, 113n.9, 114nn.11, 13, 170n.17
Mitchell, T. S., 210nn.9, 10
Momigliano, A., 17
Motyer, S., 175n.34
Moule, C. F. D., 8n.23, 119n.34
Murphy O'Connor, J., 62n.11

Neirynck, F., 164n.3, 168n.8

Painter, J., 128n.55, 133n.56
Parker, P., 168n.6
Payne, D. F., 119n.34, 199n.35
Peterson, D., 195n.15
Plummer, A., 190
Porter, S. E., 112n.4, 113n.10, 119n.32

Reicke, B., 151n.3
Reinhardt, W., 19n.13, 97n.5
Reinhartz, A., 170n.19
Riesner, R., 8, 19n.15, 23nn.2, 4, 25nn.9, 11, 14, 65n.1, 68nn.7, 8, 122n.40, 203n.47, 204n.52

Robinson, D. W. B., 63n.14
Robinson, J. A. T., 106n.17, 163n.2, 169n.14
Ruckstuhl, E., 178n.36

Sabbe, M., 164n.3
Schürer, E., 174n.28
Schürmann, H., 114n.12, 118n.29
Selwyn, E. G., 133nn.57,58, 198n.32
Shellard, B., 168n.11
Sherwin-White, A. N., 203n.50
Slingerland, H. D., 31n.11
Stuhlmacher, P., 115n.16

Talmon, S., 114n.13, 116n.18, 117nn.24, 26, 118nn.30, 31

Theissen, G., 35n.20
Tuckett, C. M., 120n.38

Vielhauer P., 196n.20
von Ranke, L., 10

Waddington, W. G., 25n.9
Williams, M. M., 200n.38
Weizsächer, C., 187
Wenham, D., 16n.9, 36n.23, 120n.38, 191n.10, 202n.43
Westcott, B. F., 175
Williams, P. J., 148
Wrede, W., 2
Wright, N. T., 3n.9, 138n.1, 143-46, 180

INDEX OF SUBJECTS

Aeneas, 103, 104
Agabus, 83
Alexander the Great, 72, 112
Alexandria, 33, 34, 37, 38, 40, 81, 108
Ananias, 76, 88, 94
Ananias and Sapphira, 197
Anatolia, 204
Annas, 197
Antioch (in Pisidia), 92, 93
Antioch (in Syria), 26, 31, 32, 34, 35, 37, 39, 40, 48, 66, 78, 79-85, 80
Arabia, 48, 61, 87, 96, 105, 117, 185, 201
Aramaic, Aramaisms, 112, 113, 118, 198-99
Aretas, 23, 24, 28, 30, 32, 62, 96, 200
Aristobulus, 35
Augustus, 12, 24, 27, 38
Azotus, 86, 101

Barnabas (Joseph), 40, 68, 70, 82, 83, 84, 105, 107, 197
Bethsaida, 104
Birkath ha-Minim, 170

Caesarea (Maritima), 31, 36, 38, 39, 40, 67, 80, 81, 82, 87, 96, 99, 100, 101, 103, 104
Caiaphas, 28, 29, 30, 66, 75, 96

Cana, 177
Capernaum, 177
Christology, 2, 8, 23, 26, 44, 48, 50, 57, 59, 67, 69, 70, 71, 76, 77, 78, 84, 86, 87, 91, 143, 183-84
Christianoi, 32, 35, 81, 82, 83
Chronology, 22, 23
Cilicia, 73, 76, 98, 117
Claudius, 11, 12, 13, 25, 27, 28, 31, 32, 33, 37, 38, 39, 40, 89, 107, 195
Corinth, 25, 26, 50, 50-54, 107
Cornelius, 36, 37, 102, 103, 104, 105, 184
Cuspius Fadus, 40, 173, 199
Cyprus, 26, 31, 32, 80
Cyrene, 32, 80

Damascus, 20, 21, 23, 24, 25, 30, 31, 32, 49, 60, 61, 62, 66, 67, 69, 74, 75, 76, 77, 78, 80, 81, 87, 88, 91, 96, 200
David, King, 185
Decapolis, 21
Diaspora, 72, 73, 74, 97, 127
Dio Cassius, 165
Domitian, 185

Egyptian Prophet, 173
Ephesus, 107
Essenes, 74, 76

Felix, 173
Fire of Rome, 21
First Thessalonians, 21, 26, 50-54
Flaccus, 34

Gadara, 113
Gaius ("Caligula"), 27, 32, 33, 34, 35, 36,
    37, 40, 81, 82, 96, 114
Galatia, 26
Galatians, Letter to the, 55-64
Galilee, 31, 32, 36, 66, 96, 98, 99-100, 102,
    110
Gamaliel, 29, 199
Gerizim, Mount, 29, 100
Gospel sources Q, L, M, 125-26, 132, 135

"Hebrews," 49, 66, 67, 68, 73, 77, 79, 96,
    98, 112
Hebrews, Letter to the, 106-9
Hellenism, 72, 83, 98
"Hellenists," 20, 31, 32, 49, 66, 67, 68, 70,
    71, 72, 73, 75, 77, 80, 80, 83, 96, 98, 101,
    107, 108, 109, 112, 197
Hellenized regions, 113
Herod Agrippa I, 16, 33, 34, 36, 37, 38,
    39, 40, 67, 81, 99, 106, 127
Herod Agrippa II, 109
Herod Antipas, 28, 29, 30, 32, 33, 36, 37,
    84, 96
Herod, King, 16, 33
Herod Philip, 29, 33
Herodians, 184
Herodias, 33, 62
Hippos, 113

James, brother of the Lord, 39, 48, 59,
    61, 64, 66, 105-6, 107, 186, 200
James, Letter of, 126-33
James, son of Zebedee, 39, 67
Jamnia, 34, 81
Jerusalem, 19, 27-41, 48, 49, 50, 59, 60,
    67, 71, 72, 73, 74, 77, 80, 84, 87, 93, 95,
    97, 98, 102, 104, 107, 109, 117, 127, 202-
    3

Jesus Seminar, 138-49
"Jews" in the Gospel of John, 177-78
Joanna, 84, 113
John the Baptizer, 5, 29, 105, 172-73
John, Gospel of, 163-79, 194
John Mark, 70
John, son of Zebedee, 32, 36, 39, 48, 60,
    66, 82, 96, 100, 101, 102, 114, 200
Joppa, 31, 101, 102, 103, 104
Josephus, 13, 14, 195
Judas the Galilean, 5, 16, 185, 199, 200
Judea, 31, 32, 36, 66, 96, 98, 99, 102, 109,
    110, 188

Lucian, 12
Luke, 12, 48, 66, 73, 97, 98, 101, 119, 190-
    95
Lukios of Cyrene, 83
Lycaonia, 57
Lydda, 31, 101, 102, 103, 104

Malalas, 34
Manaen, 83, 84
Mark, Gospel of, 150-62, 185, 194
Masada, 113
Mnason, 67, 108
Momigliano's rule, 17-18, 180
Moses-Prophet, 173
Murabbaʿat, 113

Nabatea, 32
Nabateans, 23, 29, 30, 62
Nazarenes, sect of the, 66, 76
Nero, 21
"New Perspective" on Paul, 63
Nicodemus, 175
Nicolaus, 32

Oral tradition, 97, 116
Orality and textuality, 111-36

Papias, 116, 158-61
Parousia, 47
Parthia, 29, 33

Paterculus, 165

Paul: in Antioch, 83, 84; apostle to
Gentiles, 60-62; in Damascus, 61-62,
67, 76-78, 114; "the faith," 57-59; persecutor, 60, 67, 73, 74, 75, 78, 80, 95,
97, 98, 99; pre-Christian, 60, 62, 73;
source of his beliefs, 48-50; "unknown years," 18, 45, 62; "we" passages, 15-16

Peter (Cephas), 31, 36, 37, 39, 48, 59, 60,
61, 64, 66, 67, 68, 69, 77, 78, 86-94, 89,
91, 95-105, 114, 152-62, 200

Peter, First Letter of, 133-35

Petronius, 34, 35, 38, 82

Philip, 31, 32, 36, 67, 70, 72, 77, 80, 86-87,
93, 96, 98, 100, 101, 102, 104, 110

Phoenicia, 31, 80

Pisidia, 57

Philippi, 191

Polybius, 195

Pontius Pilate, 12, 14, 28, 29, 30, 32, 40,
96, 184, 188

Priscilla and Aquila, 31, 89, 107

Ptolemais, 31, 35, 101

Q, 3, 138-49, 188, 194

Quirinius, 16, 200

Qumran, 14, 72, 118

Resurrection, 185-86

Rome, 31, 33, 99, 162, 184, 185

Samaria, 31, 32, 36, 66, 86, 96, 98, 99-101,
102, 110, 175-77

Samaritans, 29, 70, 82, 94, 102, 175-77

Scythopolis, 113

Sejanus, 27

Sepphoris, 113

Sidon, 35, 101, 113

"Sign" prophets, 173

Silvanus, 70

Simeon called Niger, 83

Simon bar Gioras, 5, 185

Simon the tanner, 103, 104

Solomon's Colonnade, 71

Stephen, 31, 32, 70, 71, 72, 73, 74, 75, 77,
78, 104, 107

Suetonius, 165

Syria-Cilicia, 57, 114

Taheb, 100

Tabitha/Dorcas, 103, 104

Tacitus, 11, 14, 165, 188

Tarsus, 32, 48, 73, 83, 96

Temple (in Jerusalem), 34, 35, 37, 70, 71,
72, 73, 74, 75, 76, 77, 104, 106, 107, 109

Thessalonica, 42-54, 93, 184, 185

Theodotus inscription, 19

Theudas, 5, 16, 40, 199-200

Thomas, Gospel of, 3

Thucydides, 195

Tiberias, 35, 113

Tiberius, 24, 26, 27, 37, 29, 30, 32, 33, 34,
96, 165

Timothy, 45, 46, 106, 107

Titus, 83

Trajan, 185

Troas, 191

Tyre, 31, 101, 113

Vespasian, 185

Vitellius, 29, 30, 32, 33

Vitrasius Pollio, 34

Written traditions, 114

INDEX OF SCRIPTURE REFERENCES

OLD TESTAMENT

Deuteronomy

6:4	52
21:22-23	69

2 Samuel

7:14	145

Psalms

2:7	145
110:1	70

Isaiah

29:18	144
35:5-6	144
42:19	144
52:13	69, 87
52:13–53:12	69
61:1-3	144

Ezekiel

47:15-17	80
48:1	80

NEW TESTAMENT

Matthew

3:7-10	146
3:11-12	144
8:11-12	146
8:20	146
10:5	100
11:4-6	144
11:5	146
11:25-27	145
12:28	144
12:40	146
16:16	86, 94
16:18	86, 94
19:28	145
22:1-10	145
23:6	144
23:37-39	145, 146
24:27	50
25:6	50
25:14-20	146
25:37-39	146

Mark

1:1	158
1:21-34	155
2:1–3:6	155
2:9	167
3:6	81
4:1-34	155
4:35–5:43	155
7:3	115
7:3-5	194
7:9-13	115
7:19	157
8:29-30	4, 6
9:42	157
9:42-50	155
11:9	146
12:13	81
12:17	157
12:35-37	70
13:1-37	155
13:1–17:25	171
13:7	157
13:14	35, 156, 157, 158
13:35-37	50
13:36	50
14:1–16:6	156
14:6	59
14:36	70

14:54	167	10:22-23	71	4:6	66
14:61-62	4, 145	12:11	168	4:10	69
		12:13	146	4:18	87, 155
Luke		12:42	170	4:26	69, 87
1:1-4	17, 118, 137, 162,	16:2	170	4:27	69, 77, 87
	193	18:1-14	168	4:30	69, 87
1:3	159	18:25	167	4:32	68
2:1-5	199	18:28-40	168	4:33	69, 70
3:8	146	20:3-10	168	4:37	68
3:16-17	144	21:15-17	94, 104	5:12	71
7:22	144, 147			5:14	97
7:36-50	168	**Acts**		5:17-40	71
8:3	84	1:3	18	5:21	87, 155
8:18-19	105	1:8	31	5:25	87
9:51-53	100	1:13	18	5:28	69, 87, 155
9:58	146	1:14	18, 105	5:30	69, 77
10:21-22	145	2:9	18	5:31	70
11:20	144	2:13	68	5:33-39	199
11:31-32	146	2:14-36	91	5:34-40	29, 115
11:43	144	2:21	77	5:42	69, 87, 155
13:28-29	146	2:22	69, 104	6:1	68
13:34-35	145, 146	2:30	69, 77, 87	6:1–7:73	170
15:24	145	2:31	69, 87	6:2	18, 68
17:16	100	2:33-34	70	6:4	194
21:34-36	50	2:36	70	6:5	32
22:28-30	145	2:38	69, 87	6:7	71, 176
22:39-53	168	2:41	97	6:8	71
23:1-4	168	2:42	59, 69, 87, 115,	6:9	68, 73
23:13-25	168		155	6:13	71, 72
24:10	84	2:42-45	68	6:14	173
24:12	168	2:47	97	7:10-11	122-23
24:36-43	168	3:1	70	7:37	173
		3:6	69	7:40	173
John		3:11	71	7:58	73
1:21	173	3:13	69, 87	8:1	73, 98, 99, 103,
1:41	6	3:15	69		110
1:49	6	3:18	69, 87	8:3	73, 74, 98
2:19-21	72	3:20	69, 87	8:4	77, 87, 98
3:23-24	24	3:22	173	8:4-24	170, 176
4:7-27	100	4:1-3	71	8:4-40	86
4:45	99	4:2	69, 87, 155	8:5	98
5:8	167	4:4	97	8:14	82, 102
6:14-14	173	4:5-6	29	8:25	102, 103, 155
9:22	170	4:5-22	71	8:26-40	170

8:27	98	13:39	63, 92	10:18-21	56
8:32-35	69	15:2	126	14:13	157
8:35	77, 87	15:3	31, 103, 155, 176	14:14	157
8:40	98, 101	15:3-8	58	15:18-20	201
9:1	74	15:6-21	40	15:19	48, 109
9:10	76	15:13	106	16:17	90, 115
9:14	122-23	15:23	51	16:17-20	88
9:18	87	15:24	117	16:21-25	88
9:20	49, 59, 69, 92	15:39	160		
9:21	31	15:41	51	**1 Corinthians**	
9:22	49, 59, 92	16:11	42	1:23	51
9:25	32	17:2-3	92	7:10	46
9:26-36	96	18:2	25, 31	8:4	52
9:27-29	201	18:5	45	8:4-6	53
9:28	87, 99, 110	18:22	32	8:6	58
9:28-29	109	21:4	32	11:2	115
9:29	170	21:7	32	11:23-25	46, 77, 115
9:31	31, 36, 95, 97, 99,	21:8	86, 101	12:3	52
	103, 104, 110, 151,	21:10	101	13:7	157
	155, 175, 176	21:17–27:1	162	14:13	124
9:31-43	79, 94	21:38	173	14:14	124
9:32	31, 98	22:4	74	14:20	124
9:36	31	22:5	74	15:1-3	46, 49, 50, 76, 115
10:14-15	109	22:12	76	15:1-7	52, 67, 77, 87-88
10:34-43	105, 152, 153	22:16	87, 88	15:3	59
10:39	69, 77	24:5	66	15:3-5	152
10:40	77, 88	26:9	74	15:3-7	6, 18, 26, 135
10:43	88	26:10	74	15:5	94
11:1	82	26:11	74	15:7	106, 127
11:19	80, 98, 110, 170	26:20	51, 87, 109	15:11	58
11:19-26	32	28:16	162	16:22	51, 52, 53, 70, 119
11:23-26	59				
11:24-25	122-23	**Romans**		**2 Corinthians**	
11:26	79	1:1-4	67, 70, 77, 88-93,	1:19	51, 58, 69
11:29-30	126		135, 186	2:11	51
12:1-3	39	1:9	70	4:5	51
12:12	160	1:11	88	11:32-33	30
12:17	106	3:24-25	44		
12:20-23	40	6:17	90, 115	**Galatians**	
13:1-4	17	8:3	70	1:1	57
13:5	160	8:15	59, 70	1:4	59
13:14–14:28	207	8:29	70	1:9	46
13:29	77	8:32	70	1:11–2:11	55-64
13:32-37	92	9:30-33	56	1:12-13	60

1:13	49, 64, 73, 74, 97
1:16	48, 57, 67, 69, 76, 201
1:16-17	17, 87
1:17	48
1:17-19	64
1:18	16, 23, 26, 30, 49, 94
1:18-19	59, 105
1:18–2:10	110
1:19	18
1:19-20	201
1:21	99
1:22	32, 45, 79, 109, 117n.27, 151, 155
1:23	31, 49, 64, 67, 76, 98
2:1	16, 23, 126
2:1-10	39
2:2	61
2:6	61
2:7-9	49, 60, 94, 99, 102, 110
2:9	61, 105
2:11-13	61
2:11-14	39
2:15-16	63
2:20	59

3:7-8	32
3:13	57, 58, 59, 77
4:4	57
4:6	57, 58, 70
5:11	58
6:13	63

Ephesians

4:5	52
4:20-21	115

Philippians

3:3	73
3:6	74

Colossians

2:6	46
4:10	160, 161

1 Thessalonians 43-54, 120-22

1:1	58
1:9-10	93
1:10	58, 69
2:14	32, 79, 99, 117n.27, 151, 155
2:15	87
4:9	46

4:11	46
5:10	59

2 Thessalonians

2:3-4	156
2:4	35
3:6	46

2 Timothy

4:11	65, 160, 161, 162

James 126-33

1 Peter 133

1:17	59, 70
2:24	77
5:11	162
5:13	160

2 John 115

Jude

3	115

Revelation

22:20	119

INDEX OF OTHER ANCIENT WRITINGS

Dio Cassius
History
59.26   33
59.28   33
60.11   40

Eusebius
Historia Ecclesiastica
3.12   186
3.19   186
3.22   186
3.39.15   159

Josephus
Antiquities
17.269   199
18.1-6   200
18.64   28
18.86   29
18.89   29
18.105   29
18.116-17   172
18.135   29
18.261-309   34
19.239   37
19.343-52   40
20.97-99   173, 199

20.167-68   173
20.168-72   173
20.200-201   40, 127

Apion
1.51   37

Life
364   37

War
2.184-203   34
2.206   37
2.232-34   100
2.259   173
2.261-63   173
7.43-45   79

Philo
Embassy to Gaius
32   33
75-77   33
93-118   33
200   34
201   34
346   33

Philostratus
Life of Apollonius
7.10   89

Suetonius
Life of Caligula
22   33
Life of Claudius
18.2   40
25.4   25

Tacitus
Annales 15.44   28, 188
Historia 5.9   27, 28

1 Enoch
48:2-10   145
62:12-16   145

2 Baruch
29:1-8   145

Talmud
Ketubim 17d   39
Ketubim 105a   19
Sota 41b   39